THE LEARNER-CENTERED
INSTRUCTIONAL DESIGNER

THE LEARNER-CENTERED INSTRUCTIONAL DESIGNER

Purposes, Processes, and Practicalities of Creating Online Courses in Higher Education

Edited by Jerod Quinn

Foreword by Flower Darby

STERLING, VIRGINIA

COPYRIGHT © 2021 BY STYLUS PUBLISHING, LLC.

Published by Stylus Publishing, LLC
22883 Quicksilver Drive
Sterling, Virginia 20166-2019

All rights reserved. No part of this book may be reprinted or reproduced in any form or by any electronic, mechanical, or other means, now known or hereafter invented, including photocopying, recording and information storage, and retrieval, without permission in writing from the publisher.

Library of Congress Cataloging-in-Publication Data
Names: Quinn, Jerod, 1981- editor.
Title: The learner-centered instructional designer : purposes, processes, and practicalities of creating online courses in higher education / edited by Jerod Quinn ; foreword by Flower Darby.
Other titles: Learner centered instructional designer
Description: First Edition. | Sterling, Virginia : Stylus Publishing, LLC, 2020. | Includes bibliographical references and index.
Identifiers: LCCN 2020045036 (print) | LCCN 2020045037 (ebook) | ISBN
 9781642670417 (Paperback : acid-free paper) | ISBN 9781642670400
 (Hardback : acid-free paper) | ISBN 9781642670424 (PDF) | ISBN 9781642670431 (eBook)
Subjects: LCSH: Instructional systems--Design--Handbooks, manuals, etc. |
 Internet in education. | Distance education--Computer-assisted instruction.
Classification: LCC LB1028.38 .L39 2020 (print) | LCC LB1028.38 (ebook) |
 DDC 378.1/7344678--dc23
LC record available at https://lccn.loc.gov/2020045036
LC ebook record available at https://lccn.loc.gov/2020045037

13-digit ISBN: 978-1-64267-040-0 (cloth)
13-digit ISBN: 978-1-64267-041-7 (paperback)
13-digit ISBN: 978-1-64267-042-4 (library networkable e-edition)
13-digit ISBN: 978-1-64267-043-1 (consumer e-edition)

Printed in the United States of America

All first editions printed on acid-free paper
that meets the American National Standards Institute
Z39-48 Standard.

Bulk Purchases

Quantity discounts are available for use in workshops and for staff development.

Call 1-800-232-0223

First Edition, 2021

To the instructional designers, developers, specialists, and technologists who spend your working days hustling behind the scenes of higher education doing all you can to help others have deep and meaningful learning experiences. I see you and celebrate your impactful work.

CONTENTS

FOREWORD   xi
Flower Darby

ACKNOWLEDGMENTS   xiii

INTRODUCTION
Always Learner Centered   1
Jerod Quinn

PART ONE: INSTRUCTIONAL DESIGN IN ACADEMIA: A COMMON CORE WITH DIFFERENT APPROACHES

1. CONCIERGE MODEL
   The Full-Service Guide   13
   Rayne Vieger

2. CONSULTATION MODEL
   At the End of the Day   27
   Jerod Quinn

PART TWO: BUILDING FACULTY TRUST: YOU CAN TRUST ME, I'M A PROFESSIONAL

3. BUILDING TRUST
   Creating a Climate of Trust, Care, and Collaboration Among
   Instructional Designers and Faculty   39
   Christopher Grabau

4. HAVING BOUNDARIES
   I'm Not Your Personal Assistant   49
   Olena Zhadko

5. FACULTY PERSPECTIVES
   A (Love?) Letter to Instructional Designers   59
   Tom Warhover

6 GROUNDED IN RESEARCH
   Be Good, or at Least Evidence Based   69
   Johanna Inman

PART THREE: FRAMEWORKS THAT TOUCH EVERYTHING: THE LENSES WE WORK WITH

7 LEARNING ONLINE
   The Internet Should be Used for More Than Just Do-It-Yourself Videos   81
   Josie G. Baudier

8 UNIVERSAL DESIGN FOR LEARNING
   Everybody Gets to Learn   93
   Carl S. Moore

9 DECENTRALIZING WHITENESS
   Where Do We Start?   107
   German E. Vargas Ramos

10 MOTIVATION FOR LEARNING
   If We Build It, Will They Come?   117
   Traci Stromie

11 METACOGNITION AND REFLECTION
   How We Know What We Know and Don't Know   129
   Kathryn E. Linder

12 INTEGRATING TECHNOLOGY
   It's New and Shiny, So It Must Be Good for Learning   139
   Bonni Stachowiak

PART FOUR: COMPONENTS OF ONLINE CLASSES: PRACTICAL EVERGREENS

13 COURSE STRUCTURE
   Spend Time Engaging With Course Materials, Not Hunting for Them   151
   German E. Vargas Ramos

14 MULTIMEDIA
   Moving Beyond Passive to Active Learner Engagement   165
   Danilo M. Baylen, Jonathan Gratch, and Linda Haynes

15	GROUP WORK Online Collaboration Isn't Always Horrible *Emily Goldstein*	177
16	SYNCHRONOUS LEARNING Good to See You Again *David Wicks and Annie Tremonte*	189
17	DISCUSSION FORUMS Our Love-Hate Relationship With Discussion Forums *Shannon Riggs*	201
18	PRESENCE Online Courses Still Have to Be Taught *Olena Zhadko*	213
19	REMOTE INSTRUCTIONAL DESIGN The Best We Can *Tammy M. McCoy and Jerod Quinn*	223
	CONCLUSION A Day in the Life *Jerod Quinn*	235
	ANNOTATED BIBLIOGRAPHY	245
	EDITOR AND CONTRIBUTORS	249
	INDEX	257

FOREWORD

This book is the most sorely needed resource I've come across in a long time. And I come across a lot of sorely needed resources.

Jerod Quinn has compiled a wonderfully useful, practical, and compassionate—yes, *compassionate*—handbook on instructional design and instructional designers (IDs). This collection of "a day in the life of an ID" essays includes countless pointers, rich theoretical frameworks, and good old-fashioned advice for getting along with faculty partners and other peers on campus. I wish I'd had this book when I started out in instructional design 7 years ago.

As I write, in June 2020, I'm reflecting on the incredible disruption to higher education caused by COVID-19. COVID-19 has succeeded in doing what I never thought possible: demonstrating the value of online instruction and motivating greater numbers of faculty than ever before to learn how to do it better. There has never been a greater need for online class support. There has never been a greater demand for the expertise instructional designers provide. IDs, your time is now. This book will help.

There is so much to recommend about the book you hold in your hands that I struggle to know where to start. But that's not strictly true. Let us start, as always, with people.

Multiple populations will benefit from this new resource. That's why I emphasize compassion as a strength of this resource; it helps the people in online classes have a more rewarding and enjoyable experience. Given the challenges we face in online courses, helping wherever we can is a top priority.

First and foremost, online and remote students will experience better, more effective learning as a result of the "behind-the-scenes" work of better equipped instructional designers. Quinn's eloquent appeal to "focus our efforts on the people we serve before the products we create" (p. 4, this volume) is an important reminder for people who work with tech all day long, people who, like I've done before, might be tempted to focus more on shiny tech bells and whistles and not so much on the people for whom we're creating meaningful learning experiences.

Faculty will create and teach better online courses based solidly on the science of learning when instructional designers, having read this book, are more consistently prepared to do their work well. Across the nation, IDs find themselves in a wide range of institutional contexts. They've had varying levels of preparation for the job. I've worked with hundreds of IDs in the amazing ID2ID peer mentoring program, which places IDs in community with IDs at other schools. Two things I know as a result of those interactions are: (a) Few people have had extensive formal training in instructional design, and (b) institutions provide different levels of professional development opportunities for IDs. This book will help level the playing field, fill in any gaps, and better prepare IDs. Their faculty partners will directly benefit as a result.

Many faculty members will further benefit from reading Tom Warhover's chapter 5, "Faculty Perspectives: A (Love?) Letter to Instructional Designers." Warhover tells of his own growing awareness of and appreciation for what IDs can do, and have done, to improve his classes. Others may benefit from this informative piece, people who may not have known about the value of working with IDs, an often underutilized resource available to them.

Finally, by virtue of this book, higher education administrators will better see the value of supporting and resourcing instructional design teams and of explicitly encouraging faculty to take advantage of these online teaching and learning rockstars. With students and faculty both enjoying better online classes, administrators are sure to observe growing enrollments and improved equitable learning outcomes in online programs and courses. Given the central role that online classes must play as a direct result of COVID-19, this is surely a good thing.

The chapters in this collection have been written by knowledgeable experts, people who can attest to Quinn's presupposition that online learning can happen, and happen just as well if not better than it does in person, people who—better yet—can show you how, step by step. Gathering this treasure trove of contributors is truly a remarkable feat in and of itself. Read on to discover the inestimable value of their practical suggestions. Investing in yourself in this way will pay off in big dividends as you find increased meaning and purpose in your work.

I truly believe that we—IDs; faculty; administrators; and other support heroes, such as librarians, media technologists, help desk colleagues, and more—make the world a better place when we create and teach better online classes. Dive into this work with me and with the contributors represented here. You will be glad you did.

Flower Darby
Flagstaff, Arizona

ACKNOWLEDGMENTS

This book never would have happened without the constant support (emotional, logistical, and proofreading) of my sweet wife, Charity. Thank you for believing in me, especially during the days when I couldn't believe in myself. And thank you to Grace and Ash, my kiddos, for being proud of me during this opportunity and never failing to miss a chance to ask me if my book was done yet.

Thank you to Katie Linder, who made the secret dream of mine to be a writer a reality. Your relentless help is deeply appreciated, and I am forever in your debt. Without your guidance, advice, encouragement, and willingness to take a chance on me, this dream would still be a secret one.

Thank you to the fantastic contributors who agreed to be part of this venture. I'm still a little baffled about why you said yes when I came calling, but I'm so glad you did. Your efforts and expertise took the vision for this book and made it an actual, physical resource for instructional designers in higher education.

And, of course, thank you to the legion of friends and colleagues who listened to my ambitions and tolerated my idea chasing, with special thanks to Chris Grabau, Debie Lohe, and Kevin Gannon for their support and encouragement. Tina Fox, thank you so much for editing my drafts and helping with the graphics. Thank you to Karen Nazario and Mary Decker for helping me think through what ideas would be most helpful to people new to instructional design in higher education. And to my friends at Saint Louis University and the University of Missouri whose camaraderie formed me into the designer I am today, thank you all very much.

The role of an instructional designer is to advocate for the learner in a process that, while targeted toward learners, rarely involves them.

INTRODUCTION

Always Learner Centered

Jerod Quinn

Explaining what exactly instructional designers do can be a tricky feat. *Instructional designer* is one of those wondrously nebulous titles that can mean everything and nothing at the same time. The benefit of this ambiguity is that we can make our work what it needs to be in different contexts. Some instructional designers will focus on the technology of instruction, using online tools to design and build new learning experiences. Some will focus on the pedagogy, helping instructors craft their courses grounded in evidence-based teaching practices. All will juggle those two approaches, often changing focus by the hour. Morris (2018) says that instructional designers "understand digital space. They understand learning. They understand teaching. *And* they understand technology" (para. 6, emphasis in original). Our work is nebulous and complicated.

I often joke with faculty about the work of design, saying I get to have those exciting conversations about how to create learning experiences, design authentic assessments that mimic real-life work, and dream up instructional approaches that communicate the value of the course content all without ever having to grade a single assignment. Most of us perfect our elevator pitches about our work pretty early in our careers. Here's mine:

> At the university, your biology teacher is a biologist. Your accounting teacher is an accountant. They know their discipline really well. But they may or may not have had any training in teaching or course design. But that's my world. I work with faculty from across the university to create engaging online classes where faculty are excited to teach, learners are excited to learn, and where evidence that learners have mastered the class material is concrete.

This introduction talks about what instructional design in higher education looks like across the country. Then we take a deep dive into defining *learner-centered teaching*. Next, we examine some of the instructional assumptions that provide the foundation for this book. Finally, I provide an outline of this book to help guide readers through the conversations.

Who We Are

A common icebreaker at instructional design gatherings is asking participants, "So how did you get into instructional design?" This is a great question, because the answers are never linear and rarely repeated. Although options for instructional design degrees are continually expanding, many instructional designers do not take a direct path to the profession. The backgrounds and skills designers bring with them to the work are diverse. When you look at the population of instructional designers in higher education, 67% are female, and the average age is around 45 years old (Intentional Futures, 2016). Almost 90% have master's degrees from a wide range of disciplines, and almost 90% have been instructional designers for 10 years or less (Intentional Futures, 2016). Designers tend to work on relatively small teams housed in information technology departments, learning technology departments, or teaching centers. And like many working in academia today, designers report feeling overworked and underresourced at their institutions (Intentional Futures, 2016). Despite the varied contexts and backgrounds, designers almost unanimously report the same primary tension: building trust with instructors (Intentional Futures, 2016).

What We Do

The work of instructional designers can vary by the hour across a wide spectrum of tasks, but the bulk of the work tends to fall into four categories: design, manage, train, and support (Intentional Futures, 2016). Design is the work of building and creating online courses, from scaffolding instruction to crafting authentic assessments. It is the creative work of generating ideas with instructors, then pragmatically constructing the ideas so that instructors can succeed in an online environment. Design is also connected to reviewing courses for a defined measure of quality standards. Instructional design also requires designers to effectively and efficiently manage multiple projects at different levels of commitment. I know designers who carry a load of six major course design projects at any given time. I know other designers who refuse to count their major projects because that would just give them a greater sense of being overwhelmed. Personally, my workload is about 13 major course redesign projects, 3 to 5 department instructional design projects, and dozens of short consultations and one-off meetings at any point in the semester. Your mileage may vary depending on your institution and other duties as assigned. Designers also play the role of trainer at times, helping instructors to master the learning management system and other instructional technology used in their courses. But that work is more than just helping them know what buttons to click; it is also having conversations about which technologies to select for specific instructional objectives. Finally, technical support is another aspect of the work as designers field emails and phone calls from instructors when something goes sideways in their courses. Providing this type of immediate support shows that we are partners in designing online courses and in their daily implementation. Although these four categories pretty well define the scope of the work, they do not define the scope of the role.

Instructional designers play a unique role in education as the mediator between the student experience and the instructor's vision. According to Morris (2018),

> It's their [designers'] job to watch out for the student, to make sure that they will be able not only to follow the course, and locate relevant information like due dates and assignment descriptions, but also that they'll *enjoy* the course, *get something* from the course, and *remember* the course as a true college experience. (para. 7, emphasis in original)

The role of an instructional designer is to advocate for the learner in a process that, while targeted toward learners, rarely involves them. That can be a tough job. It is much easier to bend to the requests of others, not challenging them and doing exactly what they ask regardless of how it will affect student learning. But that is not instructional design. Designers critically and proactively examine decisions and approaches with an eye on what will make the most effective learning experience for the most learners. We use creativity, pragmatism, and research-based course design principles in our partnerships with instructors to advocate for and develop learner-centered online courses.

On Being Learner Centered

What do I mean, exactly, by learner centered? Being learner centered is an approach to the work of instructional design and a value that grounds our decisions. As an approach, designers need to lean on the research that says the one who does the work does the learning (Doyle, 2011). Learning is not a spectator sport; it is active engagement with ideas and skills. That engagement can include writing, discussing, creating, extending, thinking, questioning, or any number of activities that spur learners to wrestle with new and challenging ideas. The goal is for the designer and the instructor to collaborate and create an environment for learning and for practicing the skills and content of the course (Doyle, 2011). But learner centered is as much a value as it is an approach. It is a person-forward approach to course design.

The great promise of online learning is the democratization of education, where geographical boundaries no longer restrict learning opportunities.

Weimer (2013) lists five areas for learner-centered teaching in her book, and I have adapted these five items to describe the practical approach and value-based approach of being learner-centered in all we do as instructional designers.

1. Include all learners in the messy work of being more responsible for their learning.
2. Motivate and empower learners by giving them some control over learning processes.
3. Facilitate connection and work to build a community where everyone shares the learning agenda.
4. Promote reflection about what the instructor and the students are learning, how they are learning it, and why it matters.
5. Include explicit learning skills instruction in content and online learning pedagogy.

This is an almost comically tall order. That being said, the value of being learner-centered (or serving the learner first) drives the instructional designer to take their role as an advocate seriously in the face of instructors who are resistant about teaching online and administrators who view online courses as merely a revenue stream to be harnessed. It is that value, serving the learners first, that reminds us our learners are taking online courses to pursue an education that will better their own lives and the lives of their loved ones. The role of an instructional designer in helping facilitate the dreams of learners takes place almost entirely behind the scenes, but it can be a deeply influential one if we focus our efforts on the people we serve before focusing on the products we create.

Assumptions in Instructional Design

Three assumptions provide much of the foundation of the chapters in this book and underlie all the efforts of designers: Online learning can work, active learning is preferred over passive learning, and learning objectives play a vital role in every aspect of course design.

Online Learning Works

The first assumption of this book is that one can learn online and can learn deeply. It seems there should be no need to say that online learning works, but given the resistance to online courses by some, it is clearly stated here. Online courses can be an effective approach to teaching and learning in higher education. It can be hard to make a fair comparison of online courses versus face-to-face courses because each class is unique. Some instructors will have better teaching preparation, some learners will be more intrinsically motivated, and some learning management systems are a usability nightmare that will sink any wholehearted attempt to use them for learning. There are so many variables in each and every course regardless of the modality, and painting a picture of general effectiveness is complicated. But there are studies that have tried to paint that picture. Generally speaking, they have found that learners in online courses do as well as learners in face-to-face courses in meeting learning objectives, and learners in blended courses do slightly better than learners in online and face-to-face courses (Bailey et al., 2018). One of the more encompassing studies found little to no difference in grade-based student performance between online and face-to-face courses but noted that learners with higher grade point averages perform better in online classes, and learners with lower grade point averages tend to perform worse (Cavanaugh & Jacquemin, 2015). Whether online or face-to-face, it really boils down to the fact that a well-designed and well-taught course is an effective course, regardless of modality.

Active Learning Over Passive Learning

The second assumption of this book is that active learning tends to be more effective than passive learning. Among the few definitions of *active learning*, in general, the emphasis in active learning is to develop the skills of the learners by asking them to do something with information as opposed to merely being presented with information (Brame, 2016). When studying the effectiveness of active learning versus passive learning, researchers generally compare a course with a constructivist design, where the learners are asked to make connections between new information and their current mental models, and the same course with an expository design, where information is transmitted to the learners primarily through one-way lecturing. Regardless of whether the course is from science, technology, engineering, mathematics, humanities, or any other discipline, courses based on active learning approaches tend to be more effective for student learning than those based on passive approaches (Brame, 2016). For instructional designers, this means applying active learning approaches that are well suited for online courses. That does not mean all the approaches need to involve sitting in front of a computer (e.g., ask yourself how to get learners engaged with their communities), but it means designers are constantly looking for ways learners can wrestle with new knowledge throughout the course.

Learning Objectives Matter

The third assumption is that having learning objectives, preferably measurable ones, is vital to the design of effective online courses. A course grounded in measurable objectives promotes a deeper level of learner engagement because naming those objectives gives you the launching point to design active learning strategies (Nilson, 2010). If your objective is for learners to be able to build a working circuit board, then by choosing the word *build* you have declared they will need to actively do the work of building to demonstrate they have met the objective. So what makes an objective measurable? It is the right verb that is aligned with how the skills or knowledge will be measured. *Discuss, demonstrate, create, identify, write, record, recite,* and *analyze* are all words that conjure up types of assessments that measure if learners are meeting the objective. *Know, understand,* and *learn* are classic examples of unmeasurable objective verbs because they can mean too many different things to accurately pair with an assessment. What's the difference between understand and identify? What about understand and demonstrate? Understand is unmeasurable because it can mean anything, and when it comes to objectives, much of their value comes from being able to explicitly point to the expectations of the instructor.

Anything you read about learning objectives will argue that they are crafted so the learners can see the purpose of the course. They help the learners grasp the value of the lesson content while hinting at their responsibility in mastering that content. That is absolutely true. At the same time, I offer a bit of instructional design heresy and claim that although objectives can be useful to learners, practically speaking that's not their primary role in course design. We would be lying to ourselves if we thought learners in the typical undergraduate online course gave anything more than a cursory glance at the learning objectives. For me, the primary value of solid, measurable learning objectives is that they draw design constraints around the focus of the course to prevent scope creep. During course design conversations, you will have countless ideas about activities and approaches for the course. The instructor will be asking endlessly if the course needs to be covering more content. Objectives are the scale used to weigh the idea against the scope of the course and see if it's a great fit for this course or a great fit for some other course and should be dropped from the current one. Objectives draw a boundary line for what gets into the course and what does not.

The Flow of This Book

The first of the four parts of this book is about the nature of instructional design work in higher education. The second part is focused on the number one tension designers face in their daily work: building trust with instructors. The third part discusses several frameworks that guide course design, and the fourth part consists of conversations about common approaches in designing online courses.

Instructional Design in Academia

Instructional design in education typically follows one of two streams: the concierge model or the consultation model. In the concierge model, faculty are often hired to write the instructional content of the course, and the instructional designers then take that content and work with the faculty to create an online course from the content. The consultation model works just as the name indicates; the instructional designers work as consultants. They ask questions, develop project time lines, offer evidence-based approaches to online learning, and help the faculty learn and master the course management system. But at the end of the day, it's the faculty's responsibility to actually build and maintain the course. Regardless of the stream, instructional designers share a core value across academia. They want all the online courses they touch to be created as learner-centered experiences, which encourage active, independent thinkers and learners.

Building Faculty Trust

Our work has not only a unifying value but also a unifying frustration. The biggest tension we instructional designers in academia face is building trust and credibility with the faculty we work with (Intentional Futures, 2016). If faculty do not trust us, they will not take our advice on appropriate pedagogical risks in creating and facilitating online courses. Learners can end up with a class that consists of little more than a slightly curated list of uploaded PowerPoint slides, an online learning experience that benefits no one. Effective online course development means that designers need to learn how to build trust with faculty quickly and with integrity.

To build trust, instructional designers need to know what they are talking about. They do this by operating with evidence-based approaches. Feelings cannot be the foundation of effective course design. Most of the general approaches to course development and online teaching have been around long enough to accrue research that helps refine tactics. As we steep ourselves in the research of online teaching and learning, our intuition strengthens, and when new ideas and approaches are dreamed up, we can then trust our gut to create novel experiences grounded in researched ideas.

We also build trust by having strong and clear boundaries on what is and what is not instructional design work. When faculty see instructional designers as tech support, then faculty go to designers with their tech support questions. We want and need them to come to us to talk instructional design.

Frameworks That Touch Everything

Volumes have been written about how people learn, and the instructional designer needs to understand how learning works online. We know a clear structure can provoke engagement, but a poor structure can force learners to spend their energy searching for what they need as opposed to engaging with content. But structure does not just mean sequencing an online course; it also includes metacognition, or how we think about thinking. We can structure in moments of reflection to encourage metacognitive approaches to instruction and help our learners transfer what they are learning in the classroom to other contexts.

Our approach to learning technology is another framework. It is all too easy to see a shiny new gadget and kick into overdrive hunting for a nail to hit with this technological hammer. Instructional designers need to be technology agnostic. Our priority is on the learning, no matter how shiny and improved that new gadget appears. Beginning with solid objectives and authentic assessments, we then scan the available technology and see the appropriate tool (assuming there is one) floating to the top.

Finally, the framework instructional designers need to have tattooed on their forearms is that everybody gets to learn. Universal design for learning is not an afterthought but an intentional approach from the very beginning. Our inclusion work doesn't end with making sure all the stuff of the course is available to all learners, but we encourage our faculty to include a diversity of voices in the content itself: Can our learners see themselves in our courses?

Components of Online Classes

Technologies come and go, but some approaches to online learning go beyond specific gadgetry. This section focuses on common approaches to creating online courses.

One approach is creating instructional media. Basic principles can help instructional designers make more effective choices about when and how to create instructional videos regardless of the tool. Mastering a few of those practical approaches can mean the difference between spending time and effort to create instructional videos and spending time and effort to create instructional videos that learners actually watch.

Another common approach is collaboration through online group projects. Some approaches to collaboration work better than others, and some work better in specific contexts. Collaboration can also take place through one of the most used tools in any institution's learning management system: the discussion forum. Designers can share practices with faculty that can encourage meaningful discussions, from writing appropriate discussion prompts to knowing how to encourage learners to dig deeper to understanding where assessment rubrics are helpful and where they reduce discussions to artificial exchanges of post-and-run comments.

Finally, a practical consideration to online teaching that is far too often overlooked reduces the course to the status of a glorified correspondence course. You still have to teach online courses. You have to engage with your learners, creating and maintaining your presence as an instructor. The sense of presence learners have can make and break online courses. A great structure, thoughtful objectives, and authentic assessments can go a long way in creating a meaningful learning experience, but if learners do not believe there is a real person on the other end of that screen who is advocating for their success, then that sense of isolation can derail even the best designed courses.

Conclusion

The role of the instructional designer is to work in partnership with instructors and help equip them with tools and learning frameworks to create meaningful learning experiences. We design courses in ways that engage the learners and always work to serve the learners above all other competing priorities.

When drafting the scope of this book, I kept returning to the consideration of what new instructional designers need to know to get their footing when working with faculty to create online classes. I have recruited friends and colleagues from across the United States to talk about different areas of our work. They are experienced designers with specific areas of expertise, all doing instructional design work at public and private universities, research universities, liberal arts universities, and everything in between. Our work looks different depending on the specific context of the specific institution, but there is a common core in how we approach our work. Everything we do during course design and implementation is founded on always being research based and learner centered. I have been an instructional designer for about 10 years, first working in a teaching center and then with an educational technology group. It took some time to get my feet under me, and I had a lot of help along the way. I hope this book can help you find your footing as an instructional designer in higher education.

References

Bailey, A., Vaduganathan, N., Henry, T., Laverdiere, R., & Pugliese, L. (2018). *Making digital learning work: Success strategies from six leading universities and community colleges.* Boston College Group.

Brame, C., (2016). *Active learning.* Vanderbilt University Center for Teaching. https://cft.vanderbilt.edu/active-learning/

Cavanaugh, J. K., & Jacquemin, S. J. (2015). A large sample comparison of grade based student learning outcomes in online vs. face-to-face courses. *Online Learning, 19*(2). http://dx.doi.org/10.24059/olj.v19i2.454

Doyle, T. (2011). *Learner-centered teaching: Putting the research on learning into practice.* Stylus.

Intentional Futures. (2016). *Instructional design in higher education: A report on the role, workflow, and experience of instructional designers.* https://intentionalfutures.com/static/instructional-design-in-higher-education-report-5129d9d1e6c988c254567f91f3ab0d2c.pdf

Morris, S. M. (2018, April 12). *Instructional designers are teachers.* Hybrid Pedagogy. http://hybridpedagogy.org/instructional-designers-are-teachers/

Nilson, L. (2010). *Teaching at its best: A research-based resource for college instructors* (3rd ed.). Jossey-Bass.

Weimer, M. (2013). *Learner-centered teaching: Five key changes to practice* (2nd ed.). Jossey-Bass.

PART ONE

INSTRUCTIONAL DESIGN IN ACADEMIA: A COMMON CORE WITH DIFFERENT APPROACHES

A savvy instructional designer should be able to identify an instructor's individual teaching approaches and help structure experiences that reflect these in the design.

I

CONCIERGE MODEL

The Full-Service Guide

Rayne Vieger

Graduate school has wrapped up, and you've landed a new job as an instructional designer in a concierge-style instructional design office at a large university. You know you'll be supporting instructors in the design and development of fully online and hybrid courses from start to finish. You know that you'll also be in charge of training instructors on best practices of online learning and on educational technologies. You've just been assigned your very first project, a fully online undergraduate history class, working with an instructor who has taught on campus for more than 15 years but is brand new to online learning. How do you go about initiating this project? How do you bring the instructor onboard and collaborate together? What role or multiple roles do you play in this process? What does it even mean to work in a concierge instructional design office?

The concierge model of instructional design consists of a full-service, highly personalized approach where designers guide instructors throughout the entire process of online course development, much like a hotel concierge guides a guest in an unfamiliar city (McCurry & Mullinix, 2017). This may include "reviewing, editing, making recommendations, training, building learning objects, consulting, course reviews, quality assurance reviews, and course deployment" (Outlaw & Rice, 2015, p. 1). One of this model's strengths is that it takes into account that "teaching is a highly individualized and personal process" (McCurry & Mullinix, 2017, p. 1) and that instructors have varying levels of familiarity and readiness for online teaching. Although there is often a defined course development process in place with associated quality standards, actual collaboration in the model is tailored to instructors' individual needs and skill levels. In this model, instructors still retain full ownership and decision-making for the course; however, it is the designer's responsibility to build the course and ensure that instructors are trained to teach it.

How the Concierge Model Begins

Often the collaboration in this model begins with an initial intake meeting so that the instructional designer can meet the instructor; introduce the course development process, which is likely unfamiliar to the instructor; and ask questions about the instructor's overall vision for the course. This is also a great opportunity to build trust with the instructor, especially if they are new to developing online courses and are hesitant about the work ahead. Imagine that in your initial meeting with the undergraduate history instructor, she comments that because she's juggling a lot, she's concerned about completing the entire course development before the start of the quarter. The instructor says that she usually develops her course along the way in her face-to-face classes, and she'd rather take the same approach in her online course. This comment may elevate your anxiety a bit, but you know that as her instructional designer, it's your job to advocate for her students by explaining why we fully design ahead of time while assuaging her concerns by providing course development tools to make the process less daunting.

As a strategy for framing the online course development process and setting the stage for the requirements of your work together in that initial meeting, consider providing a schedule that breaks up the development into manageable deliverables. This is a helpful way to allow the instructor to visualize the overall process and keep the course development on track to achieve a fully developed course prior to the start of the quarter. This time line may not be contractual, but at the very least it adds accountability and eases instructors' anxiety about their ability to complete the work along with all their other responsibilities. No matter how you map out the time line, be sure to emphasize that although the process can require extensive time to plan and create course elements, you will be there as a guide and supportive presence throughout.

Roles and Responsibilities

Instructional designers often take on a number of roles, which can vary depending on other support services available at their institution. Examples include pedagogy expert, educational technology adviser, media designer, trainer, project manager, and course builder. As a designer working in this model, you should determine which of these roles you will play and which will be played by others in the organization to ensure that instructors receive full support when developing their course.

Similarly, it's helpful to identify instructor roles in this model, including which tasks instructors will be required to complete and what their level of ownership or decision-making may be. This is an important piece of bringing instructors onboard, especially if they are new to the university and are accustomed to other course development models that give them more freedom and also responsibility in the process. Instructional designers should consider how they intend to communicate these roles to ensure a positive and productive collaboration that sets development expectations and conveys the value of collaborating with a designer while also respecting instructors' experience. One method is to create a handout for faculty outlining roles and responsibilities of each person (Table 1.1). Designers can lean on such documentation to help frame how they will collaborate as a course design team and communicate the specific expertise they bring.

Backward Design

In the overall structure of the concierge model, designers also employ a curriculum design model to help faculty plan and design their specific course. One model commonly used in higher education instructional design is backward design or, very simply, designing with the end result in mind and the learner always at the center.

Wiggins and McTighe (2005) boil down the approach to three main stages:

> Stage 1: Identify desired results
> Stage 2: Determine acceptable evidence
> Stage 3: Plan learning experiences and instruction (pp. 17–18)

In this design model, instructional designers work closely with instructors to first identify the major outcomes for the course and the key things learners should be able to do after completing the course. This conversation may take place in either an initial planning meeting or a course development workshop. From there, designers ask questions to identify the type of acceptable evidence instructors need to see to determine if learners have successfully met the outcomes and the assessments that will deliver this evidence. Once

TABLE 1.1
Instructional Designer and Instructor Responsibilities

Course Development Phase	Instructor Responsibilities	Instructional Designer Responsibilities
Course development workshop	Enroll in and complete course development workshop, submit required course assignments	Facilitate course development workshop, provide feedback, help shape plans for the course to optimize the online asynchronous format
Collaboration	Collaborate ongoing with instructional designer and media developers	Collaborate ongoing with instructor, bringing in other personnel as needed (e.g., media developer, videographer, testing coordinator)
Course content, accessibility	Provide course content to instructional designer on agreed-on time line (e.g., outcomes, assessments, activities, discussion prompts, readings, videos, tutorials, lectures, demonstrations)	Build content into learning management system, ensure that materials are posted in an accessible format using research-based best practices in course design
	Incorporate feedback and modify course content as needed to meet research-based best practices in course design	Provide recommendations to instructor about online class management that factors in design (e.g., how to set up asynchronous discussions to ensure they are robust)
Copyright and permissions	Track and cite origins of any third-party content to obtain copyright permission if needed	Request copyright permissions
		Consult with librarian about fair use determinations and assist instructor with documentation
Administrative tasks	Order textbook, schedule course, and request a learning management system course site	Remind instructor about housekeeping tasks as needed
Course finalizing	Review course build in learning management system, proofread	Explain learning management system functionality, and ensure instructor is comfortable with the controls
Ongoing support and continuous improvement	Request help or training on technology and online pedagogy as needed	Provide help, resources, and training as needed
	Document ideas for future iterations, collect student feedback on design	Assist with course revisions based on student and instructor feedback

Note. From Ecampus Course Development Agreement by S. Riggs (2019). Copyright 2019 by Oregon State University Ecampus. Internal document, adapted with permission.

outcomes and evidence are clearly defined, designers help instructors craft online learning experiences and instructional materials that support learners meeting these outcomes. As Wiggins and McTighe (2006) note, this is often a time-intensive process that, although seemingly intuitive, may feel unnatural to some, and a quality course design is dependent on allowing enough time to work through any questions an instructor has.

This model may differ from the design approach faculty use in their face-to-face courses, such as designing for content coverage. Suppose the undergraduate history instructor tells you she is used to starting with the course textbook when designing a class, then mapping assessments to the textbook content that she needs to get learners through in the 11-week quarter. In this situation, it's helpful to acknowledge that this is a tall order and a lot of pressure for her to get through centuries of content in 11 weeks. Moving away from the sheer amount of content she needs to cover and instead focusing on what she hopes learners will be able to do as a result of her class will help narrow the scope to only the essential content that will support her students' learning.

That being said, although backward design is presented as a linear approach, it can be cyclical or nonlinear, too (Wiggins & McTighe, 2006). The important piece of the process is to ensure that the three main stages of learning outcomes, instructional activities, and assessments are aligned throughout the course architecture, regardless of how you navigate through them. This ensures that learners have the necessary support to master outcomes, and it ensures that instructors are achieving what they set out to do when they first envisioned the course.

Once instructional designers have helped instructors craft a big picture plan of their course, they begin filling in the gaps by assisting instructors in sequencing modules. This may involve a template to guide faculty through the creation of aligned weekly introductions, outcomes, learning content, activities, assessments, and all the learner support and context needed to guide students through the module. This collaborative back-and-forth process spans the bulk of the development cycle (Li & Shearer, 2005).

Instructors as Partners

Subsequent collaboration with instructors will vary depending on the instructor's availability and location as well as the overall workload of designers. Some collaboration can occur asynchronously; however, much can be accomplished by sitting down face-to-face with instructors in regular meetings so that designers can help instructors draw out key details about their course design, problem solve, and advocate for the needs of online learners.

Regular meetings also allow time for designers to build relationships with instructors, which is an important and ongoing part of the job (Campbell et al., 2009; Outlaw & Rice, 2015). As Campbell et al. (2009) note, "Instructional designers find themselves working with novice instructors who may enter projects with reasonable levels of confidence about their content, but who are much less confident about their teaching skills" (p. 650). It's the designer's job to help bolster this confidence by building "an atmosphere of trust that relates to the client's professional identity, and that can be nurtured throughout the design process, and sometimes long after" (p. 650). For more information on ways to build this trust with instructors, see chapter 3.

Project Management

A concierge instructional designer may act as the project manager in charge of keeping all assigned course projects on track. Even if designers aren't trained in traditional project management methodologies, there are tools and strategies designers can employ to manage their own time as well as keep track of all assigned projects. According to Kumar and Ritzhaupt (2017), "to manage the course development cycle at their institution, [instructional designers] . . . [can] create a schedule to manage the courses and the roles played by different team members" (p. 382). Because instructional designers are often acting as a single point of contact in this model, it's important for them to be detail oriented and excel at communicating to all internal and external collaborators.

Project time lines and processes will vary at each university, and the academic schedule (e.g., semester or quarter) can further dictate how much time instructors have to design courses. Li and Shearer (2005) describe a 2-week cycle used at Pennsylvania State University, where in a 6-month period, instructors deliver a new week of content every 2 weeks, and designers build the content for the instructor before the next 2-week milestone. This project management cycle encourages regular contact with the designer and spaces out deliverables to keep projects on track. Outlaw and Rice (2015) describe a six-phase project cycle that includes an initial meeting, content delivery, training, building, quality assurance, and revision. In the content delivery phase, the designer provides templates for weekly content, and after the instructor delivers the content on paper, the designer provides feedback, and the instructor revises accordingly. This process continues until the content is in a final format, and at that point the designer begins to build the content in the learning management system (LMS). Instructors are often not used to being project managed, so designers should be mindful of their large role in keeping the project on track within tight time lines.

Training and Development

The online modality presents unique design and delivery challenges, even for the most experienced instructor. According to Outlaw and Rice (2015), instructors are "educated experts in their content discipline; however, they may not particularly know how to integrate and/or teach with technology, nor are they usually trained to transform classroom strategies into an online format" (p. 2). Instructional designers play a key role in helping instructors adopt new educational technologies that support an engaging, learner-centered online experience by focusing on training opportunities that integrate technology and learning theory. As Kumar and Ritzhaupt (2017) gathered from their survey of higher education instructional designers, designers are often in charge of training instructors on pedagogy and "demonstrating LMS functionality or technologies during workshops" (p. 383).

Whether or not designers also formally share responsibility as a technology and pedagogy trainer, training is infused in all their interactions and meetings with instructors. McCurry and Mullinix (2017) recommend that designers focus on improving the course rather than developing the instructor. Over time, as instructors and designers build rapport and they collaboratively make decisions about the course design, instructors will develop new skills that improve their future ability to design online courses.

Course Design Standards

Many institutions have a rubric containing a minimum set of standards that course designs must meet to run online, and the instructional designer is often a safeguard to educate and ensure compliance with these standards. These include federally mandated items, such as accessibility, copyright, and regular and substantive instructor interaction, and pedagogical design standards, such as active learning requirements and student-to-student engagement. Designers may use the rubric as a tool to coach instructors throughout the course design process and also as a quality assurance metric at the end. Quality Matters and the Online Learning Consortium are two examples of organizations that support online course quality by providing ready-made course design rubrics detailing standards that promote learner-centered course designs. The rubrics published by these two organizations are backed by current research, so everyone can feel confident taking them off the shelf and integrating them into their design process. Quality Matters (2018) is considered the gold standard in many instructional design offices and offers a course review and certification process for institutions willing to pay for this service. The Online Learning Consortium's Open SUNY Course Quality Review (OSCQR) Course Design Review Scorecard (shown in part in Table 1.2) is openly licensed, meaning institution administrators may adapt the rubric to fit their own unique needs, adding, removing, or modifying standards as needed.

Whatever rubric is used at a particular institution, it's also helpful to understand how closely instructors must stick to, or be able to deviate from, that set of standards. Standards that are too flexible may lead to quality concerns in a course, and standards that are too rigid may impede creativity or innovation. To ensure that the process is personalized and each course design is as unique as the instructor designing it, it's important to be flexible to ensure that an instructor's preferred pedagogical approach and teaching philosophy shine through in the course design. A savvy instructional designer should be able to identify an instructor's individual teaching approaches and help structure experiences that reflect these in the design.

Ongoing Support

After a course development project wraps up, instructors often need help in the initial weeks of the quarter or semester (Kumar & Ritzhaupt, 2017). It's helpful for designers to monitor the course at this time to intervene in any major design issues they can assist with. Ideally, designers should also gather formative feedback on the efficacy and impact of the new design from learners and instructors; however, as Kumar and Ritzhaupt (2017) observed in their study of instructional designers working in higher education, this rarely happens in practice. Feedback during the delivery phase, however, can be a useful tool for future iterations and continuous improvement.

TABLE 1.2
Instructional Designer and Instructor Responsibilities

OSCQR Course Design Review

OLC Quality Scorecard Suite: OSCQR 3.1

Need ideas? See standards below for explanations and examples from https://OSCRQC.suny.edu	Sufficiently Present	Minor Revision	Moderate Revision	Major Revision	Not Applicable	Action Plan
Estimated time needed for revision:		1/2 hour or less	1/2–2 hours	2+ hours		
1. COURSE OVERVIEW AND INFORMATION						
1. Course includes Welcome and Getting Started content.						
2. An orientation or overview is provided for the course overall, as well as in each module. Learners know how to navigate and what tasks are due.						
3. Course includes a course information area that deconstructs the syllabus for learners in a clear and navigable way.						
4. A printable syllabus is available to learners (PDF, HTML).						
5. Course includes links to relevant campus policies on plagiarism, computer use, filling grievances, accomodating disabilities, etc.						

(*Continues*)

Table 1.2 *(Continued)*

6.	Course provides access to learner success resources (technical help, orientation, tutoring).					
7.	Course information states whether the course is fully online, blended, or web-enhanced.					
8.	Appropriate methods and devices for accessing and participating in the course are communicated (mobile, publisher websites, secure content, pop-ups, browser issue, microphone, webcam).					
9.	Course objectives/outcomes are clearly defined, measureable, and aligned to learning activities and assessments.					
10.	Course provides contact information for instructor, department, and program.					

Note. The OSCQR Rubric, Dashboard, and Process are made available by Online Learning Consortium, Inc. (OLC -https://onlinelearningconsortium.org/) under the Creative Commons Attribution 4.0 International License (CC By 4.0). To view a copy of this license, visit https://creativecommons.org/licenses/by/4.0/. The OSCQR Rubric, Dashboard and Process were originally developed by the State University of New York, through the Open SUNY® Online Teaching (https://innovate.suny.edu/onlineteaching/). Open SUNY and its logo are registered trademarks of the State University of New York. Content also from Quality Matters (2018).

Ongoing support can vary depending on the institution's specific processes, resources, and personnel. Nevertheless, it's helpful to determine the designer's role in the ongoing support of course projects after they launch. As a designer's portfolio of courses grows, it will be difficult to maintain the same full-service approach on all past projects. This requires a delicate balance of maintaining positive instructor relationships with past collaborators, while also moving to the next group of instructors who need help now.

Considerations and Recommendations

The concierge model is not perfect, so designers should be aware of some of the challenges they may face. For example, the model requires designers to juggle a number of job duties, some of which they may lack formal training in, which can often be surprising and potentially overwhelming. From the instructors' perspective, the model can be challenging because instructors may not have the same level of control they would like to have or are accustomed to, so it may be hard for them to share or hand over certain responsibilities to their designer. From the institutional perspective, this model is expensive, especially if instructors are being compensated for their time and the organization has a robust team of instructional designers. The financial model needs to be carefully planned to ensure it's sustainable in the long term. Despite these challenges, there are many efficiencies and benefits in this model, especially if institution administrators want to support a high volume of work while also maintaining quality.

One tip to help concierge instructional designers thrive in this context is for them to know how and when to choose their battles. There is always more work to be done, and there is always room for improvement. Designers may be tempted to focus on all the things that are wrong with a design or the ways an instructor rejected their advice. The thing to remember is that instructors are still learning. They come to this process from all different levels of motivation and readiness, and it's perfectly acceptable for them to take small steps to improve their craft. Being too heavy handed may damage relationships or trust, so designers should focus instead on continuing the conversation in the long term, during which instructors will come back to iterate and improve their course.

Summary

Concierge instructional designers fulfill a number of essential roles to provide instructors with a full suite of services when designing their online and hybrid courses, such as pedagogy expert, technology adviser, trainer, project manager, and course builder. These roles ensure that instructors can spend their time focusing on the content rather than worrying about the technical implementation. In this model, designers guide the course development process from start to finish, typically using backward design to help faculty align learning outcomes, instructional activities, and assessments that will provide the necessary framework for students to succeed. Designers often use an established set of design standards and templates to maintain quality and consistency across courses, while also differentiating their approach and suggestions to ensure that each course feels personal to the instructor developing it. Instructors still retain full decision-making in this model, so if they are not ready to adopt a designer's suggestions, instructional designers should instead focus on maintaining a culture of trust and encouraging continuous improvement. After all, many instructors are approaching online learning for the very first time and are still learning about this new modality, so designers should remember to meet all instructors where they are in their unique learning process.

References

Campbell, K., Schwier, R. A., & Kenny, R. F. (2009). The critical, relational practice of instructional design in higher education: An emerging model of change agency. *Educational Technology Research and Development, 57*(5), 645–663. https://doi.org/10.1007/s11423-007-9061-6

Kumar, S., & Ritzhaupt, A. (2017). What do instructional designers in higher education really do? *International Journal on E-Learning, 16*(4), 371–394. https://www.learntechlib.org/primary/p/150980/

Li, D., & Shearer, R. (2005). Project management for online course development. *Distance Learning, 2*(4), 19–23.

McCurry, D. S., & Mullinix, B. B. (2017). A concierge model for supporting faculty in online course design. *Online Journal of Distance Learning Administration, 20*(2), 6. https://www.westga.edu/~distance/ojdla/summer202/mccurry_mullinix202.html

Online Learning Consortium. (2019). *OLC OSCQR Course Design Review Scorecard (version 3.1)*. https://onlinelearningconsortium.org/consult/oscqr-course-design-review/

Outlaw, V. & Rice, M. (2015). Best practices: Implementing an online course development & delivery model. *Online Journal of Distance Learning Administration, 18*(3).

Quality Matters. (2018). *Specific review standards from the Quality Matters higher education rubric, 6th edition.* https://www.qualitymatters.org/sites/default/files/PDFs/StandardsfromtheQMHigherEducationRubric.pdf

Wiggins, G., & McTighe, J. (2006). *Understanding by design* (2nd ed.). Pearson Education.

Consultations are things, much like writing effective learning objectives, that look really easy from an outside perspective but actually take far more skill than is obvious to an onlooker.

2

CONSULTATION MODEL

At the End of the Day

Jerod Quinn

Online teaching is still a relatively new world as more higher education instructors are by choice or force beginning to teach online. Instructional designers working in the consultation model collaborate with instructors to enhance their skill level and comfort with course design, online pedagogy, and authentic assessments with the goal of improving online learning for all learners (Border, 2012). It's about moving the needle forward on the effectiveness scale, not about crafting the illusionary perfect course where everyone always learns everything and is always excited to do so. It's also about connecting and empowering instructors. As Stommel (2019) states,

> At many institutions there's a problematic divide between instructional designers and teachers—between those building online courses and those teaching them. Expert teachers need to build their own online courses or we need to create closer collaborative relationships between teachers and instructional designers. (para. 13)

The consultation model is about building those closer collaborative relationships.

This chapter walks through approaches of consultation-based instructional design in online courses in higher education. Although many, dare I say, even most instructional designers have no formal training in consultations, it is a method that can be learned and developed. This chapter begins by looking at the criteria that make effective consultations, then discusses what designers do during consultations and how to lean into backward design in small and large projects. Finally, the chapter concludes by exploring how to end a project by preparing instructors to move forward on their own and how the designer can use that consultation experience to intentionally build professional expertise.

The Consultation Method

Consultations are things, much like writing effective learning objectives, that look really easy from an outside perspective but actually take far more skill than is obvious to an onlooker. They require a broad and deep skill set that combines pedagogical knowledge, active listening, reflection, problem-solving, critical thinking, and the ability to rapidly find solutions to real teaching and learning problems. Designers have to learn how to quickly build trust with a total stranger before tackling more than surface-level course design tensions. So if consultations are such slippery creatures, why take that approach in the first place? Because instructors are more likely to change their teaching and learning practices when evidence and approaches are discussed with a consultant (Brinko, 1997). As instructors continually work to be more learner centered in their teaching, ultimately the learners are the ones who benefit. This is the core value of the learner-centered instructional designer: They consult with instructors because it helps create more meaningful learning experiences. Instructors bring to the consultation a deep knowledge of the course subject and a picture of who their learners are. Designers bring an understanding of how people learn online and a practical, evidence-based approach to course design. That collaboration of shared expertise is where the possibility of creating something new and innovative emerges. But what makes an effective consultation?

Border (2012) discusses seven factors that are the essentials of effective educational consultations. Although they are specifically about educational or faculty developers, the first four of these factors, which regard the work of instructional designers in consultation contexts, are choosing the consultation method, establishing trust and roles, clarifying procedures and norms, and agreeing on goals of the session.

Choosing the Consultation Method

Choosing the consultation method means deciding on how to approach working with the instructor. For designers, a typical approach is the collaborative process model in which "the consultant and client may identify, diagnose, and suggest solutions to problems; however, it is the client's prerogative to accept or reject the consultant's contributions" (Brinko, 1997, p. 6). In this context, the instructor is ultimately responsible for what happens after the consultations. The role of the designer in setting up these conversations is to create an environment in which the instructor is relaxed enough to explore new ideas, identify issues, and generate creative solutions with the designer for online courses (Border, 2012). As with creating learner-centered online courses, the consultations designers facilitate need to be instructor centered, not consultant centered.

Establishing Trust and Roles

Establishing trust with instructors is the biggest reported tension instructional designers face in their profession. Part Two of this book is devoted to building trust, but there are some aspects of building trust that are directly connected to the consultation model. Consultants can lay the groundwork for a trusting relationship by being supportive of the instructors, meeting them where they are in their teaching, and emphasizing that the meetings will be nonevaluative (Border, 2012). Course design is difficult work, and instructional designers damage the trust-building process by *shoulding* the instructor, or couching their advice as a correction, as in, "You should have done this instead, that's the wrong approach," or "Your assessments should read like this." Every decision made in the course has to be something the instructors are empowered to act on, because at the end of the day, it's their course, not the instructional designers' course. That's the freedom of the consultation model: There's never a question of ownership. When that ownership is made explicit at the beginning of the consultation process both parties can relax, knowing that the designer is there to support and encourage the instructor, not to commandeer the course. By acknowledging the instructor's goals, choices, and expertise, the designer can build on the strengths of the instructor to make the course a compelling experience for the instructor and the learners.

Clarifying Procedures and Norms

An instructional designer is a systematic problem solver. Designers excel at creating processes of investigation and evaluation, planning the smallest of details, and making sure no assessments are without a rubric. The goal of clarifying procedures and norms is to communicate those processes clearly with your team. Take a few minutes to explain the instructional design model that will be used and specify roles and expectations as the team works through that model. Discuss deadlines for work that happened during the meetings but also in between a series of meetings. Working with a designer is likely to be a new experience for instructors as will designing an online course. There is no need to be mysterious about the process.

Agreeing on Goals

Nothing can take the wind out of a designer's sails faster than an instructor in the middle of a meeting saying, "Wait. What I really need is just some help figuring out how to put my PowerPoint slides on the LMS." It's vital to be in agreement with everyone involved on the scope of the project. The designer may be ready to craft something brand new that will revolutionize online education, whereas the instructor is more interested in learning how to make instructional videos learners will actually watch. Often the programs departments create have specific outcomes, and it's important to go over those with the instructors to make sure their goals match the program's goals. But what about those more casual conversations? How to you establish goals over a cup of coffee?

Designers can still set goals for one-off consultations. If instructors ask to meet with the designers, there's often a tension they want to address. Goals for a one-off meeting could be as simple as naming that tension, crafting a few options to address that tension, and deciding on a time to report the results. These casual meetings are vital for designers; they are small risks the instructor can take in testing if the designer proves to be a helpful ally. If designers can demonstrate their value in these small consultations, the instructors begin to see that the designers' role is to bring options, identify strengths and weaknesses, and craft practical plans for improving teaching and learning (Border, 2012). So now that we know some of the components of an instructional design consultation, what do we actually do during a consultation?

Backward Design

There are many instructional design models, from the ubiquitous analysis, design, development, implementation, and evaluation (ADDIE) model to the more agile successful approximation model (SAM). These different models often work well in certain contexts. ADDIE is likely the most well-known model in instructional design but is rarely adhered to in educational contexts where analysis is usually a less formal triage approach, and proper evaluation is a rarity. SAM is a more collaborative and iterative approach, but its prototyping and redeveloping cycles just don't cooperate with semester-based time lines that university environments are typically bound to. When it comes to online course design, the vast majority of instructional designers in higher education use backward design. Backward design can feel a bit like old hat, but its endurance in higher education is because of its simplicity and flexibility. It can be adapted to most university contexts and circumstances.

Backward design is often described as designing a course where the results are the priority as opposed to the content. It is all about taking your learners where you really want them to go while making sure all your course components are aligned with that goal. The objectives, assessments, and learning activities all work together to move the learners to the same destination. And although it is easy to just start revising content from previous semesters or looking at the chapters of the textbook as a beginning point, using backward design means beginning at the end.

Objectives: Where Are You Going?

For instructional designers, the end is never the end of the semester. That's too short term. When I talk with instructors about where to begin, I adapt Fink's (2003) approach and say to them,

> Two years after this course is done, grades have long been submitted, and the learners have moved on to other classes or their future professions. What do you want your learners to still know or be able to do from your class? What do you want them to still be using long after their time at university is done?

These are difficult questions. Most instructors are not accustomed to thinking beyond the 16 weeks of a semester. But if instructors can internalize that question of what they want their learners to still know and be able to do 2 years after the course ends, it moves them beyond the pressure of what content they need to cover. I've been asking the 2-years-after question for 10 years, and I have never had a faculty member answer, "Two years after this course I want learners to have read and remembered all 16 chapters of their textbook." I have noticed that by framing the ultimate goals of the course in a time outside the semester, it gives the instructors permission to design their course to provide what they ultimately think is valuable for their learners.

Fink (2003) shares a framework for creating objectives that can be particularly useful in online course design. His taxonomy of significant learning asks instructors to create learning objectives for their courses in the following categories:

- Foundational knowledge, knowledge about the subject, and the ideas and theories connected to it
- Application, skill development and putting new knowledge to work in context
- Integration, connecting the course content to other areas of life
- Caring, developing interests, feelings, and values
- Human dimension, learning to interact with others and yourself more effectively
- Learning how to learn, the skills and strategies to continue learning after the course ends

Not many instructors I work with end up wholeheartedly adopting Fink's taxonomy and crafting objectives in all six categories, but I continue to use this taxonomy for a specific reason: This taxonomy challenges instructors to think about objectives in richer ways beyond content coverage. I remember speaking with a physics instructor about objectives for her introductory physics course and saying, "What would it look like for your learners to care about your content?" She was quite stunned at that question, and then said it would change the whole dynamic of the classroom. I replied, "What can we do throughout your course to demonstrate that physics is something worth caring about?" There is power and freedom in thinking about objectives beyond content coverage.

Assessments: What Would It Look Like to Get There?

Although objectives help instructors know where the course will take the learners, assessments provide opportunities for learners to demonstrate they can meet those objectives. Online classes have a hearty amount of quizzes, discussion forums, and papers as assessments and for good reason; these common assessments work well as measurement tools. But the designer is in a prime position to push the conversation past the obvious cast of assessment characters by asking the instructor what the work of the discipline looks like in the real world and then emulating that. These assessments that mimic the deliverables of the profession are often called *authentic* assessments. They can be more motivating to learners, because they not only look more like real-world work than an online quiz but also often require more autonomy and creativity to complete. Learner autonomy and creativity combined encourage motivation.

I used authentic assessments in an online laboratory course redesign. The course was connected to environmental practices, and one of the instructor's objectives was to help her learners see how their personal choices affect the environment. We designed the water conservation lab for the learners to measure and gather data on their own water use. Afterward, they made a change, continued to gather data, and then compared the results. For this online course the learners were not bound to the 3-hour time constraint of a traditional laboratory space; instead they gathered their water usage data over weeks. In an evaluation at the end of the course, one of the learners stated, "I really liked that part . . . where you could do the labs and they're really related to you. . . . I learn more from that than if it was in a random laboratory sink or something." This lab assessment was meaningful because it was authentic to the discipline and authentic to the lives of the learners.

Learning Activities: What Do the Learners Need?

The last step in backward design is figuring out the kinds of instruction and preparation the learners will need for them to do well on assessments. As mentioned in the introduction of this book, the learner-centered instructional designer works to create active learning experiences over passive ones. Although there certainly is a role for lecture videos in online courses, that is not the only method of preparing learners. The designer collaborates with the instructor to uncover methods of getting the learners to interact with, not just observe, the instructional artifacts. An engineering instructor I work with likes to say, "If I can get my learners to see fluid mechanics outside the classroom, I win." He asks his learners to take pictures of where they see fluid mechanics in the real world and explain the engineering principles at work in what they are seeing. These aren't formal assessments but activities to get his learners to make connections in content from inside the class to life outside class.

Ending the Conversation

In the consultation model, ending an online course design project can often feel anticlimactic. Designers spend months working with instructors to craft and build an exciting learning experience, and just like that, it's over. The design decisions made and the effectiveness of the course after learners have been able to experience it over time should be evaluated. But practically speaking, that rarely happens. Systematic follow-ups and evaluations are few and far between. Quite frankly, the need for instructional designers to jump into the next course design project is often the more pressing priority than evaluating the outcomes of just finished projects. Many teams do a course structure evaluation, like Quality Matters (https://www.qualitymatters.org), but those types of rubrics aren't designed to evaluate the teaching of the course or the effectiveness of the instructional design decisions. When a course is complete, we generally just shoo those little birds out of the nest to make room for new eggs.

But in the consultation model, the designers share their course design tool kit with the instructors. The instructors don't leave empty-handed; the designer has walked them through the process of crafting meaningful objectives. They have collaborated on authentic assessments and weighed the pedagogical risks of their choices. Instructors have learned how to use the technology and how to navigate the online learning environment while seeing evidence-based research about how learning works. In a productive consultation approach, the instructor leaves after having experienced a bit of an apprenticeship in instructional design. The fact is, from that point on the designer isn't needed as much. And when designers do hear back from instructors, they often ask deeper instructional design questions or ask about a new idea as opposed to asking about specific quiz settings in the learning management system.

Building Expertise

Although the conversation may end for the instructor when the course goes live, it doesn't have to end for the instructional designer. This is when designers can intentionally evaluate their own efforts and work to build expertise, which for an instructional designer isn't so much about how to master a specific technology (although that may be part of it) but to develop efficient ways of solving course design problems (Tiberius et al., 2012). The thing about expertise is that it takes time and deliberate practice to develop, and it is always tempting to move directly on to the next project without reflection or hesitation. Few individuals engage in deliberate professional practice in their careers, but having obtained just enough skill to appear competent in most familiar situations they instead lean on well-worn activities and approaches in their practice (Ericsson, 1996). Instead of building new skills and tools, designers tend to keep the same handful of tricks and apply them to every situation without considering if it's the right tool for the job: "Hey, let's put a rubric on it!"

No set routine equates to deliberate practice for an instructional designer. The routine will vary based on the individual approach to the work and how individuals reflect on their actions. Chapter 11, "Metacognition and

Reflection," offers more details on the value of metacognition and reflection in learning but also in the life of an instructional designer. The following is my approach to practicing expertise in my daily work.

During meetings with instructors I take lots of notes by hand in a small notebook. I feel that having a screen between me and the instructor impedes our connection. I write down my interpretations of how the instructor feels about shared ideas. Finally, I make notes on the next steps to complete before our next conversation. That's my approach to data collection, but data alone won't build expertise. I schedule times in my week, literally blocking out time on my calendar, to type my handwritten notes and document the project. This gives me a chance to reflect on what happened during the meeting, note ideas I need to research, and craft a plan of action. This reflection time is crucial to expanding my skills and identifying my own knowledge gaps. I repeat this cycle throughout the life of the project. Every 2 weeks I read through my current notes and then develop my task list for the next 2 weeks. At the end of the project I have documentation that explains why we made the decisions we made for the course. I read through the whole thing, reflect on the choices made, and wrap it all up into a PDF file in case I need to refer to it in the future. My approach has evolved over time, and your approach may be completely different. The important factor is to have a process that pushes your practice forward. As consulting instructional designers, our expertise develops as we commit ourselves to lifelong learning in our discipline, building our capacity and efficiency in progressive problem-solving as opposed to always returning to familiar approaches (Tiberius et al., 2012).

There's one last step in the consultation process after the project has ended: Celebrate! The continual pace of instructional design work does not encourage practitioners to pause to celebrate the good work they have done. Celebrating the end of a project is an intentional choice to acknowledge hard work and to fight against long-term burnout that comes from unrecognized progress. Brown (2018) discusses how pausing to recognize good work fights burnout and combats a sense of foreboding:

> We've got to stop and celebrate one another in our victories, no matter how small. Yes, there's more work to be done, and things could go sideways in an hour, but that will never take away from the fact that we need to celebrate an accomplishment right now. (p. 84)

Conclusion

Instructional designers working in the consultation model are responsible for creating a consulting environment in which the instructors know they will be supported in their course design and pedagogy. Designers build trust by defining their role as nonevaluative while asking questions that encourage instructors to deeply explore their teaching process. They clarify procedures for projects and demystify the experience of systematic course design. Together with the instructor, they collaboratively set goals for consultation and conversation.

As the project ends, designers may or may not have the opportunity to evaluate the effectiveness of their design decisions, but they can intentionally reflect on their work and practice developing expertise. The instructors have been shown many tools to further develop their own instructional design experience independently and move forward to teach the course, which was developed in collaboration. The instructor has full ownership of the course in the consultation model, whether it goes on to win online course design awards or ends up faltering as a learning experience. Again, at the end of the day, it's the instructor's course. Designers have labored to empower, encourage, and challenge the course design and pedagogy of the instructors, and they know their work is to support teaching and learning, not to own it. To be a learning-centered instructional designer is to empower others' teaching and learning.

References

Border, L. L. B. (2012). Understanding and implementing effective consultations. In K. T. Brinko (Ed.), *Practically speaking: A sourcebook for instructional consultants in higher education* (pp. 8–15). New Forums Press.

Brinko, K. T. (1997). The interactions of teaching improvement. In K. T. Brinko & R. J. Menges (Eds.), *Practically speaking: A sourcebook for instructional consultants in higher education* (pp. 3–8). New Forums Press.

Brown, B. (2018). *Dare to lead: Brave work, tough conversations, whole hearts*. Random House.

Ericsson, K. A. (1996). The acquisition of expert performance: An introduction to some key issues. In K. A. Ericsson (Ed.), *The road to excellence: The acquisition of expert performance in the arts and sciences, sports, and games* (pp. 1–50). Erlbaum.

Fink, L. D. (2003). *Creating significant learning experiences: An integrated approach to designing college courses*. Jossey-Bass.

Stommel, J. (2019). Online learning: A manifesto. In S. M. Morris & J. Stommel (Eds.), *An urgency of teachers: The work of critical digital pedagogy* (pp. 60–64). Hybrid Pedagogy.

Tiberius, R. G., Tipping, J., & Smith, R. A. (2012). Developmental stages of expertise in educational consultation. In K. T. Brinko (Ed.), *Practically speaking: A sourcebook for instructional consultants in higher education* (2nd ed., pp. 161–163). New Forums Press.

PART TWO

BUILDING FACULTY TRUST: YOU CAN TRUST ME, I'M A PROFESSIONAL

Approach your interactions with instructors with the perspective that they have the agency to find the best solution to their needs. You are simply facilitating the process to help them decide.

3

BUILDING TRUST

Creating a Climate of Trust, Care, and Collaboration Among Instructional Designers and Faculty

Christopher Grabau

Instructional designers often create collaborative partnerships with instructors in nearly every aspect of their work. Whether helping roll out new technologies, designing new courses, or coaching instructors on learning pedagogies, the collaborative opportunities instructional designers create with instructors can benefit all learners (Kumar & Ritzhaupt, 2017). However, one of the biggest challenges designers face is a lack of understanding and trust in the instructional design process. A survey examining the role, workflow, and experiences of instructional designers in higher education found that the number one obstacle designers face in their work is lack of instructor buy-in (Intentional Futures, 2016). Another study found that only one in four faculty members reported working with an instructional designer for online and face-to-face courses (Jaschik & Lederman, 2018).

Although most instructional designers report that they work with faculty multiple times a day (Intentional Futures, 2016), some of the resistance and lack of trust is a familiar component of our work with instructors. Perhaps one reason for this resistance is that our interactions with instructors often do not happen under ideal circumstances. With increasing institutional demands combined with a lack of time and resources, instructors can experience feelings of stress or disempowerment that threaten even the best intentions for collaboration.

To build trust and develop impactful collaborative interactions with instructors, we as instructional designers must be prepared to ask a number of tough questions regarding our work. How do we as consultants, designers, or specialists treat others? Do we offer scripted responses, watch the clock, or turn to the same bag of tricks? Or do we model a more humanistic, person-centered orientation to our work that considers the uniqueness of the individual by striving to make visible the authentic talents, perspectives, and teaching styles of every instructor we strive to serve? To do so, I believe we must strive to intentionally model behaviors in our work that support learner-centered teaching in a manner that is genuine, free from judgment, and empathetic to needs of instructors.

This chapter shows how a person-centered focus in instructional design can help encourage a better sense of trust between designer and instructor while also inviting opportunities for true collaboration. I address how an environment of empathy, genuineness, and congruence can invite collaboration through the use of interpersonal competencies or soft skills. I also discuss some of the essential competencies and strategies needed for successful collaborative partnerships between faculty and instructional designers. Finally, I offer a few practical tips to help instructional designers work with purpose, empathy, and kindness to facilitate deeper and more gratifying educational experiences for academia.

Person-Centered Teaching

As an educational developer with a background in counseling and educational psychology, I often think about the work of Carl Rogers, one of the founders of humanistic psychology. Rogers is often celebrated for creating client-centered therapy, a model for therapy that places value on the individual by emphasizing empathy, acceptance, and genuineness toward the client (Patterson, 1977). Over time, Rogers's client-centered approach toward therapy expanded to other helping professions, including nursing and education (Patterson, 1977; Rogers et al., 1989; Rogers & Freiberg, 1995).

Like his work in psychology, Rogers's views on education seek to fully support the education of the whole individual (Rogers & Freiberg, 1995). His person-centered perspectives for education complement many of the earlier constructivist learner-centered perspectives, which trust learners' ability to actively construct knowledge while learning in an accepting and empathic educational climate.

Although instructional design is not therapy, the deeply personal exchanges that can take place during instructor consultations can be supported by some of the skills Rogers discusses in his person-centered approach to education (Rogers & Freiberg, 1995). Rogers seemed to think so as well.

In a brief statement, Rogers (1967) succinctly articulated his beliefs regarding the importance of the relational aspect of teaching:

> We know that the initiation of such learning rests not upon the teaching skills of the leaders, not upon scholarly knowledge of the field, not upon curricular planning, not upon use of audiovisual aids, not upon the programmed learning used, not upon lectures and presentations, not upon an abundance of books, though each of these might at one time or another be utilized as an important resource. No, the facilitation of significant learning rests upon certain attitudinal qualities that exist in the personal relationship between the facilitator and the learner. (p. 2)

Rogers's (1967) comments beautifully underscore that the teacher-learner relationship is the bedrock everything else is built on. Teaching is not just a pedagogical approach, a body of knowledge, or a technology; it is a relationship with others through the lens of an educational experience.

With that in mind, I believe that faculty do not come to us for teaching tools, instructional strategies, or course design tips. Instead, what they really come for is to find ways to make a greater connection to learners. The relationship aspect of learning is at the heart of their desire to seek our support. The tension they feel in their work is not only the lack of instructional clarity or efficiency but also the difficulty of teaching in a manner that elicits authentic connections with their learners.

So how do instructional designers help build trust and support instructors at the same time? One way is to consider instructional design work as a learner-centered profession that complements the humanistic theoretical perspectives found within Rogers' views on education (Patterson, 1977; Rogers et al., 1989; Rogers & Freiberg, 1995). Just as we champion learner-centered experiences in the classroom so too must we model learner-centered experiences in our interactions with instructors. We must not only possess a cache of tools to help instructors learn new approaches to teaching but also strive to develop several interpersonal skills that can help us connect with instructors. These skills can humanize our work as instructional designers. They help facilitate a relational orientation to working with instructors that not only creates trust but also respects their own relationship while still prioritizing students' relationship with learning.

Building Collaborative Partnerships With Faculty

Often called soft skills, interpersonal skills are an essential tool kit instructional designers need to build trust and rapport with faculty. They can include good listening skills, cultural sensitivity, open-mindedness, and flexibility. In a learner-centered collaborative partnership, these skills are as important as the technical and methodical competencies often associated with instructional design (Ritzhaupt & Kumar, 2015). They are often associated with not only good practices related to serving others but also a deliberate enactment of kindness, empathy, and care that serves the greater good of working for others.

A phenomenological student study by Richardson et al. (2018) investigated what constitutes effective collaborations between an instructional designer and faculty. Their study found six elements to building collaborative partnerships with instructors. Although these elements are good examples for any professional practice, they also help identify a few concrete approaches designers can consider to create greater connections with faculty. Each of the following elements prioritizes the faculty-designer relationship, encourages dialogue, and helps articulate professional roles:

1. Building trust and rapport
2. Actively listening
3. Acting as a coach and facilitator
4. Remaining open-minded and flexible
5. Setting boundaries
6. Considering cultural and academic differences

The following is a brief summary of each element and a few ways to incorporate them with the hope that they will help you build trust and develop greater collaborative partnerships with instructors.

Building Trust and Rapport

Although building trust and rapport may seem like an obvious start when working with instructors, how we build trust and rapport can be a bit of an art. Consider the following comment from an instructional designer:

> It's not enough that you are very knowledgeable in course curriculum design. If you cannot connect to faculty; if you cannot create that rapport and make them feel comfortable with you to really explore different options it's not going to work. It really doesn't, even if you have great collaborators; but if you don't create that space where the faculty feels excited and actually safe and these things combined, you're not going to have a productive collaboration and you're not going to have a productive consultation. (Richardson et al., 2018, p. 866)

There are many of ways instructional designers can build trust and rapport with instructors. First, taking time to get to know instructors as people is a great place to start. If meeting in a one-on-one consultation, slow down and briefly greet them first before addressing their needs. Show you care for the person, not just the process. Actively listen to the instructors' responses and demonstrate that you understand where they are coming from.

When meeting faculty for the first time, I often try to find a place to meet where they are the most comfortable. However, most prefer to meet in my office. As a result, I try to make sure my office is clean, my computer is closed, and my phone message notifications are turned off. I do this for two reasons. First, these actions are a subtle demonstration that their presence is my priority, and second, they help ensure that I am practicing confidentiality for other instructors who wish to meet with me.

When meeting instructors virtually, building trust and rapport can be a little trickier. One approach is to strive to be as organized as you would be in a face-to-face meeting. Promptly respond to emails and offer dates and times when you will follow up. Keep a log to track your responses and tasks. Also, don't be afraid to ask their preferred method of communication. Some instructors now prefer to use video conferencing for meetings. When doing so, consider using the same models for professional candor that you may encourage instructors to use when using online multimedia. Use conversational language, but speak with enthusiasm, make sure the video frame is free from distractions, face the camera, and make sure your audio is clear and easy to hear (Guo et al., 2014).

Actively Listening

One of the most important skills an instructional designer can use to build trust and rapport is to actively listen. Coined by Rogers (1989), the term *active listening* is often defined as a technique of listening when the listener and the speaker are actively communicating with one another. Active listening is an active and collaborative practice in which the listener demonstrates concern, paraphrases to show understanding, and uses nonverbal cues (nodding, eye contact, learning forward). Active listening can often be confused with verbal affirmations (e.g., "Uh huh, I see," and "Thank you"). Although verbal affirmations are important components of listening and conducting conversations, providing your full attention and emotional presence is the only way to demonstrate that you are actively listening during a conversation (Grogan, 2013; Richardson et al., 2018; Rogers & Farson, 1987).

Several skills can help a person become an active listener, but the most important skills are listening for total meaning, noticing and responding to feelings, and noticing all cues communicated by the speaker (Grohol, 2018).

Most people do not arrive with a fleshed-out outline of their needs. Therefore, it is important to consider not only the content of the communication but also total feelings or attitudes of the conversations. Next, have the courage to respond to feelings. In some conversations, the content is not as important as the feeling that underlies it. Strive to remain sensitive to the total meaning behind a conversation. Ask about what, specifically, they are trying to tell you. What does it mean to them? How do they see the situation?

Finally, note all cues. Remember that not all communication is verbal. Active listening requires awareness of more than the words being spoken. For instance, the way a speaker hesitates in speech, body language, or facial expressions can communicate a lot about feelings of apprehension, stress, or discomfort. Pay attention to the speaker's nonverbal cues to get a sense of their feelings about what they are communicating (Rogers & Farson, 1987).

Acting as a Coach and Facilitator

Maintaining teaching autonomy is an important value for most teaching centers. Teaching autonomy is linked to teaching motivation, job satisfaction, stress, and feelings of empowerment (Pearson & Moomaw, 2006). How we approach supporting instructors is a key component to building trust. Strive to respect others as they are, without judgement or evaluations. Rogers (1989) calls this perspective "unconditional positive regard" (p. 225). Approach your interactions with instructors with the perspective that they have the agency to find the best solution to their needs. You are simply facilitating the process to help them decide.

I have found that in some cases, simply giving people a chance to talk through their thoughts can be an extremely rewarding experience for the instructor. Because our consultations are confidential, I often remind instructors that our conversation is between the two of us and that we have the freedom to explore options. I remind them that this is their course, and we are only exploring their ideas.

When working with instructors on online course design or new learning technologies, I often preface our training with the goal that they should be able to perform each function without my help. I try to make it as hands-on as possible, guiding rather than showing. Sometimes I will simply sit beside them while they click the options on the computer screen to build course material. I often tell faculty, "It's just the two of us, give yourself permission to be a novice." I think this statement is important for two reasons. First, it relieves instructors from feeling they will make a mistake. Second, it also helps instructors see what a novice student may experience when working for the first time. My hope is that by assuring faculty that mistakes are not only okay but encouraged, I provide a space for trust and collegiality.

Finally, another way to empower instructors is to offer time for feedback on your work together. Surveying instructors to gather their input on your work together tells them their perspective matters. It opens a dialogue about their needs and may uncover some blind spots in your professional habits when working with others.

Remaining Open-Minded and Flexible

As the saying goes, "The best-laid plans of mice and men often go awry." Sometimes the realities of our work force us to abruptly change our plans, improvise, or abandon them altogether. An instructor may not be ready to implement a new idea or process. Additionally, an unseen variable may force you and the instructor to change your plans at the last minute.

When working with instructors on a new technology, teaching strategy, or course module, I often think through the potential risks involved with each situation. For example, an instructor wanted to incorporate an online polling tool into an online course. However, after spending hours discussing and planning how to incorporate the tool, the instructor admitted being nervous about doing it for the first time. As a result, we scaled back the amount of times the polling tool would be used, and we practiced the tool together until the instructor was comfortable using it alone. We even decided on a low-tech option for polling.

Don't be afraid to throw out the playbook every once in a while. Remain present as a guide, provide encouragement, and be patient.

Setting Boundaries

It is also important to communicate the scope of work you and the instructor will be doing together. A collaborative partnership can be flexible and open-minded, but it requires some boundaries to be productive. Be clear about what work you are willing do to and what work is beyond the scope of your relationship with faculty. There will always be moments when saying no to something is just as important as saying yes.

One easy way to set boundaries is to try to keep your meetings to a set amount of time. Time management is an important aspect of our work, especially when juggling multiple projects at once. If meetings are scheduled for an hour, limit them to an hour and ask to schedule another meeting if necessary.

Also, consider providing a statement of practice for your work for first-time meetings with instructors. The statement should provide the scope of your collaboration, describe some of the work you will be doing together, and tell faculty what to expect when working with an instructional designer. For example, my teaching center offers a statement of practice for a fellowship program that offers instructors an opportunity to design or redesign new courses. The statement describes the instructional designer's role, how the course design phase will be conducted, and how an instructional designer will support the implementation of the course. This statement is an excellent tool to start a conversation about the fellowship and also provides an opportunity to inform faculty about my work as an instructional designer (Reinert Center, 2014).

Considering Cultural and Academic Differences

As learner-centered instructional designers, we must remain conscious of how stereotype threats can inhibit educational environments. We all have to work to understand our own bias and strive to work from a deeper place of understanding and compassion. Strive to create an identity-safe working environment that invites all people to collaborate.

Also, keep in mind the differences in academic disciplines and organizational cultures. For example, instructors from a science discipline may have a different set of needs compared to instructors from humanities. Shulman (2005) defined these differences as "*signature pedagogies. . .* , types of teaching that organize the fundamental ways in which future practitioners are educated for their new professions" (Shulman, 2005, p. 52, emphasis added). Signature pedagogies include surface structures, which are concrete acts of teaching and learning (what learning looks like); deep structures or assumptions about how to impart knowledge (how teaching will be taught); and implicit structure or the attitudes, values, and beliefs associated with a discipline (Shulman, 2005). Work to become conversant in the different pedagogical approaches used in different academic disciplines. Do your homework before meeting with instructors, and be willing to ask questions.

Conclusion

To build trust and truly support instructors, we must consider the personal relationship between faculty and instructional designers. If we are truly striving to champion a learner-centered educational environment, we must approach our work with instructors in the same way we hope they will conduct themselves in the classroom. We must look at our collaborative partnerships as an opportunity to invite authentic support through deliberate attention and kindness. Furthermore, we must remind ourselves that working in support of others is a process more than a product, for "the good life is a process, not a state of being. It is a direction not a destination" (Rogers et al., 1989, p. 411).

References

Grohol, J. (2018). *Become a better listener: Active listening.* Psych Central. https://psychcentral.com/lib/become-a-better-listener-active-listening/

Grogan, J. (2013). It's not enough to listen. *Psychology Today*. https://www.psychology today.com/us/blog/encountering-america/201303/its-not-enough-listen

Guo, P. J., Kim, J., & Rubin, R. (2014). How video production affects student engagement: An empirical study of MOOC videos. In *Proceedings of the first ACM conference on Learning@ scale conference* (pp. 41–50). ACM Ed Board. Association for Computing Machinery.

Intentional Futures. (2016). *Instructional design in higher education: A report on the role, workflow, and experience of instructional designers*. https://intentionalfutures.com/insights/portfolio/instructional-design/

Jaschik, S., & Lederman, D. (2018). Faculty attitudes on technology. *Inside Higher Ed*. https://mediasite.com/wp-content/uploads/2018/11/2018-Faculty-Survey-Mediasite.pdf

Kumar, S. & Ritzhaupt, A. (2017). What do instructional designers in higher education really do? *International Journal on E-Learning, 16*(4), 371-393. Waynesville, NC USA: Association for the Advancement of Computing in Education (AACE). https://www.learntechlib.org/primary/p/150980/

Patterson, C. H. (1977). Carl Rogers and humanistic education. *Foundations for a theory of instruction and educational psychology.* Harper & Row. http://www.sageofasheville.com/pub_downloads/CARL_ROGERS_AND_HUMANISTIC_EDUCATION.pdf

Pearson, L., & Moomaw, W. (2006). Continuing validation of the teaching autonomy scale. *The Journal of Educational Research,100*(1), 44–51. www.jstor.org/stable/27548158

Richardson, J., Ashby, I., Alshammari, A., Cheng, Z., Johnson, B., Krause, T., Lee, D., Randolph, A., & Wang, H. (2018). Faculty and instructional designers on building successful collaborative relationships. *Educational Technology Research and Development, 67*(4), 855–880. https://doi.org/10.1007/s11423-018-9636-4

Ritzhaupt, A., & Kumar, S. (2015). Knowledge and skills needed by instructional designers in higher education. *Performance Improvement Quarterly, 28*(3), 51–69. https://doi.org/10.1002/piq.21196

Reinert Center. (2014). *The role of instructional developers in the innovative teaching fellowship*. https://www.slu.edu/cttl/docs/itf/id-statement-of-practice-2014.pdf

Rogers, C., & Freiberg, H. (1995). *Freedom to learn* (3rd ed.). Merrill.

Rogers, C. R. (1967). The interpersonal relationship in the facilitation of learning. In R. Leeper (Ed.), *Humanizing education* (pp. 1–18). National Education Association for Supervision and Curriculum Development.

Rogers, C. R., & Farson, R. E. (1987). Active listening. In R. G. Newman, M. A. Danziger, & M. Cohen (Eds.), *Communicating in business today*. D.C. Heath & Company.

Rogers, C. R., Kirschenbaum, H., & Henderson, V. L. (1989). *The Carl Rogers reader*. Houghton Mifflin.

Shulman, L. S. (2005). Signature pedagogies in the professions. *Daedalus, 134*(3), 52–59. https://doi.org/10.1162/0011526054622015

One of the most challenging tasks is communicating expectations to instructors, helping instructors understand the scope of instructional designers' work.

4

HAVING BOUNDARIES

I'm Not Your Personal Assistant

Olena Zhadko

This chapter explores how instructional designers can work to define and enforce professional boundaries of their often nebulous titles and responsibilities. Advice to supervisors about how to protect their instructional designers' time is also offered.

If you have the title *instructional designer*, you might frequently get the following requests:

> Would you be able to help me record my videos? Can you assist me with building my course? Can you upload my syllabus? I think I need to make my course materials accessible, can you do it? I can't access my email on my phone, can you help?

Your work experience, education, personality, workload, and institutional context (i.e., whether other units are available to offer support) could potentially define how you respond to such inquiries. When you are new to your role, you might be inclined to say yes to every request, attempting to help all instructors. After you gain some experience, you might feel frustrated when asked to troubleshoot, as your primary role is not tech support. By establishing professional boundaries, you can become more effective at your job and improve your work-life balance. In this chapter, we explore various aspects of an instructional designer's role and offer several practical strategies on how to establish boundaries and not become someone's personal assistant.

Defining the Role

Let's start with defining the role and responsibilities of an instructional designer. According to Intentional Futures (2016), there are about 13,000 instructional designers in the United States, and for the most part, instructional designers "bridge the gap between faculty instruction and student online learning" (p. 2). According to the report, the role of an instructional designer can be broken down into four major categories of responsibilities:

1. Design instructional materials and courses, particularly for digital delivery
2. Manage the efforts of instructors, administration, information technology, other instructional designers, and others to achieve better student learning
3. Train faculty to use technology and implement pedagogy effectively
4. Support faculty when they run into technical or instructional challenges (para. 3)

I have worked closely with a number of instructional design professionals while facilitating the Instructional Design Mastery Series, an online professional development program offered by the Online Learning Consortium (OLC, n.d.) and accordingly have observed some similarities as well as differences in the scope of instructional designers' work. In some cases, the scope of work responsibilities is as different as if the instructional designers worked in different industries. In one case an instructional designer offered consultations on course design, in another the instructional designer oversaw multimedia and video production, and in another the instructional designer was primarily an accessibility or an open educational resources (OER) expert. Lujean Baab, a senior director of learning experience design at Virginia Tech University, said that "roles for those designing responsive and effective learning experiences are evolving rapidly" (EDUCAUSE, 2018, p. 2). EDUCAUSE (2017) names instructional designers as one of the seven leading professions evolving in higher education. Christopher Blaire Bundy, from the University of Wisconsin, said that "instructional designers need to assume leadership roles to help design and deliver impactful learning online, in the classroom, and with community and/or outside agencies" (EDUCAUSE, 2017, p. 1). Institutional context and the size of the unit that houses instructional designers define the scope of their work.

As an instructional designer, to help you plan how to handle instructor requests that might be outside your primary work responsibilities, you may want to separate your work projects into the four major categories of responsibilities previously mentioned and see how your day-to-day activities align with the defined categories of responsibilities (see the introduction for a review). Consider reviewing your job description as part of this exercise and then discuss your results with your supervisor to ensure that your day-to-day activities are in alignment with your role.

What Do Instructional Designers Do?

Instructional designers often lead instructor professional development programming in the form of consultations, workshops, institutes, and other program formats. In many cases, these initiatives introduce instructional concepts and practices related to teaching and learning, often with technology. When instructors experience technical difficulties, they are inclined to contact those who led professional development initiatives for support. Although some requests might be somewhat technical, these tech support meetings can also provide an opportunity to discuss the pedagogy being applied.

It is easier for an instructional designer to design, manage, train, and support when instructors know what kind of support and services instructional designers can provide. However, most instructors are simply unfamiliar with the role of an instructional designer. Not every institution has instructional designers, and the scope of their work might vary from institution to institution. According to a survey, only 25% of instructors have worked with an instructional designer to design an online or a blended course, and only 22% have worked with an instructional designer on a face-to-face course (Jaschik & Lederman, 2018). For instructional designers to be effective in their roles, and for instructors to make the most out of the support from instructional designers, it is essential to ensure that instructors know what designers can offer.

Although other units on campus (besides the office that offers instructional design support) might be able to assist instructors with technical issues, it is important to remember that instructors might feel frustrated or possibly less likely to innovate in teaching and learning when they have to contact different offices for support. Thus, it is important for offices providing instructor development and instructional technology support to work collaboratively to ensure that instructors can easily get answers to their questions and get the help when they need it.

Saying *No* and Redirecting

When instructional designers are asked to assist with tasks outside the scope of their responsibilities, they can politely point out that it is not something that they normally do, assist instructors with the matter at hand, and advise where to find support in the future. There is always a way to say *no* while still being helpful. After all, being an instructional designer is a service profession requiring a customer service approach. Blair Goodlin, an instructional designer at Manhattan College, related how he handles such requests for support:

> I say "no" but still offer support. I offer to help find someone on campus who does perform the service that the instructor needs. Or, I offer help to the instructor but I will simply tell the instructor, "That's something instructors typically do themselves." It's helpful to know other people at the institution who could potentially do the work that the instructors are asking about. For example, you can tell the instructor to inquire if the department's administrator can do the work, or suggest that the instructor ask the chair for a graduate student to do the work. That way, if they insist on not doing the work, at least you have given them yet another option. (Personal communication, August 8, 2019)

As long as instructors get answers to their questions in an efficient manner, it might not matter to them which unit is providing that service. It is important for instructors be familiar with the skillset instructional designers have and services of support they can offer so that instructors can make appropriate requests. There are several strategies that instructional designers can apply to empower instructors to make the most of their expertise and ensure that instructors request support that is within the scope of an instructional designer's work.

Meeting Preparation, Resource Sharing, and More

There are many things designers can do to prepare instructors for a productive meeting. First, create a template email message to remind instructors about what they should do before a scheduled meeting. This email can offer several reminders about logging into the system, securing the wireless connection on their device, and running computer updates. You can also name the office that can provide support if needed. Second, when working on course design and development, ask instructors to send you a course syllabus or provide access to the course site prior to the scheduled meeting. When an institution has a process in place for course development, use a course development schedule or time line to facilitate the process and communicate with instructors.

When helping instructors prepare to teach online, be sure to share useful resources. Your school might already have compiled or developed resources to share with instructors, from guidelines to instructional guides, tutorials, and more to help instructors plan their courses and teach intentionally. These resources can help instructors plan ahead and prepare before the semester starts. An instructional designer often becomes responsible for driving instructors to these resources, sharing updates, and sending these as a follow up.

In addition, instructional designers can empower and teach instructors how to find a solution to a problem when instructional designers are not available. The idea is to create opportunities for instructors to become less dependent on the support from instructional designers. One simple technique is to encourage instructors to take advantage of the power of a simple web search, by modeling and showing how to quickly find an answer to an instructor question while you are working with them. Be prepared for some hesitation or doubt when you first suggest it, show instructors how to find answers to a technical question, and offer contextual commentary and instructional design expertise to help instructors apply what they learned.

Furthermore, consider offering professional development programming for instructors on topics for which you are often contacted to provide support. For example, a 2-week workshop or a week-long institute on teaching online can create a learning path and introduce instructors to institutional resources, refresh their knowledge, and provide an opportunity for them to get started and learn more about your instructional design expertise (that certainly goes beyond technical support!).

These simple strategies can lead to a decrease in troubleshooting inquiries and ensure that instructors consult instructional designers primarily for support with instructional design matters.

Productivity: Meetings, Scheduling, and Time

Not all meetings are created equal. In some cases, a meeting is simply an opportunity to check in and share updates, usually scheduled for about 30 minutes. A working meeting requires more time, 45 minutes but no more than 90 minutes to help everyone stay focused and on task. When planning a meeting or a working session with a large group, you might end up using breakout sessions, and scheduling time accordingly to ensure that the meeting is productive.

Draft an agenda for the meeting, even if it is an informal one sketched at the beginning of your meeting. As the meeting begins, ask the instructor what questions they have. Although there might not be enough time to answer all questions, listen and take notes, and then prioritize. Explain how you would like to proceed. First, address questions that do not take much time to answer, and then identify and delegate those that another unit or colleague can assist with. Then, note that you will follow up on the items that need to be researched further. Do all this before diving into the items to be addressed during the meeting. It is not uncommon for instructional designers to work on multiple projects simultaneously and have very busy days. To avoid burnout, schedule at least 15 minutes between meetings to catch a breath, stretch, hydrate, or just take notes on what needs to be done for a follow-up or in preparation for another meeting. Remember to build in some time for drop-ins and "open doors" periods when instructors can stop by and ask for advice or assistance. It is important to have a balance between scheduled meetings and unscheduled or unplanned events (as those will certainly appear on your calendar when you least expect them!). To be efficient, instructional designers need to review their calendar at the end of the week and for the week ahead and plan accordingly to not overbook themselves with tasks they can teach instructors do on their own or that can be delegated to other colleagues or units.

Ensure the Success of Your Team

When supervising an instructional design team, there are a few things you can do to protect their time. For example, review each team member's job description, especially if you are new to your role, noting what you already know about their specialized skill set. This will refresh your memory and assist with required annual performance reviews. Note that the scope of instructional designers' work continuously evolves, in some cases due to the changes in institutional priorities or advancements in educational technology and in other cases simply as things become outdated. For example, instructional designers hired 15 years ago might not be performing the tasks they were hired to do. As a result, those supervising instructional designers need to stay up to date and redefine the scope of work for their instructional design team and each instructional designer individually. Additionally, supervisors are responsible for ensuring that instructional designers are not stretched too thin as more and more instructors become aware of their expertise and skill set. Brian Udermann, director of online education at the University of Wisconsin–La Crosse, offered the following three approaches he takes in his leadership role:

> [First,] whenever possible I make it clear to instructors what our instructional designers (IDs) do and do not do. I think when instructors know what IDs do, they tend to respect the time of our IDs and don't attempt to stretch the boundaries and ask our IDs to do things they shouldn't be doing.

[Second,] when one of our IDs comes to me and tells me about a scenario where an instructor asked them to do something they shouldn't have (this just happened yesterday!), I always support our IDs and will often have a follow-up conversation with the instructor to make sure they are clear on what it is our IDs do.

[Third,] I see our IDs doing something that is a bit outside of their job description, I ask them about it. If it is something they want to do—for example, if they were asked by an instructor to help or do something that would not be required of them, but they (our IDs) want to help out, that is certainly okay. But in this case, I usually reinforce the idea that they don't need to be doing things outside of their job descriptions for instructors if they don't want to. (Personal communication, August 18, 2019)

An instructional design supervisor can apply a few simple strategies to ensure that the instructional design team is effective and efficient. First, communicate to instructors what they can expect from instructional designers. Second, establish clear channels of communication with your designers so that they won't be hesitant to communicate with you as their supervisor. And third, like any good supervisor, engage with your team by being present and empowering them to succeed.

Inform Your Audience

One of the most challenging tasks is communicating expectations to instructors, helping instructors understand the scope of instructional designers' work, making the most of their instructional design expertise, and introducing instructors to other support services available on campus. Jaschik and Lederman (2018) emphasized the central role of instructional designers in creating and building quality courses in academia and the lack of awareness among instructors about what instructional designers actually do. In my current role as director of online education at Lehman College, City University of New York, I continuously communicate the support services and programming we offer to instructors and leadership, including support for teaching and learning, instructional and course design, and teaching with technology. Before the start of every semester we send an email to all deans, chairs, and instructors with updates and reminders. You can adapt the template in Figure 4.1 to meet your office needs.

Sending an email with essential information on whom to contact allows you to reconnect with instructors prior to the start of the semester and connect with new instructors. You will be able to introduce or remind instructors

Figure 4.1. Essential communication template.

Dear Colleagues,

Technology is not the only way to be innovative in your teaching—a change in instructional design or the adoption of new approaches to teaching and learning can increase student engagement and enhance student learning while refreshing your own teaching experience as well.

We invite you to contact the Office of Online Education for support. (We can meet with you in person and online.)

For assistance with designing your course and making the best use of our learning management system (LMS; Blackboard) and other educational technologies to support student learning, contact our educational technologist and instructional designer [Insert name and contact info].

For questions and consultation on teaching online, hybrid and technology-enhanced courses, and best practices on digital pedagogies, contact our faculty development consultant designer [Insert name and contact info].

For questions about online education, please contact our director of online education [Insert name and contact info].

For other support services, please contact the Division of Information Technology. For questions about email, log-in, hardware and software technical assistance, please contact the Information Technology Center by telephone at [Insert phone number], email at [Insert email address], or in person at the help desk in [Insert location].

For technical questions about our LMS (Blackboard), contact our [Insert name of your LMS] administrator [Insert name and contact info].

We appreciate your dedication to creating engaging learning experiences for our students.

---

of the available resources and services. It is also important to inform and keep up to date program directors or department chairs, sometimes also new to their roles, to ensure they know where to direct their instructors for support.

In conclusion, instructional designers play an essential role in supporting student success by assisting instructors with teaching and learning matters. By applying a few simple strategies in your role as an instructional designer, you can continue to be efficient and effective. Those in leadership roles can also be of assistance and enable instructional designers to succeed.

References

EDUCAUSE. (2017). *7 things you should know about the evolution of teaching and learning professions.* https://library.educause.edu/resources/2017/3/7-things-you-should-know-about-the-evolution-of-teaching-and-learning-professions

EDUCAUSE. (2018). *7 things you should know about the 2018 key issues in teaching and learning.* https://library.educause.edu/resources/2018/1/7-things-you-should-know-about-the-2018-key-issues-in-teaching-and-learning
Intentional Futures. (2016). *Instructional design in higher education.* https://intentionalfutures.com/insights/portfolio/instructional-design/
Jaschik, S., & Lederman, D. (2018). Survey of faculty attitudes on technology. *Inside Higher Ed.* https://www.insidehighered.com/news/survey/conflicted-views-technology-survey-faculty-attitudes
Online Learning Consortium. (n.d.). *Instructional design mastery series.* https://my.onlinelearningconsortium.org/s/community-event?id=a1Y1U000001DMBYUA4#Program_Overview

You want to educate your professors without creating a power struggle. Battling may help someone's ego, but ultimately the student suffers the collateral damage of such a fight.

5

FACULTY PERSPECTIVES

A (Love?) Letter to Instructional Designers

Tom Warhover

Dear designers,

I have this exercise in my journalism semantics class that helps students understand the different ways people perceive words and images. I call it "Painting the Roses Red," because I like *Alice in Wonderland*, the animated Disney version, when the deck-of-cards guys dance around the white rose bushes with buckets of paint while singing (Geronimi et al., 1951).

Here are the instructions to students: Get a paint swatch from your favorite paint shop, show it to five people, record how they name the color, and describe their emotions about it.

Participants will describe the paint swatch color Salute as red or maroon or burgundy. They will associate it with blood or stop signs. Kentucky Blue (where do paint companies get these names?) is called blue steel or sea green or desaturated teal. One student wrote in her report that a participant teared up while describing the color because of the memories it evoked. "While each person looked at what was on its face a universal symbol," the student wrote, "they each held something personal inside that was the lens they were looking through."

The exercise rocks my students' worlds. They write responses that begin with phrases like "I never knew" or "I never thought." The course objectives promise to improve critical reading and thinking. So I can pretty much do a mic drop after this exercise and go home. Except this is the second week of class, and there are six more ahead.

It's my course all right. That's my name on the class schedule. But it's not my creation, not solely. And it's certainly not my exercise. My department's instructional designer came up with the color swatch activity while we were moving through my course modules.

By that time we had worked together enough that she felt she could just shoot straight, stating bluntly that this was "a great exercise" instead of hedging with a bunch of nonthreatening adjectives and adverbs.

After struggling through course objectives, after sifting through Bloom's taxonomy for the right active verbs, after taking a class in how to teach an online class, after suspending disbelief that teaching online would be an utter bore and a poor substitute for the real thing, after all that investment, I still wanted to scream (insert favorite 11-year-old voice), "You're not the boss of me!" I had spent a lot of time reading and thinking about the content I wanted for the course. I had reviewed syllabi and lessons from the revered professor who taught the class before me, and he had reviewed the syllabi and lessons from the revered professor who created the course decades ago. Here was this instructional designer who knew nothing about the materials telling me what I should do.

Fortunately for me and for my students, my temper tantrum stayed in my head.

You probably know this already: Professors can be the worst students. After all, we know everything. We've been teaching for years. We were hired because we are experts in our field. Why do you want us to do things this way? Why can't we just teach the way we always have in the classroom? Did we mention we are experts? That we have degrees and worldwide experience and awards? We don't want to change.

Why can't we just paint the roses red?

Your professors might come to online teaching through ambition; the writing is on the digital wall, and smart academics looking for career advancement would do well to notice. They might come in a departmental forced march, victims, they think, to tyrannical deans and administrators driven by budgets or new visions and made worse by consultants and surveys. They might be among the professorial retirees who accepted buyouts or were forced out but still have something to give.

It doesn't matter. It is all the same task for you, dear instructional designers, and it has nothing to do with technology or pedagogy. Your first task is building trust. Well, no. Your first task is creating a human-to-human relationship. Well, yes, but really, your job is even more simple and challenging: You must look that belligerent instructor in the eye and still be able to smile.

Learning to Learn

Take heart: When it's all over and done, the instructors will like you. The fall survey of more than 2,000 instructors by *Inside Higher Education* (2018) shows that 70% of those who worked with instructional designers thought they "improved the quality of their courses" (p. 6). The same number said designers "shared helpful tips and effective practices for fostering student engagement" (p. 15).

The following are other numbers of note from *Inside Higher Ed* (2018):

- 44% of respondents had taught an online class, up from 30% five years earlier
- 45% had professional development about course design
- 25% had help from an instructional designer in an online or blended course

You might be depressed by how few instructors have benefited from your expertise. The reasons vary and include a lack of communication in administrators of universities. We need to get the word out that what you do matters. Other respondents to the *Inside Higher Ed* (2018) survey viewed online learning as inferior, and one third acknowledged that online courses could be equivalent to in-class learning. (See the introduction for more on how to respond to the argument that online equals inferior learning.)

My initial approach to online learning was this: I couldn't teach it if I hadn't experienced it. I was in a foreign land, not particularly excited to be there but willing to keep an open mind. So I enrolled in Online Teaching Foundations, taught by Jerod Quinn. (Check the cover of this book if the name sounds hauntingly familiar.)

Quinn smiles a lot in his writing. He's definitely sneaky in the way he provides constructive criticism wrapped with a Socratic approach. He stays positive. My undergraduate professors and my professional journalism colleagues started with what was wrong with my idea or plan or essay or story while occasionally giving the most oblique of attaboys, things like, "Well, this doesn't suck." Quinn had me on my heels from the outset. Eventually I adopted this approach in my semantics class. I try to celebrate even the most lame-brained submissions before asking questions and giving nudges to get the students on the right track, and, by golly, it seems to have made an impact (Benson, 2016).

We spent the first week of the course sharing our thoughts on the work ahead in the class and in our teaching. It seemed like too much time for an 8-week class. But we know that the best part of any class, including and maybe especially online, is the discussion between students and teacher. Introductions matter more in online classes. In fact, a quantitative study by Martin and Bolliger (2018) found that "students rated the icebreaker discussion as the most important" (p. 216) strategy in learner-to-learner engagement. That first week becomes critical in establishing the rest of the course, not just for students, as I would learn later, but also for the instructor reading those thousands of words. You can tell when students are writing for the assignment versus writing for their fellow students.

Quinn's introduction assignment came with a parable about three bricklayers—one laying a brick, one building a wall, one building a cathedral, and a challenge: What did I want to get out of this course? I needed to build all three: a cathedral, because this class didn't exist online before; a wall, because there were no objectives or outcomes listed; and a brick, laid one at a time with each lesson of the course.

I also announced my skepticism. There is a common phrase in journalism: If your mother says she loves you, check it out. The idea is that assumptions should be left behind when you research and report a story. It's not unlike the mentality of my friends in the hard sciences: We need to test ideas before saying, yep, that makes sense. Facts are friends here. Researchers like to know the pedagogy is backed by research. At the same time, we're humans, and we can be influenced just like anyone else through a conversation with a bitter or fearful colleague. A debate won't do. Instead, as you deal with instructors, acknowledge and embrace their need for skepticism; the alternative is blind trust or blatant rejection. Skepticism can too easily lead to cynicism, a much harder hurdle to overcome.

Another journalism adage: Design follows content. You can't design a gorgeous print newspaper page that doesn't match the content in mood, importance, urgency, and other factors. (You might be more familiar with "Form follows function," a more universal maxim.) You can imagine my skepticism, then, when I learned that instructional designers start with outcomes and goals and objectives. I lump them all into this question asked by my semantics class design partner: What do you want your students to know at the end of the class? I thought I was prepared, having taken Quinn's class on how to approach online learning. Still, it seemed foreign, uncomfortable. I wanted students to know the material from the class. We don't really need to discuss outcomes, do we?

We did, and we do.

The questions forced me to think hard. What I really wanted was for my students to read more critically and write more intentionally. It didn't really matter if 2 years from now they couldn't remember whether some politician's statement was a strawman logical fallacy or a special pleading; what mattered was whether the warning bells went off in their heads when they heard the statement. It didn't matter whether they could attribute the idea that you can never enter the same river twice (the river changes, and you also change both times) to Heraclitus; what mattered was for them to recognize the impermanence of language and other symbols.

That was a big moment for me. I had to acknowledge that many of my practices as a teacher were unintentionally reinforcing old paradigms like encouraging student strategies for getting an A rather than learning for the sake of knowledge and understanding.

Concentrating on outcomes is important. But your instructors will probably say it's hard to start with outcomes. It is simply foreign to the way we learned in school and the way we pass along our knowledge as teachers.

To be fair to instructors, instructional design carries the danger of all areas of expertise: the specialization of language. It might be important to differentiate among goals and outcomes and objectives. Your job as instructional designers, though, is to start where your teachers start, even if you don't end there. You must be the linguist translating the language of instructional design into either the language of the particular expert (science folk, say, versus humanities professors) or at least a layperson's language. Similarly, I imagine most professors will bristle if you start with a form and say, "We have to fill this out." You can get there, eventually, but forms can feel like make-work, not creative design of topics intrinsically important to the people who teach them.

To be fair to instructional designers, you really are experts, and some instructors don't understand that your strategies and tactics are based on a body of work of best practices and research on how people learn. I'm not suggesting you dumb down your work or offer design-light suggestions. You know things I don't. And yet, "Often faculty don't take us seriously," an instructional designer wrote in the comments section of an *Inside Higher Ed* article, "even though many of us have advanced degrees in education or years of work experience in instructional design" (beeethousand, 2017, para. 1). I don't believe this is something you can fix alone. It takes some serious cheerleading from above. The deans and provosts of the world need to get out front and show your value.

One-on-one conversations between instructors and designers can be tricky. You want to educate your instructors without creating a power struggle. Battling may help someone's ego, but ultimately the student suffers the collateral damage of such a fight. As we developed the journalism semantics course, my instructional designer would repeat often: "This is your course, Tom." She was reaffirming my role as the content expert. After all, I'm the one who had to make it work—in other words, who had to live with the results of the design. At the same time, she demonstrated design expertise over and over through suggestions and ideas like the Painting the Roses Red assignment.

French politician Alexandre Auguste Ledru-Rollin has been credited with the saying, "There go the people. I must follow them, for I am their leader," and a variation of this has also been attributed to Mahatma Gandhi. You are the leader when it comes to designing a course, even if you must lead from behind.

Learning to Teach

I've taught my online journalism semantics course four times now, enough to know that it's working even as we continue to tweak assignments. Students have cited the discussions in evaluations, which have pleasantly surprised me, such as:

- "Tom . . . engaged and encouraged us to foster relationships with one another despite this being an online class."
- "Definitely was easier to connect with Tom online than in some in-person classes."
- "The group discussion aspect of the class was cool. I liked bouncing ideas and opinions off one another."

The credit is misplaced. The interactive nature of the course didn't just happen. It was designed that way. Making me look good was just a side benefit.

I still have worries about the class. Can students game the course without doing the readings? Sometimes it feels as if they are simply pinging off other students rather than adding their own ideas and opinions. Are they really interested and involved in the discussions or simply making a good show of it? Is everyone participating? Is anyone pissed off by me or their colleagues or the content?

Then again, those are the same concerns that nag at me with other classes.

I have begun incorporating some of my instructional design lessons into my in-seat seminar in advanced reporting. The following are some of the challenges:

- It's already highly successful, at least according to the course evaluations (We could have a long discussion about their merits.) and anecdotally. Do I risk eroding that success by making these changes?

- Most of an 85-minute class is off script. I ping off students' blog posts, and we go deep on fears, hopes, dreams, and frustrations in reporting stories. How do I incorporate that spontaneity into the highly structured methods of course design?
- The class is predominantly lab work, writing stories for a community newspaper, and only 25% of students' grades are based on our seminar portion. How do I get buy-in from the lab instructors, who are professional editors?

Small hurdles, really, that don't prevent me from asking important questions. What do I want my students to know and experience that will help them a year from now? How can I align one week with another and with the goals of the course? How can I be more explicit in my teaching?

At the end of my Online Teaching Foundations course, Quinn had us create postcards. It's a cool assignment, by the way. Rather than, or in addition to, a longer essay or assignment, the student creates a postcard with a photo or illustration and adds just a few words to illustrate a point. Mine is a good summary of not only where I was at the time but also what I continued to experience while implementing and refining my work.

My postcard was presented as a series of tweets (OTF in the first tweet refers to Online Teaching Foundations):

First reaction: Learning outcomes? Objectives/outcomes aligning with every activity? OTF or WTF? #dazed

Then: Oh, so maybe student perception might be valid when they say they haven't been taught what we know was covered.

And: Content drives design. Alignment ALSO drives design. Everything is connected.

Finally: I'm all in.

Teaching to Teach

I hope you'll create more teachers who are all in, too. Remember, designers: Relationships, not technology or pedagogy, are your biggest challenge. Forget about all the smart techniques and tools you want to convey. Forget about the fact that you know more than the professor in front of you when it comes to how to teach. Look for the human being, who might be mad or scared or, like me, simply ignorant. Listen, and then listen some more, and then:

- Stay positive: Lead with a celebration of your instructors' steps, no matter how small. Consider the critique sandwich: Begin with positive feedback, add suggestions for change, and end with a positive thought.
- Show students the power of introductions: It's counterintuitive for an instructor to invest a lot of time that's not directly related to content. You know how critical that first module can be.
- Acknowledge that starting with outcomes is hard: Instructors weren't brought up that way. But you can help them envision the student as being more than a vessel for downloading information. Ask them, what do you want your students to know 2 years from now? What do you want them to be able to do with that knowledge?
- Embrace their skepticism: The academy is built on a bedrock of skepticism. Acknowledge your instructors' need to test assumptions and turn their own assumptions into questions to be tested. Online learning is inferior, they say? Hmmm, well, let's take a look at that.
- Don't get caught in the weeds. What might be the language of instructional design to you could be undecipherable jargon to your instructors. What's a module except a set of lessons, after all? Eventually we'll catch on to the lingo. But break out a worksheet as the first thing you do and you'll have a professor fleeing or fighting.
- Lead from behind. I'm sure your work has been compared to coaching. Maybe. But there are lots of famous, highly paid coaches out there who are bigger in reputation than their players. That's not you, dear instructional designers, much as I wish it were. You are most successful when instructors like me get the praise. I know, it's weird. But that's the gig. That's what success looks like. So, a nudge here, a prompt there, and you'll turn that recalcitrant professor into a star.

I'll be cheering you on every step of the way.

References

beeethousand. (2017, May 4). Emily, this is a very thoughtful piece [Comment on the article "Easing instructional designer-faculty conflicts"]. *Inside Higher Ed.* https://www.insidehighered.com/digital-learning/article/2017/05/03/easing-conflicts-between-instructional-designers-and-faculty#comment-3288405112

Benson, J. (2016). The power of positive regard. *Educational Leadership, 73*, 22–26. http://www.ascd.org/publications/educational-leadership/jun16/vol73/num09/The-Power-of-Positive-Regard.aspx

Geronimi, C., Jackson, W., & Luske, H. (Directors). (1951). *Alice in wonderland* [Film]. Walt Disney Productions.

Jaschik, S., & Lederman, D. (2018). 2018 survey of faculty attitudes on technology. *Inside Higher Ed.* https://mediasite.com/wp-content/uploads/2018/11/2018-Faculty-Survey-Mediasite.pdf

Martin, F., & Bolliger, D. U. (2018). Engagement matters: Student perceptions on the importance of engagement strategies in the online learning environment. *Online Learning, 22*(1), 205–222. https://doi.org/10.24059/olj.v22i1.1092

It is important to address feelings about the evidence as much as it is to share the evidence.

6

GROUNDED IN RESEARCH

Be Good, or at Least Evidence Based

Johanna Inman

Educational technology professionals in higher education have sometimes been criticized as tech enthusiasts with a general lack of critical perspective (Selwyn, 2011). And yet, as enrollments in online courses grow (Seaman et al., 2018), data from the National Survey of Student Engagement (2017) show that students have high expectations regarding their interactions with faculty. This reveals a need for college instructors to design effective learning experiences, including online, that intentionally improve these interactions. In Brigance's (2011) argument for instructional designers to take a greater leadership role in higher education, she says,

> Professors who are accustomed to being able to make adjustments in their courses based on student feedback are generally unable to do so in an online format. Online learning requires an emphasis on underlying pedagogies and the technological designs that will support these pedagogies. Having professors put their courses online without giving them the necessary support to do so results in ill-structured design that inhibits student learning. An instructional designer for online learning can provide that needed support. (p. 44)

This chapter explores what it means to work from a research foundation and why this approach is especially critical for instructional designers in higher education. It examines ways that research can help instructional designers better understand their role as well as the importance of acknowledging the expertise and experience of the college instructors they work with. Finally, it discusses the importance of contributing to and engaging with emerging research in the field, along with the opportunities for instructional designers and instructors to work as partners on educational research projects.

Start With the Research

When I started working in educational development, one of the first tasks I was given was to put together a workshop for a group of dental faculty about using blogs and wikis to improve and extend student learning. I remember the moment my director at the time told me that I would be facilitating this workshop and the sense of apprehension I felt. I had been teaching college-level courses for 12 years and had accrued plenty of firsthand experience in the classroom. I had also previously worked as a technology trainer, teaching instructors how to use technology tools. But this was somehow different.

This time I was asked to show dental faculty not only how to use teaching tools but also *why* to use these tools and maybe even convince them that it could be beneficial. Furthermore, my disciplinary background was in the arts. I did not teach, had not even studied, dentistry, the health sciences, or the learning sciences, for that matter. I began to ask myself why this group of clinical experts would listen to anything I had to say about how to teach dentistry. I did not know it, but I was suffering from something common in higher education among academics and administrators alike: imposter syndrome.

Imposter syndrome has been well documented throughout higher education (Parkman, 2016). Clance and Imes (1978) first wrote about imposter syndrome to describe characteristics of a group of high-achieving female academics who were struggling to acknowledge their success. Since that time, this term has been more widely adapted to describe feelings of professional self-doubt, an overall fear of being uncovered as fraudulent or of not deserving a particular professional role or rank.

Similarly, my concerns stemmed from a lack of specific content expertise. But as I began to raise concerns with my director, she reassured me that indeed I was an expert, not in the content (dentistry) perhaps, but in pedagogy and technology. She also provided me with some sage advice: Read the literature, know what the research says, and start with the evidence. She went on to explain that although the instructors in that workshop were dental clinicians and experts in their field, very few, if any, had the time to read, evaluate, and interpret research on teaching. Instead, that was my charge and what these instructors wanted—someone to summarize the research and help them find practical ways to implement it in their context.

At that point, I got right to work researching the implementation of blogs and wikis in college courses. To my surprise, I found studies on the use of these tools in various professional courses, such as nursing and premed, and I put together a workshop that led with the research and included examples of case studies where blogs and wikis were used in health sciences. I will never forget the words of my director as we walked out of the workshop that day. "You were really made for this work—you might even be better at it than I am!" I beamed as she talked about the confidence I had when I fielded questions and my command of the research. I asked, "But do you think they took me seriously?" She said, "If that was even a question at all, it evaporated the moment you started speaking." My heart raced with excitement and a renewed conviction that this was the right position for me.

Know Your Audience

The workshop I just described was successful because I approached the topic from a place of evidence—not opinion, not anecdote. As clinicians, these instructors placed value on what I had to say because I provided evidence for my claims. However, from my research, I also discovered that health professionals promote evidence-based practice themselves. In fact, the term *evidence-based practice* was first used in medicine (Biesta, 2007). Explicitly using that language helped me develop a rapport with these instructors.

As an instructional designer, it is incredibly important to put yourself in the shoes of the instructors you work with, or better yet, put yourself in their classrooms. A brief discussion with a department chair, a quick review of the department website, or even a discussion with a colleague who previously worked with the same group can be critical to your success. Knowing the situational context of their teaching is key. Do they teach large classes? Is their online program synchronous or asynchronous? Are the students in state, out of state, or international? What are the challenges they expect to face in moving courses to an online environment? Are the faculty excited about teaching online, or are they approaching it with trepidation, or, worse, are they doing it only because they were told they have to? Spending time answering these questions before you meet with instructors can help position you to better understand where they are coming from and prepare you to focus on points that may get you better buy-in, especially if you address their concerns.

In building instructional design credibility, Summers et al. (2002) discuss the importance of including "both data and feelings" (p. 28). The term *data* refers to accuracy of the information presented, whereas the term *feelings* takes into account the way the audience connects with, interprets, and responds to those data. In this way, it is important to address feelings about the evidence as much as it is to share the evidence. With faculty this may just be sharing a few reassuring words or recognizing their concerns are valid. In the case of the dental faculty, through conversations I had with the program director, I knew their concerns were mostly focused on finding time to implement change and the likelihood of facing student resistance to those changes. As a result, I was prepared to acknowledge those concerns, validate them, and provide some ways to mitigate them.

Recognize Your Value

College instructors are typically hired because of their disciplinary or professional expertise; however, many lack formal pedagogical training. Therefore, it is important for instructional designers to explain that the strategies and recommendations you provide to instructors are not just helpful tips. Rather, they are consistent findings across multiple studies that can be used to guide decision-making (Kirkwood & Price, 2013).

The term *evidence-based practice* may have originated in the medical field, but it has become common in other disciplines, including its widespread adoption in the literature on teaching in higher education (Groccia & Buskist, 2011). Educational theorist and higher education scholar Paul Ramsden (2003) describes evidence-based teaching simply as the idea that teaching can be improved when evidence from the research about student learning is implemented by instructors. Instructional designers serve an important role providing this evidence, but they are also a part of a much larger movement in higher education—helping instructors learn and implement the research and cognitive science regarding teaching and learning.

Be Collaborative

Grounding one's work in research is a great strategy to foster trust and earn credibility with college instructors and so is taking a collaborative approach. It is important to remember that many instructors have several years of experience teaching in the classroom before they begin teaching online. Although that experience may not translate exactly to online teaching, it should be used as a foundation to build on, not discredited or ignored. One theoretical framework that can guide instructional designers to better understand their role as partners with faculty is the technological pedagogical content knowledge (TPACK) model (Mishra & Koehler, 2006). TPACK is a framework that extends Shulman's (1986) seminal work identifying the need for higher education instructors to gain what he termed *pedagogical content knowledge* (see Figure 6.1). Shulman argued that instructors' knowledge of their discipline does not automatically equate to pedagogical knowledge. Rather, these types of knowledge are separate, but when both are learned together, they can be reinforcing. In the TPACK model, Mishra

Figure 6.1. The TPACK framework.

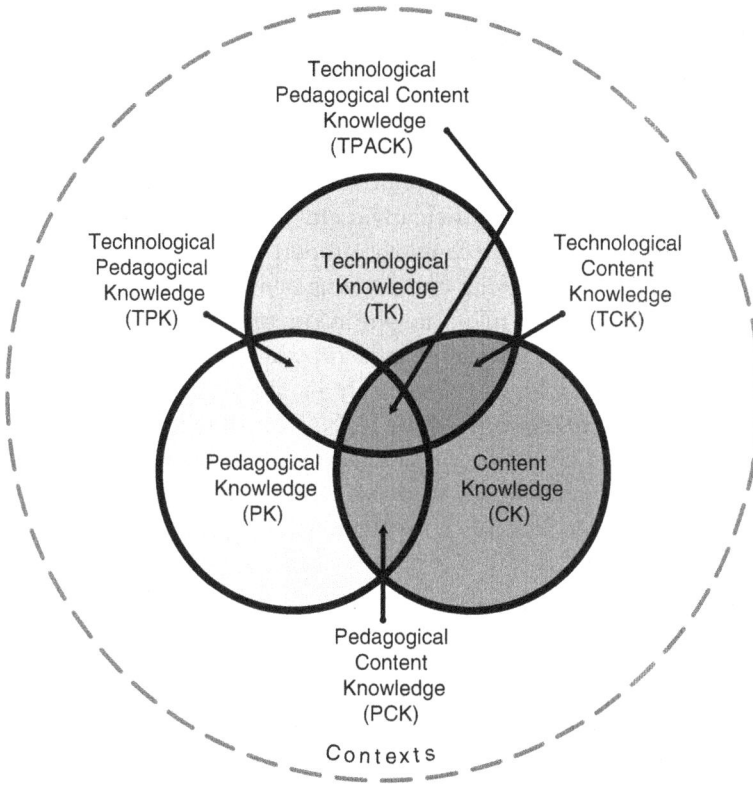

Note. Reprinted with permission from TPACK ORG, http://www.tpack.org/ © TPACK, 2012.

and Koehler (2006) took Shulman's work and added another layer: technological knowledge. In this model, the goal of teaching with technology is the alignment of an instructor's content knowledge, pedagogical knowledge, and technological knowledge in order to achieve the best possible success for student learning.

This framework can also be helpful to instructional designers and instructors to identify the particular expertise each party brings to the partnership. Clearly, the instructor brings the content knowledge, and the instructional designer brings the pedagogical and technological knowledge. Of course, depending on the instructors' experience and background, they may also contribute to the pedagogical knowledge. Possibly the most important aspect of this model is identifying the need for training that integrates all three branches of TPACK (Mishra & Koehler, 2006) to build an effective online learning experience for students. As a result, discussions with instructors should focus on the pedagogical potential for technology (Will this tool improve student learning?) and the potential for it to teach the content (Could this technology be used effectively to illustrate a specific concept or facilitate student practice of a particular skill?). Instructional designers need a command of technological knowledge and pedagogical knowledge, but they must remain open to input from content experts about how that research best applies to teaching specific content knowledge.

This model can also be particularly useful in distinguishing the instructional designer from other technology support staff in higher education. Prior to working in a teaching and learning center, I held a position as a technology trainer. In this role, I taught instructors how to use technology, but there was no expectation for me to incorporate pedagogical research into that training, placing this position firmly in the technological knowledge part of the TPACK framework (Mishra & Koehler, 2006). As a result, teaching tips in the training ended up focusing on improved user experience or clean-looking interfaces—useful aspects of technology to consider, but they should not be the sole focus of an instructional designer.

Keep It in Perspective

It is important for instructional designers to ground their work in the research on effective teaching and learning, but instructional designers should not succumb to idealism regarding how research and theory translate to the reality of teaching online. Unfortunately, most higher education instructors are working in less than ideal conditions, and a little pragmatism can go a long way.

Although many college instructors distrust technology or online learning (Carmean & Friedman, 2014), their resistance is often rooted in valid concerns. One study found that what comes across as resistance to online learning is often the result of a range of concerns that include fear of learning new technologies, apprehension that faculty-student relationships will degrade, and misconceptions that online learning lacks rigor (Mitchell et al., 2015). Additionally, instructors are often dependent on student evaluations for decisions such as tenure and promotion or contract renewals; therefore, they face a serious risk when implementing new strategies and teaching in new formats (Kember et al., 2002). For the past few decades, scholars have also been discussing the ratcheting of faculty in higher education and growing demands for research productivity (Massy, & Zemsky, 1994). With greater expectations for research production, there is simply less time to spend on the improvement of teaching, let alone preparations to teach online.

Luckily, the research regarding online learning can also be used to mitigate some of these concerns. Research can be a great way to point out the potential value of the tools, techniques, and strategies instructional designers often recommend. For instructional designers, this means starting with the identification of the benefits for the students and also the instructor: How has this strategy been shown to improve students' learning and transfer learning to future courses? How might it be used to improve feedback but also save time grading? What strategies can foster a positive learning community and reduce student conflicts? In addition, providing case studies with real-world examples or success stories from instructors who have previously implemented these techniques helps concretize the value. The practical application of these strategies is often at the forefront of the instructor's mind.

Furthermore, when introducing instructors to theory and research on teaching and learning, it helps to scale back on the jargon, hyperbole, and buzzwords. Whenever possible, use unpretentious terminology that instructors without a PhD in educational psychology or instructional design will understand. Remember that college instructors come from a wide variety of backgrounds, disciplines, and professional fields. Although accuracy is important and the research is valuable, consider the most important concepts about that literature for instructors to know and then lay it out for them, clearly and in plain language.

Finally, there is a big caveat to all of this: Be careful not to oversell the research. It is important to help instructors approach teaching, especially online teaching, as an iterative process. One of my biggest pet peeves is when faculty say, "I tried that once and it didn't work, the students hated it." I usually respond by asking them to tell me more about how they implemented the technology, what their students said, and exactly how many of them said it. It is funny to me that no one expects to get on a bike and ride it perfectly the first time, but with instructional technology immediate perfection is the exact expectation. Whenever possible, introduce online teaching as an art and a science, which require planning, practice, implementation, and continual adjustments based on experience. Prepare instructors to be reflective as they make the transition to teaching online. Set the expectation that they should plan to adjust in future courses.

Step Up Your Research Game

The next step is encouraging instructors to engage in reflection in a more formal way by conducting their own research, which can help instructors identify evidence from their own courses that reinforces the positive changes they make in their teaching. It can also be helpful to tell them they need to make additional improvements. But perhaps more important, engaging in the scholarship of teaching and learning can improve an instructor's sense of fulfillment in teaching (Bishop-Clark & Dietz-Uhler, 2012). I argue this is also true for instructional designers.

As some instructional designers do not have experience conducting firsthand research, a great way to get started is working with faculty. Many college instructors are conducting research in their field, which can be an advantage as the process and procedure for conducting the scholarship of teaching and learning are similar, especially if the research is in the social sciences.

Another common strategy that can help instructional designers get started is to begin sharing experiences in an informal blog post or by presenting preliminary findings at a professional conference.

Keep On Learning On

As academic degree programs that focus on educational technology grow, it is likely that more instructional designers will enter the field through this path than before (Ku et al., 2012). But the reality is that not all instructional designers enter the field through one of these programs. For some, this means they do not always know where to find research, let alone how to evaluate it. Moreover, for those instructional designers who begin their careers with this knowledge, many claim their lack of preparation to vet new technologies as they continue to emerge (Ritzhaupt & Kumar, 2015).

The good news is there are a number of professional organizations and networks that can help. For example, the Association for Educational Communications and Technology (AECT.org), the Professional and Organizational Developers Network (podnetwork.org), and the Online Learning Consortium (onlinelearningconsortium.org) are just a few of the national and international organizations that provide conferences, workshops, webinars, and other resources for instructional designers. These organizations can provide a way for instructional designers to build a network of supportive colleagues committed to the improvement of teaching and learning in higher education.

Conclusion

When I started working in educational development, I feared that my academic background in the visual arts would be challenged by instructors outside that field. But almost a decade later, I have not found that to be the case. Instead, I have used my experiences as an artist and educator to develop rapport and camaraderie with the hundreds of college instructors I've had the pleasure of working with throughout my career. That said, intentional relationship building and my firsthand experience as a college instructor have only taken me so far. As this chapter suggests, an essential key to my effectiveness in this work—and for all instructional designers—is to start and remain grounded in the research.

References

Biesta, G. (2007). Why "what works" won't work: Evidence-based practice and the democratic deficit in educational research. *Educational Theory, 57*(1), 1–22. https://doi.org/10.1111/j.1741-5446.2006.00241.x

Bishop-Clark, C., & Dietz-Uhler, B. (2012). *Engaging in the scholarship of teaching and learning: A guide to the process, and how to develop a project from start to finish*. Stylus.

Brigance, S. K. (2011). Leadership in online learning in higher education: Why instructional designers for online learning should lead the way. *Performance Improvement, 50*(10), 43–48. https://doi.org/10.1002/pfi.20262

Carmean, C., & Friedman, D. (2014). Conjecture, tension, and online learning. *Educause Review and Academic Affairs Publications, 16*. https://digitalcommons.tacoma.uw.edu/academic_affairs_pubs/16

Clance, P. R., & Imes, S. A. (1978). The imposter phenomenon in high achieving women: Dynamics and therapeutic intervention. *Psychotherapy: Theory, Research & Practice, 15*(3), 241. https://doi.org/10.1037/h0086006

Groccia, J. E., & Buskist, W. (2011). Need for evidence-based teaching. *New Directions for Teaching and Learning, 128*, 5–11. https://doi.org/10.1002/tl.463

Kember, D., Leung, D. Y., & Kwan, K. (2002). Does the use of student feedback questionnaires improve the overall quality of teaching? *Assessment & Evaluation in Higher Education, 27*(5), 411–425. https://doi.org/10.1080/0260293022000009294

Kirkwood, A., & Price, L. (2013). Missing: Evidence of a scholarly approach to teaching and learning with technology in higher education. *Teaching in Higher Education, 18*(3), 327–337. https://doi.org/10.1080/13562517.2013.773419

Ku, H. Y., Plantz-Masters, S., Hosler, K., Diteeyont, W., Akarasriworn, C., & Lin, T. Y. (2012). An analysis of educational technology-related doctoral programs in the United States. In M. Orey, S. A. Jones, & R. M. Branch (Eds.), *Educational media and technology yearbook* (pp. 99–112). Springer.

Massy, W. F., & Zemsky, R. (1994). Faculty discretionary time: Departments and the "academic ratchet." *Journal of Higher Education, 65*(1), 1–22. https://doi.org/10.1080/00221546.1994.11778471

Mishra, P., (2018, September 18). *The TPACK diagram gets an upgrade.* Punya Mishra's Web. https://punyamishra.com/2018/09/10/the-tpack-diagram-gets-an-upgrade/

Mishra, P., & Koehler, M. J. (2006). Technological pedagogical content knowledge: A framework for teacher knowledge. *Teachers College Record, 108*(6), 1017–1054. https://doi.org/10.1111/j.1467-9620.2006.00684.x

Mitchell, L. D., Parlamis, J. D., & Claiborne, S. A. (2015). Overcoming faculty avoidance of online education: From resistance to support to active participation. *Journal of Management Education, 39*(3), 350–371. https://doi.org/10.1177/1052562914547964

National Survey of Student Engagement. (2017). *Engagement insights: Survey findings on the quality of undergraduate education.* Center for Postsecondary Research, Indiana University. https://nsse.indiana.edu/NSSE_2017_Results/pdf/NSSE_2017_Annual_Results.pdf

Parkman, A. (2016). The imposter phenomenon in higher education: Incidence and impact. *Journal of Higher Education Theory and Practice, 16*(1), 51–60. https://doi.org/10.33423/jhetp.v16i1.1936

Ramsden, P. (2003). *Learning to teach in higher education.* Routledge.

Ritzhaupt, A. D., & Kumar, S. (2015). Knowledge and skills needed by instructional designers in higher education. *Performance Improvement Quarterly, 28*(3), 51–69. https://doi.org/10.1002/piq.21196

Seaman, J. E., Allen, I. E., & Seaman, J. (2018). Grade increase: Tracking distance education in the United States. *Babson Survey Research Group.*

Selwyn, N. (2011). In praise of pessimism—the need for negativity in educational technology. *British Journal of Educational Technology, 42*(5), 713–718. https://eric.ed.gov/?id=ED580852

Shulman, L. S. (1986). Those who understand: Knowledge growth in teaching. *Educational Researcher, 15*(2), 4–14.

Summers, L., Lohr, L., & O'Neil, C. (2002). Building instructional design credibility through communication competency. *TechTrends, 46*(1), 26–32.

PART THREE

FRAMEWORKS THAT TOUCH EVERYTHING: THE LENSES WE WORK WITH

When learners are both prepared for and excited by a learning challenge, like deliberate experimentation, they are in their zones of proximal development—the space where deep learning can occur.

7

LEARNING ONLINE

The Internet Should Be Used for More Than Just Do-It-Yourself Videos

Josie G. Baudier

Imagine the following scenario: You are meeting with an instructor to help design and develop an online course. As you brainstorm the course, the instructor begins to get nervous and ask questions, sending the conversation in several different directions. The instructor feels online learning is subpar and questions whether it can be as productive as face-to-face learning. Hesitation regarding the outcomes of online learning is a common dilemma you will face as an instructional designer. In this scenario, you are cool under pressure because you know the process and research on teaching and learning and are ready to help your instructor create a great online course.

You point out to the instructor how you can learn just about anything from the internet—for example, just this week you learned how to fix the drain in your shower, change the headlight in your car, and sharpen the blade on your lawnmower, all by searching online. At this point the instructor is still skeptical, so you ponder a few challenging questions with the instructor. Can online learning be something more than do-it-yourself home repairs or cat videos? Cat videos are cool, but do they really help learners achieve their learning goals?

Now you explain that as the online learner population continues to grow, learners' needs should be at the forefront of online course design and delivery, similar to our traditional, face-to-face classes. Supporting students in online learning requires intentional planning—that is, course design, which takes considerable time to do effectively. You continue to explain to the instructor that most learning principles, approaches, and research in traditional teaching and learning still apply. The instructor begins to understand the success of the course hinges on the design of the online course and that despite the apparent initial complexity of intentional online course design, the outcome of a well-planned course provides the learners with exceptional educational experiences.

This chapter provides examples and approaches to support the learning process. Similar to traditional face-to-face learning, learning research stems from a few key concepts: prior knowledge, mastery, memory, and social learning. In this chapter we talk about these learning principles and how they apply to the online environment. These are approaches that may begin to shape your instructional design philosophy. Additionally, we explore common issues designers encounter when working with instructors to develop online courses.

Learning Online

To create these exceptional educational experiences for learners, instructional designers and instructors need to consider how online learning happens and how to support learning through course design. Uncovering prior knowledge, activating memory, creating opportunities for mastery, and encouraging social learning all contribute to the process of learning (Ambrose et al., 2010; Bandura, 1977; Conrad & Donaldson, 2012). Through intentional course design, consultations, and other professional development, a designer can work with instructors to encourage these same learning processes in the online environment.

Prior Knowledge

Prior knowledge includes the past experiences learners retain, experiences related to what they have learned, and also the knowledge connected to their social and cultural roles (National Research Council, 2000; Vygotsky, 1978). Prior knowledge can be insufficient or lacking to the point that students may not know enough to begin working at the level the instructor needs. Instructional designers should encourage instructors to establish the baseline of students' prior knowledge. Through automatic online quizzing or self-assessment surveys, commonly found in learning management systems, instructors can determine learners' knowledge baseline. It is important for the instructor to use that information to adjust the delivery of content. Once prior knowledge baselines are determined, instructors may need to reteach basic skills or provide supplemental materials for learners to address their misconceptions or lack of knowledge. Instructional designers assist instructors in determining the changes that might need to take place at the beginning of or during a semester.

Additionally, misconceptions can exist in prior knowledge, and these can create roadblocks in learning, regardless of modality (Ambrose et al., 2010; National Research Council, 2000). Current learning scientists lean on the early work of Piaget and Dewey regarding inquiry learning, in which some learners need to discover concepts for themselves to understand or change a misconception (National Research Council, 2000). In the online classroom, a few ways to encourage the exploration of prior knowledge are critical thinking discussion questions, intensive and authentic assignments, or collaborative projects.

Mastery

Mastery of learning content involves helping learners make long-lasting connections with content. Instructional designers can help embed opportunities in the content for students to demonstrate they have made these connections. According to Ambrose et al. (2010), there are three phases to mastery: acquire, practice, and apply. Through these three phases, students determine when and where to use the component skills of knowledge and eventually progress to mastery of knowledge.

In the online classroom, students can acquire component skills by interacting with content through readings and presentations and also by interacting with classmates in discussions. Additionally, instructional designers should encourage instructors to incorporate practice throughout their course. Activities that allow the student to practice skills in isolation, and are also realistic and authentic to the content, will likely help learners move toward mastery of skills. Finally, the application of skills in the online classroom can be measured through different assessments. An alternative to the usual summative evaluations is creating deliberate experimentation opportunities (Cannon & Edmondson, 2005), learning moments when students are faced with a failed attempt or experiment that they must resolve on their own. Through this process, the learners have to apply the skills they know and eventually find a solution. Csikszentmihalyi (1997) argued that when learners are both prepared for and excited by a learning challenge, like deliberate experimentation, they are in their zones of proximal development—the space where deep learning can occur. Instructional designers need to become familiar with failure research because instructors are often apprehensive about allowing students to fail in their class, much less using class time to do so.

Let's return to the earlier scenario. The hesitant instructor is intrigued about allowing learner failure in the online course as one way to increase mastery and asks how to do this. You explain that by allowing failure, the instructor is shifting the focus of learning to the student away from the teacher. This is considered "messy work" (Weimer, 2013, p. 15). The instructor is not encouraged by this explanation, realizing it will increase the workload. You explain to the instructor that the course design and delivery can support these opportunities to fail. Learners need the opportunity to return to their coursework to improve their outcomes. You provide examples, such as offering multiple attempts on weekly quizzes in which the learners get automated feedback from an online quizzing system before making another attempt. Similarly, the instructor can offer a way to improve a writing assignment grade by allowing learners to earn a percentage of points after making corrections based on their feedback. Another way is allowing learners to correct any incorrect exam questions to prove mastery. Varying these opportunities between summative and formative assessments can also improve learner outcomes. When the instructor hesitates on these suggestions because it will consume a considerable amount of time, you say that when learners persevere and excel after failure, they are learning to not only make connections and master the course goals but also take on life's challenges and continue to persist.

Memory

Memory organization has been researched to explain how we learn. Regardless of modality, the learner's memory needs to be aroused in their learning process. Bain (2014) suggested that "the best college teachers" (p. 27) help students build on the schemas they come to class possessing instead of assuming students are a blank slate. Therefore, through the course design, learners can begin to "stimulate construction" (p. 27) of schemas. Instructors and students need to reframe their mind-set from learners acting as a sponge or blank slates to learners reconstructing their mental models, which supports the importance of thoughtfully and intentionally designing an online course.

The instructional designer should consider fundamental course design strategies that assist learners in organizing knowledge, therefore supporting the construction of memory. Backward design and alignment are core to an instructional designer's toolbox and can provide the framework for course development to support the organization of content. Providing an alignment chart or course map that shows the alignment of the core course components helps the learners build the schemas and make connections by explicitly organizing the content for them. A second way of supporting memory through course design is in the organization of the online course. The module structure mainly provides a framework for the course. Learners will not need to make mental models about the hierarchy or complexity of the content because that will be explicit through the organization of the material in the modules.

Social Learning

Bandura (1977) described social learning theory as a way of learning through observations and modeling. He stated that students learn best through interactions with other learners and are influenced by cognitive, behavioral, and environmental factors. In this case, collaborative learning events support interaction in the online classroom and are vital to improving social learning and the overall educational experience.

An instructional designer will quickly learn that instructors are leery of online collaborative assignments because they usually cause concern for the responsible learners, anxiety for the introverted learners, and relief for the slackers. Conrad and Donaldson (2012) provided suggestions for the designer to encourage the instructor to address these concerns in the course design. First, the design of the project needs to be transparent and include information about why the assignment is intentionally collaborative. Why does this project require a team approach? The answer to this question cannot be that the instructor wants to grade as little as possible. Collaborative assignments should require shared knowledge and come to a conclusion on an assignment based on the different experiences of the group members (Kuh, 2008). Additionally, Conrad and Donaldson discussed the inclusion of assignment rubrics to specify grading criteria and peer evaluation so that all group members feel represented and heard.

Opportunities for learners to discuss the content of the course freely should be embedded in the course design to support social learning. This can be done using the discussion boards or other dialogue tools. Additionally, collaborative documentation tools, video conferencing applications, and communication options should be embedded in the online course, so that interactions can occur seamlessly. Doing so shows the learners how important interactions are to that particular educational experience.

The instructor should consider designing a course that includes interactions between instructor and learner, learner and content, and even among the learners. These types of interactions increase engagement, improve motivation, and promote social learning (Barkley, 2010).

The Asynchronous Environment

Let's return to our starting scenario. The instructor has now bought into the theory and research supporting learning and begins to wonder if the same engagement in an online class that is in a face-to-face class can be created. The instructor insists that lectures are the cornerstone to students learning the content in the course. The instructor uses interactive polling during lectures to gauge student understanding and adjust the lectures accordingly. Small-group discussions are used, so students have an opportunity to practice with the content and get feedback from their peers and the instructor. The instructor is concerned that these teaching practices will not transfer online; this is correct, and you have to tell that to the instructor. Luckily, you can explain how the asynchronous online learning environment will become an outstanding classroom for student learning and that the learners will still achieve the course goals, just in a different way. Your confidence in the asynchronous online environment will comfort the instructor, who will be ready to listen and participate in the online course design process with you.

When we say *asynchronous learning*, we really mean that learning is happening without real-time instruction. The content, assignments, and interactions are built into the course design so the learner can proceed through each area or module guided by the organization of the course. Synchronous online instruction is when the instructor delivers content live using an application or software that all enrolled students can access. (For more information on synchronous instruction, see chapter 16.) Asynchronous learning provides a space for students to consume and engage with content at different times and in different locations (Boettcher & Conrad, 2016). However, to support a learner-centered approach to instruction, students should be provided with a schedule identifying the topics, tasks, assessments, homework, and due dates (Habanek, 2005; Weimer, 2013). The course schedule allows students to set expectations with time management to be successful in the course. Without a course schedule, learners will not be able to look ahead in the semester to accommodate for planned life events or even a weekly work schedule.

Often asynchronous online learning is the default approach to online instruction because it provides time for the student to process information, develop thoughtful responses, collaborate with peers, and have a somewhat flexible schedule to achieve the course goals. Although synchronous learning can accomplish some of that, to really affect how students learn through prior knowledge, mastery, memory, and social learning, the students will also need supplemental asynchronous learning opportunities.

Pros of Asynchronous Learning

There are several reasons why asynchronous instruction supports learning. From flexible schedules to providing time to process information, learners can benefit from a course designed in this way. Even though some asynchronous courses are structured with a course schedule and due dates, students usually have some flexibility in their online modules. This allows learners to decide on their own when they will study, participate, and complete assignments. Encouraging this kind of autonomy in the course design increases student motivation (Vansteenkiste et al., 2006). Also, allowing students to contribute to decisions about the schedule and due dates shifts control to the students and promotes learner-centered practices (Weimer, 2013).

In an asynchronous course, there is time for learners to truly engage with the content at every turn. Learners will have time to stop and process information, and possibly rewatch or reread learning material. Additionally, they will have time to provide meaningful, fruitful, and thorough responses to discussions, interactions, or assignments. The extra time to process and then formulate a response is an advantage over face-to-face classes. Also, learners have the time and space to participate in collaborative learning experiences. Although group work can be challenging to design and deliver in the online environment, it does provide an opportunity for students to delve deeper into a project, and it contributes to their progress of mastering content and social learning.

There is no back row in an asynchronous course. In face-to-face classes and even in synchronous courses, learners can blend into the background of the class, lurk, and not participate. In an asynchronous course, learners are expected to participate, albeit in a delayed manner, through assignments, discussions, and interactions.

Cons of Asynchronous Learning

Although there are several perks with the asynchronous online environment, there are also some cautionary tales of asynchronous course design. A designer needs to be aware of these pitfalls to steer instructors toward creating a more effective course. As mentioned previously, instructors often try to emulate exactly what is happening in their face-to-face course. There is no easy transition to translate that type of learning environment. This mentality tends to create a course that is either too text heavy or too video heavy. Circumventing that type of design takes a great deal of time to develop and build.

When a course becomes too text heavy, students may lose interest in the content or find it difficult to process. There is nothing wrong with learning from text; however, using varied types of materials, such as multimedia and learning objects, creates a more engaging learning environment (Boettcher & Conrad, 2016). Additionally, using different kinds of materials can encourage memory building and eventually mastery. In contrast, when videos drive the course, the concern is how learning takes place. The designer needs to determine if the videos are relevant to the content and aligned with the learning objectives and therefore not overloading the student with unnecessary information. This can happen when using third-party sources or even when faculty have created the videos themselves. Additionally, videos need to include embedded tasks or be accompanied with an activity or assignment. In other words, the video should not be a totally passive event. Assisting faculty with their first view of video recordings and providing best practices will help establish the video parameters.

Other Considerations When Designing

Online instructors may arrive at your door looking for answers about why students are not mastering the course objectives and, therefore, not passing their class. Desperation and fear will consume them and permeate your entire office space. By asking the instructors questions, reviewing their online course design, and possibly surveying some of the students, you may arrive at a few different conclusions. This section discusses a few common issues that create poor learning experiences in the online course and offers possible solutions.

Expert Blind Spot

The expert blind spot occurs when instructors are teaching above the level of the course and the learners. Because instructors are subject matter experts in their field, it is sometimes difficult for them to recognize when this happens. Ambrose et al. (2010) reminded instructors to ask themselves questions about how the component skills in the course content lead to mastery. If the content consists of complex procedures in which the basic component skills are not provided, or high-level instruction is expected that is too advanced for the level of the learners, then an expert blind spot is likely built into the content of the online course (Ambrose et al., 2010; Quality Matters, 2016). A quick way for the designer to decide if the course has expert blind spots is to determine if the course content is aligned with the goals of the course. If there is misalignment, a thorough audit of the course content will need to be conducted, and revisions of content are possible.

Clear Course Design and Expectations

Another area of concern is clarity in the course. Although it is common to experience bottlenecks when learning something new, these blockages should not be caused by the course design (Land et al., 2005). Because of the asynchronous nature of the online classroom, students are sometimes unsure about content, course materials, assignment expectations, or even navigation. They are stuck and uncertain about how to move forward in the course. In any case, a designer can analyze the course for these types of blockages or bottlenecks. One way to do this is to examine the scaffolded instruction (Ambrose et al., 2010; Clarke et al., 2005). Identifying the practice skills, as well as the supporting instruction, can detect any potential roadblocks in learning. Second, the designer can evaluate using Ambrose et al.'s (2010) approach of acquire, practice, and apply to determine if the learning is designed for memory making and eventually mastery.

Interaction

Another common issue is that the course lacks interaction. One way online instructors attempt to create interaction and include social learning is through the discussion board, which is usually embedded in a learning management system. Designers need to determine the purpose of the discussion board. Sometimes instructors use discussion boards for students to submit papers or other type of writing assignments. However, discussion boards are intended for students to create dialogue on a topic or questions and are to be used to support social interaction in the online environment. Additionally, designers need to ensure that the discussion prompts are suitable for promoting interactions among students as in a dialogue and encourage different responses from each learner potentially connecting to their life experiences. Appropriate interactions among students create engaging online courses, which produce an effective online course for the online learner (Conrad & Donaldson, 2012).

Conclusion

Instructional designers need to support instructors in creating a course design beneficial to how students learn. By identifying the students' prior knowledge, they will be able to gauge students' learning progress. Mastery and memory can be supported by scaffolded learning, critical thinking assignments, and explicit mapping of course content. The organization of the physical space of the course supports students' organizational needs, providing logistical connections in the online classroom. Addressing learning issues in the course design, such as eliminating expert blind spots and possible bottlenecks, creates a supportive environment and effective online course design. Now when another instructor seeks a course design, you will have the foundational information of prior knowledge, mastery, memory, and social learning to guide your work and meet the needs of the instructor.

References

Ambrose, S., Lovett, M., Bridges, M., DiPietro, M., & Norman, M. (2010). *How learning works: Seven research-based principles for smart teaching.* Jossey-Bass.

Bain, K. (2004). *What the best college teachers do.* Harvard University Press.

Bandura, A. (1977). *Social learning theory.* General Learning Press.

Barkley, E. (2010). *Student engagement techniques: A handbook for college faculty.* Jossey-Bass.

Boettcher, J. V., & Conrad, R. M. (2016). *The online teaching survival guide: Simple and practical pedagogical tips.* Jossey-Bass.

Cannon, M. D., & Edmondson, A. C. (2005). Failing to learn and learning to fail (intelligently): How great organizations put failure to work to innovate and improve. *Long Range Planning, 38*(3), 299–319. https://doi.org/10.1016/j.lrp.2005.04.005

Clarke, T., Ayres, P. & Sweller, J. The impact of sequencing and prior knowledge on learning mathematics through spreadsheet applications. *Educational Technology Research and Development, 53*(3), 15–25. https://doi.org/10.1007/BF02504794

Conrad, R. M., & Donaldson, J. A. (2012). *Continuing to engage the online learner: More activities and resources for creative instruction.* Jossey-Bass.

Csikszentmihalyi, M. (1997). *Finding flow: The psychology of engagement with everyday life.* Basic Books.

Habanek, D. V. (2005). An examination of the integrity of the syllabus. *College Teaching, 53*(2), 62–64. https://www.jstor.org/stable/27559222

Kuh, G. (2008). *High-impact educational practices: What they are, who has access to them, and why they matter.* Association of American Colleges & Universities.

Land, R., Cousin, G., Meyer, J. H., & Davies, P. (2005). *Threshold concepts and troublesome knowledge: Implications for course design and evaluation* [Paper presentation]. Improving Student Learning Conference, 12th Annual Meeting. Oxford Centre for Staff and Learning Development.

National Research Council. (2000). *How people learn: Brain, mind, experience, and school.* National Academies Press.

Quality Matters. (2016). *Specific review standards from the QM higher education rubric, sixth edition.* https://www.qualitymatters.org/sites/default/files/PDFs/StandardsfromtheQMHigherEducationRubric.pdf

Vansteenkiste, M., Lens, W., & Deci, E. (2006). Intrinsic versus extrinsic goal contents in self-determination theory: Another look at the quality of academic motivation. *Educational Psychologist, 41*(1), 19–31. https://doi.org/10.1207/s15326985ep4101_4

Vygotsky, L. S. (1978). *Mind in society: The development of the higher psychological processes.* Harvard University Press.

Weimer, M. (2013). *Learner-centered teaching: Five key changes to practice.* Jossey-Bass.

My contention is that the design of the learning experience is often what is unprepared or lacking, and not the student, as is frequently made out to be.

8

UNIVERSAL DESIGN FOR LEARNING

Everybody Gets to Learn

Carl S. Moore

What does the phrase, "Everybody gets to learn" really mean? "Everyone getting to learn" translates to broadening opportunities for learners to share accountability with instructors in the learning process. Much work has been done in granting physical access to educational experiences for varying constituencies through policies and procedures in higher education, but that does not always result in learners learning. We still have an educational system that privileges some while disadvantaging others (Guinier, 2015). Let's take the online space, for instance. The growth of digital education in general has been one of the greatest milestones in the history of education. However, granting access to enrolling in college classes, even if the course is fully online or a hybrid, does not guarantee that learning will take place. In fact, granting access to courses in the digital arena disadvantages those learners who do not have access to devices or the internet. As instructional designers (IDs) it's part of our job to help instructors understand the intricacies of access in this regard. We should help instructors understand that the promotion of learning in any course rests on the nuances of how courses are designed. Thus, access to education and access to learning are different, and this is why inclusive teaching is important: It drives us to continue to better understand how to provide that access in an instructional sense so that every student gets to learn.

The most commonly used term when referring to providing instruction for a broad range of learners is *inclusive teaching*. Although familiarity is growing, a term like *inclusive teaching* can be just as daunting as it is nebulous; therefore I use the universal design for learning (UDL) framework for much of the chapter as a scaffold to help you better understand how one can assist instructors in creating opportunities that cast the widest instructional net. It is important for readers to understand that the intention of this chapter is not to promote any one lens or altruistic strategy that can make an instructor feel like they are doing a good deed by teaching to learners who are otherwise limited, but to invite thinking on impactful approaches to constructing learning experiences for all learners. The goal is to better envision how to create learning spaces that strengthen education for all rather than only privileging some (Guinier, 2015).

Though this chapter will indeed discuss implications for work of online instructional designers (IDs), it would be false to think that technology is needed for an approach that is universally designed. Technology can absolutely enhance one's instructional approach but only if done in a way that is in alignment with learner-centered research and best practices. I strongly agree with Ladson-Billings (1995) that inclusive teaching is good teaching. Inclusive teaching is not only quality teaching but also effective teaching, as it promotes an approach that aligns directly with research-informed best practices in instruction. In fact, courses designed to address learner variability are more rigorous than courses that are not. Inclusively designed courses include but are not limited to strategies like bringing multiple voices into the conversation; diversifying assessments; and challenging learners to draw from more areas of their mental, social, and emotional capacities. Therefore, the notion that diversifying one's instructional approach dumbs down the course material is a misguided thought.

Think to yourself: How can you guide instructors to become adept at proactively addressing inequities in the classroom with their instructional approach? In the learning design world, we know these as *situational factors* (Fink, 2013). What time does the class take place? Is it synchronous or asynchronous? Are the learners adults or mostly nontraditional? When guiding faculty in building courses it's important to help faculty look at the situational factors and think about how they will uniquely provide opportunities for learners to learn in their course context. In doing so, you must have a capacity-based mind-set and foster one in the instructor you are working with so that the situational factors or any perceived barriers are viewed as opportunities for innovation and continuous improvement for the course.

UDL and the Opportunity to Think Differently

Many conversations around inclusive teaching reveal a blind spot, a failure to realize that the vast majority of learners may need and benefit from more inclusive teaching. Reading the work of Giroux et al. (1988) on critical pedagogy initially helped expand my understanding of how the structures and traditions of educational settings disadvantage *all* learners from the learning process and even more so those from marginalized backgrounds. I have also been inspired by the work of Ladson-Billings (1995), who coined the term *critically relevant pedagogy* as a means of addressing classroom inequities by honoring cultural differences of learners through practices that are validating and affirming, comprehensive, multidimensional, empowering, transformative, and liberating. Though Ladson-Billings's work is now generally referred to as being culturally responsive and sustaining pedagogy for all learners, there are many educators in largely homogenous institutions of higher education who ignore any conversation about teaching with culture in mind because they do not always view their White student constituent as cultural beings. Though we should play close attention to and continue to champion the works of critical pedagogy and culturally relevant (sustaining) scholars, I am purposefully using UDL in this chapter to provide IDs with a framework that will not be ignored in some settings. The great thing about UDL is that it overlaps with many of the aforementioned approaches and can serve as an entree for inviting instructors and leadership to dig deeper into all literature on inclusive teaching.

UDL is rooted in both neuroscience and learning science. It promotes flexible learning environments and accommodates individual learning differences (independent of any culture salient to students' identity) (Rose & Meyer, 2002). Some may mistake UDL as an attempt at providing a one-size-fits-all education, where all learners learn the same way. Instead, the framework promotes a proactive approach to the design of learning experiences through functional integration of comprehensive instructional methods. UDL addresses a wide range of learning needs by encouraging educators to engage students in learning information and ideas and to assess their learning in a tactical variety of ways. It advances the universal design framework originally developed in architecture and informs designers how physical environments can be made accessible to a range of people. Even with UDL's broad intentions, there is still much room in higher education to move beyond discussions centered on students with varying abilities (the word *disability* is not used here because of its deficit implications) and underrepresented minority students.

As the conversation about inclusive teaching grows, so does the complexity of the issue. The term *inclusive* has become a moving target, making it difficult for educators to understand educational issues and create solutions to remedy them. A common understanding is needed in the nature of inclusive instruction and its potential efficacy in increasing the quality and reach of education. The word *inclusion* also promotes a power dynamic that some may be sensitive to and we all must be aware of. To include, one must have some type of power dominance to allow others to be in any given space. In my opinion, we should recognize the hierarchical nature of our education systems and spaces so we can better work within them to best include learners. Our journey as educators has brought us to a nexus, where we have to move beyond simply employing inclusive instructional strategies so students can learn in their own right to creating a space for learning to take place. IDs have a critical role in helping instructors develop micro-level strategies in a certain context.

A Brief History of Inclusive Teaching in Higher Education

Although universal design came from a desire for more accessible spaces, its roots are deeply connected to the fight for civil rights in America. Even though laws have been passed and policies promoted, these provisions themselves are limited. We must move beyond them to forge a better understanding and demonstration of inclusion. The topic of inclusion has been a struggle for this nation since its beginning. When a society is built on the premise of benefiting a particular subpopulation, there will come a time when other groups continue to grow despite fewer advantages and opportunities and begin to need more access than before. This then leads to inclusion issues.

When thinking about access to learning, it is important to recognize the structural barriers at play in our context. We live in a classist, racist, sexist, and homophobic society, and that environment has certain assumptions and certain rules for learners in and outside the classroom. It is important to note that depending on the context, this marginalization could occur to a greater or lesser degree. When intersectionality is factored in, the makeup of any individual student is not one specific identity. The intersection of students' unique aspects of identification can either privilege or marginalize them at any given turn.

One such concern left from the remnants of the past is traditional singular teaching strategies, meaning that college instructors simply deliver information for students to absorb (Bok, 2009). This can occur with any direct instructional method where one simply provides information to learners without eliciting active or engaged learning. For example, having learners view a number of videos can be similar to having them attend a lecture as a video does not denote a higher degree of learning (see chapter 14 for best practices on multimedia usage).

Overall, the history of inclusive teaching in higher education calls for a shift in thinking. Scholarship on teaching suggests that even students of identical demographic backgrounds and academic preparedness can benefit from inclusive teaching techniques (Burgstahler, 2008; Center for Applied Special Technology, 2020; Rose & Meyer, 2002). Therefore, discussions of teaching strategies that currently focus primarily on marginalized students ought to address a much wider constituency of learners. These conversations currently reveal institutions' blind spots when providing inclusionary practices for classrooms; they are missing the point that there is neurodiversity across learners in every context (Pollak, 2009).

Let us now shift our focus to the overall institution. My contention is that the design of the learning experience is often what is unprepared or lacking, and not the student, as is frequently made out to be.

Unprepared Educators and the Need for UDL

Conversations about improving teaching have positioned learners as the issue as opposed to instructional practices (Rose & Meyer, 2002). Often the theme is how educators and institutions can better serve underprepared learners. Some of these conversations may also touch on how to serve learners with varied abilities. I and some other professionals who believe in holding institutions accountable in this regard feel it is the educators and institutions that are often underprepared and differently abled at meeting the needs of a diverse range of learners.

Perhaps an example will bring about more clarity. Suppose you are going to a restaurant to eat a meal and the chef can only prepare food for a certain type of diet. Would you think the customers are disabled or underprepared because they did not fit in the chef's culinary bandwidth? Some may realize that in this example the chef is limited in the ability to prepare food for a diverse range of people. As you may surmise, we can apply this model to higher education as follows: Our institutions are the restaurants, with the chefs as educators and our learners as the patrons who need to be able to digest what we are providing them educationally. I have found that such analogies are helpful in inviting instructors to see the need for continuing to refine their skills.

UDL is not a new idea or a specific template for creating content. It is an approach, a way of thinking about the needs of learners in every part of the learning process, from content acquisition to practice to skill demonstration to engagement and to the learning life cycle. UDL takes into account the fact that no two individuals have the same exact social, physical, mental, and experiential combinations. Therefore, even in the most homogeneous of environments, there is still a great extent of diversity. Considering the variation inherent in a group's neurodiversity and different social identities (e.g., race, gender, ability) adds to the complexity of diversity and the need to pay particular attention to being as proactive as we possibly can. According to CAST (2018), the best way to address variation is to meet the needs of the various aspects of our brain, which consists of three networks: affective, recognition, and strategic. These networks correspond to the why (affective network), the what (recognition network), and the how (strategic network) of learning. UDL calls for a proactive design of instructional goals, assessments, methods, and materials to meet the needs of learners across these networks.

Using UDL for Intentional Course Design

Understanding how to strike a balance among being a high-quality educator and incorporating new technology, being inclusive, and meeting all the other competing needs can be daunting for some instructors. One of the most important things to recognize when building a course in any mode is that beyond structuring the course design in a way that is standard, an educator cannot be everything to everybody. In fact, trying to do too much in any course could lead to fatigue in another way. Have you ever seen a movie with too much action or been overwhelmed by a bunch of flashing lights when out in public? That could be what a course looks like or feels like to students when they have a professor who is aggressively trying to be everything for them. I know this because I was that professor, especially in my online courses. My courses would have everything, all the bells and whistles, and it would be too much for the learners. I did not improve until I started to think more about the intentionality behind the learning design and how the tools I would use fit in to the course in a way that benefited learning. The substitution, augmentation, modification, and redefinition (SAMR) model provides a great framework for being purposeful with technology use and invites instructors to think of how any tool would substitute, augment, modify, or redefine the learning experience (Romrell et al., 2014). For example, if you plan to use Twitter in place of a discussion board, think about the ways it could transform the learning experience. If it's just a replacement, is it worth the change? Using the SAMR model as a lens has helped me cut out the unnecessary use of technological tools and saved me time.

Beyond the use of tools, for instructors' intentionality to be enhanced over time, it is important for them to continue to expand and refine the way they think. This is why a big chunk of this chapter covers aspects of diversity and equity and inclusion to help you think better about learning spaces. Without the expanded understanding in thinking, one tends to be aggressively inclusive versus systematically intentional. This is equivalent to people who are really at their core uncomfortable being around any other group, and through that discomfort, they are excessively nice or apologetic. These tendencies are microaggressions, which are "brief and commonplace daily verbal, behavioral, or environmental indignities, whether intentional or unintentional, that communicate hostile, derogatory, or negative racial slights and insults toward people" (Sue et al., 2007). Unfortunately, there isn't a quick fix for erasing microaggressions or stereotypes. In fact, the best way for an instructor to not allow these items to negatively impact their interactions with learners is through increased exposure to different groups and situations that challenge their preconceived notions. People do not necessarily lose those negative thoughts that have been engrained on their mental record through socialization through exposure, but they become more aware of when those thoughts are at play. Increased self-awareness also allows more agency over responses after any stimulus. For example, although a person may, innocuously or otherwise, be impressed at a certain student's score, with increased self-awareness they might avoid uttering something like, "Wow, this is unbelievable! I am surprised you did this well on the test; good job!" Imagine a world where people actually did in fact think before they spoke. It's not the answer to all diversity, equity, and inclusion challenges, but it could mean a world of difference in the classroom. The ID's goal is to expose instructors to these types of self-discovery scenarios. Beyond helping with the specific course design elements, part of an ID's role is to assist instructors in being intentionally inclusive in the ways they think about themselves as builders and facilitators of learning. When the conversation extends to self-discovery items that are not explicitly linked to course elements, IDs must be sure to pose questions and provide concrete examples. This guidance helps instructors connect the dots and enables them to build a learning environment that will provide the learners with a greater opportunity to meet the course objectives.

Obviously, there are many layers to inclusive teaching, and UDL does indeed provide a tight framework that helps put in place a system for inclusion in one's course. However, it is important to note that an instructor's mindset and self-work will either strengthen or derail their ability to be effective at creating welcoming learning spaces. UDL's major tenets of engagement, representation, action, and expression stem from brain research on how to provide instruction that stimulates the affective, recognition, and strategic networks of the brain. Using the brain as the center point provides the opportunity for an inclusion conversation that doesn't inadvertently exclude the learner. Guidelines are developed as a means of providing checkpoints and offer a set of concrete suggestions that can be applied to any discipline or domain to ensure that all learners can access and participate in meaningful, challenging learning opportunities (CAST, 2018). For a visual representation of the principles, see CAST (2018).

I agree with Novak and Thibodeau (2016) that "translating these guidelines will not result in a universally designed course for learners" (p. 623). They assert that "translating these guidelines into effective design practices requires training, time, and perhaps new technical development" (p. 624). There could not be a truer statement. UDL is a marathon, not a sprint, and it requires continued learning, application, and reflection. Their book is a great resource in providing practical tips for instructors.

Universal Design Principles in Practice

In the meantime, to get you started on your path, I offer the following brief definitions and a key question to ask instructors you are working with, three key strategies I have isolated from my own practice and various sources, and a personal best practice.

Representation

How do you plan to present essential course content to your learners? Learners access information in a variety of formats. Consider varying the ways you present essential course content to increase the likelihood of information access and comprehension. According to CAST (2018),

> For example, those with sensory disabilities (e.g., blindness or deafness); learning disabilities (e.g., dyslexia); language or cultural differences, and so forth may all require different ways of approaching content. Others may simply grasp information quicker or more efficiently through visual or auditory means rather than printed text. (para. 1)

Key Strategies

The following are simple strategies for representing materials in multiple ways to learners:

- Provide digital alternatives for all print materials and include captions and educationally relevant descriptions or transcriptions or flexible access

- Present material in redundant ways (e.g., images, graphical representations, slides presented with verbal reinforcement and online version for later reference)
- Provide physical books, digital readings, field trips, speakers, websites, and even other learners as a means of delivering the information

Personal Best Practice

I use VoiceThread, an interactive multimedia slideshow tool that enables users to hold conversations around images, documents, and videos (Brunvand & Byrd, 2011), for discussion boards and activities for learners (Novak & Thibodeau, 2016). In addition, the discussion board should have an option for learners to provide a text response to their peers and a video or an image in some cases.

Assessment

How do you plan to allow learners to show what they know? Learners have preferences for how they express themselves orally, written, and visually. Consider providing multiple ways for students to demonstrate their competency, which increases the likelihood of their success and, ultimately, the effectiveness of how you measure their learning. It should also be recognized that action and expression require a great deal of strategy, practice, and organization, and this is another area in which learners can differ. Montenegro and Jankowski (2017) inform us that assessment is perhaps the most critical area to promote inclusion, because it is the ultimate determining factor of whether learners are able to progress in the course. The authors posit that the assessment of learning should be as culturally inclusive as possible. Beyond cultural differences that many may associate with race and ethnicity, this may also include differences in the way learners take in information. How learners learn is based on not only what information we were exposed to throughout our formative years but also how we were exposed. For example, a household that read frequently would advantage learners who have to read and write for exams, whereas oral exams may benefit learners from more verbal home environments.

Key Strategies

The following are simple strategies for allowing learners to express what they have learned:

- Use assessment data to inform instruction (i.e., pretest, formative assessments, weekly and midcourse adjustments using student feedback)

- Create assessments that address the affective domain (i.e., values, learning how to learn, metacognition) in addition to higher-order thinking skills (i.e., creation, analysis, evaluation)
- Provide flexibility or choice in evaluation methods through assignment options

Personal Best Practice

I provide low-stakes activities (formative assessments) in the learning management system that allow learners to build their learning muscles for more summative assignments and exams. This is not exclusively for competency-based courses; every module in the course should have some type of mechanism for learners to be able to build knowledge. Activities can be as straightforward as using surveys created in Google Forms to requiring learners to react to material through EdPuzzle, a digital tool that allows for the creation of interactive videos. For learning designers who are familiar with adaptive learning, customized learning activities that meet the unique needs of the learners in the learning management system can be triggered by the level of achievement the learner demonstrates on assessments (Paramythis & Loidl-Reisinger, 2003).

Engagement

How do you plan to involve your learners in the learning process? Active participation is key to learning. Consider adopting various ways that students can actively participate in class. Variation is key as learners respond differently to the same stimuli. What excites one learner may very well not receive any response from another.

Key Strategies

The following are simple strategies for engaging learners in multiple ways:

- Encourage active learning and learner-to-learner feedback, and provide learners with the opportunity to set personal goals, including self-assessment
- Use discussion boards, email, social networking sites, or other communication tools to keep learners connected and engaged
- Incorporate humor, field trips, office hours, group work, experiential activities, case studies, and projects (problem-based learning)

Personal Best Practice

I use virtual office hours, community agreements, and placement in learning clusters with two to four other classmates. Feedback for assignments is provided by video messages sent to individual students, virtual meetings, and weekly unit summaries sent to the entire class that highlight themes found across the work of each student. Virtual meetings with the instructor allow the learners to interact with the instructor in a way that provides the same authentic and genuine connection as face-to-face interaction. The overall course promotes student motivation by increasing students' sense of value in the subject matter, belief in their own abilities, and feelings of a learning environment (Ambrose et al., 2013).

An online course can seamlessly adhere to UDL principles and learning design best practices. The overall learning design should allow learners to show what they know in varied and diversified ways. In an effort to make design more intentional and less overwhelming, scholars like Tobin and Behling (2018) have championed a plus-one approach, which invites building on what has been done in the past by adding one additional approach that addresses a UDL principle. For example, beyond using written papers to assess learners, an option can be added for a verbal presentation or video. One notable thing I have found in my research and instructional practices is that when seeking to meet the multiple means of representation principle of the UDL model, the same strategy used could also meet the other two principles: assessment and engagement. For example, if an ecology teacher asks learners to go to a nearby forest to observe the different types of organisms in their environment as an experiential learning option, it is important to recognize that this additional activity also serves as another way to engage learners and can give them another opportunity to show what they know.

Conclusion: Moving Toward a Mode-Neutral World

The future of online education is not necessarily online, hybrid, or face-to-face; it is mode-neutral. Education will focus on outcomes, not the mode of delivery, and then leverage the different modes to heighten outcome. This new reality will heighten the importance of IDs. The core of learning design is (and will become increasingly focused on) determining how the mode of delivery can be best leveraged to achieve objectives in a diversified and inclusive way. The IDs who understand this will excel.

Furthermore, as access to education expands, the IDs and instructors who are skillful at inviting all learners into learning spaces and allowing them to show and demonstrate what they have learned across modes will benefit and continue to take education where it needs to go. The use of frameworks like UDL is great as a scaffold to help guide one's thinking. However, IDs will benefit from an approach that instinctually applies the principles of models like UDL but remains framework agnostic and fluid with what is needed for a positive impact on designing learning spaces.

So what does all of this mean for IDs, instructors, and enhancements to modular objectives, course activities, or assessments? It means a lot of fun work ahead for individuals in the profession, and the likelihood of being gainfully employed is probable. As we prepare for the work ahead, I thank you for reading this chapter and leave you with the following questions: How might you think differently about your approach to guiding individual learners you interact with (instructor, administrator, student) to greater outcomes, understanding that they are unique learners as well? How might you grant greater access to your programs and access to learning in nontraditional settings? What self-reflection and discovery work does this entail for them and you? How will you do your part in making sure everybody gets to learn?

References

Bok, D. (2009). *Universities in the marketplace: The commercialization of higher education* (Vol. 49). Princeton University Press.

Brunvand, S., & Byrd, S. (2011). Using VoiceThread to promote learning engagement and success for all students. *Teaching Exceptional Children, 43*(4), 28–37. https://doi.org/10.1177/004005991104300403

Burgstahler, S. (2008). *Universal design in higher education: From principles to practice*. Harvard Education Press.

CAST. (2018). Provide multiple means of representation. *UDL Guidelines.* http://udlguidelines.cast.org/representation

Center for Applied Special Technology. (2020). *About Universal Design for Learning.* CAST http://www.cast.org/our-work/about-udl.html

Center for Applied Special Technology. (1998). What is universal design for learning?.

Fink, L. D. (2013). *Creating significant learning experiences: An integrated approach to designing college courses*. Wiley.

Giroux, H. A., Freire, P., & McLaren, P. (1988). *Teachers as intellectuals: Toward a critical pedagogy of learning*. Greenwood Publishing Group.

Guinier, L. (2015). *The tyranny of the meritocracy: Democratizing higher education in America*. Beacon Press.

Ladson-Billings, G. (1995). But that's just good teaching! The case for culturally relevant pedagogy. *Theory Into Practice, 34*(3), 159–165. https://doi.org/10.1080/00405849509543675

Montenegro, E., & Jankowski, N. A. (2017). *Equity and assessment: Moving towards culturally responsive assessment* (Occasional Paper, 29). NILOA. https://learningoutcomesassessment.org/documents/OccasionalPaper29.pdf

Novak, K., & Thibodeau, T. (2016). *UDL in the cloud!: How to design and deliver online education using universal design for learning.* CAST Professional Publishing.

Paramythis, A., & Loidl-Reisinger, S. (2003). Adaptive learning environments and e-learning standards. *Second European Conference on e-Learning, 2*(1), 369–379.

Pollak, D. (Ed.). (2009). *Neurodiversity in higher education: Positive responses to specific learning differences.* Wiley.

Romrell, D., Kidder, L., & Wood, E. (2014). The SAMR model as a framework for evaluating mLearning. *Journal of Asynchronous Learning Networks, 18*(2). https://doi.org/10.24059/olj.v18i2.435

Rose, D. H., & Meyer, A. (2002). *Teaching every student in the digital age: Universal design for learning.* Association for Supervision and Curriculum Development.

Sue, D. W., Capodilupo, C. M., Torino, G. C., Bucceri, J. M., Holder, A. M. B., Nadal, K. L., & Esquilin, M. (2007). Racial microaggressions in everyday life: Implications for clinical practice. *American Psychologist, 62*(4), 271–286.

Tobin, T. J., & Kirsten T. Behling. (2018). *Reach everyone, teach everyone: Universal design for learning in higher education.* West Virginia University Press.

Instructional designers can play a central role in the perpetuation or stamping out of inequality in higher education.

9

DECENTRALIZING WHITENESS

Where Do We Start?

German E. Vargas Ramos

The relationship among race, privilege, and education is deeply ingrained in our society. Instructional designers can play a central role in the perpetuation or stamping out of inequality in higher education. Our work puts us in a key position in regard to instructors, learners, and administrators, with the means to have an impact on teaching, learning, and access in higher education. This chapter discusses the negative impact of the centrality of Whiteness in higher education in the United States in addition to several principles and strategies instructional designers and instructors can adopt to resist its influence and to promote social justice in college education. Knowing that hatred, prejudice, and inequality are a problem in online learning spaces as much as in face-to-face classrooms, instructors and designers have an ethical responsibility to address them. Although our unique position in higher education is in itself a form of privilege, being conscious of it and of the potential impact of our behavior gives us control over our agency. This requires an earnest commitment to making inclusivity and social justice a central goal of teaching and learning, and it begins with design.

Critical Education, *Whiteness*, and *Privilege* Defined

The *critical* portion of terms like *critical literacy*, *critical pedagogy*, and *critical consciousness* refers to various things, such as the push to identify, describe, and attempt to resolve flaws, incongruities, and inefficacies in objects, processes, institutions, or other entities. *Critical education*, the first term, is more than its functional aspects, however. It seeks to promote a greater sociocultural purpose, empowering learners to construct a society that is more equitable, sustainable, and nurturing. It also challenges any individuals, institutions, discourses, and dynamics that seek to preserve systemic inequalities in society. It is important to understand that although the language in this definition of critical education seems to describe a level of impact that seems to be beyond the reach of any one individual, this is only seemingly true. In fact, critical education is founded on the principle that the actions and relationships of individuals, like instructional designers, have a collective societal impact through the interconnected nature of the institutions and communities we are associated with. In other words, the work that we do every day and how we do that work have the potential to transform the fabric of our society. To understand inequity and injustice and one's own relationship with them is known as critical consciousness, and the subsequent will to act to address these issues is known as critical action or praxis (Freire, 2000, 2003).

The second term we should understand is *Whiteness* or *White privilege*. In the field of critical race theory, Whiteness is understood to mean more than a literal designation of race (Donnor, 2013; Lopez, 2006). Instead, Whiteness or being White refers to an arrangement of racial, ethnic, social, cultural, and economic markers and values that have been historically and socially constructed, perpetuated, and exploited primarily by White people of European descent—hence the reference to skin color. These markers grant the people who embody them a disproportionate measure of social advantage over others who are not White. For example, even when they are admitted into postsecondary institutions, Black, mixed-race, and Hispanic students are less likely to graduate when compared to their White peers (National Center for Education Statistics, 2019b). White privilege refers to the advantages White people enjoy over people of color and to the conditions that perpetuate those advantages. Historically, the system of values, beliefs, relationships, institutions, and entitlements that comes with White culture is so widespread and prevalent that it seems invisible or normal to some, particularly in the United States. This is problematic in innumerable ways, but it can be summarized in the following three statements.

First, even though White people are the majority in many communities throughout the United States, their privilege comes at a great social cost to people of color and to White people themselves. Privilege takes participation, resources, and opportunities away from people who don't possess it. Examples of White privilege in education can be seen clearly at an institutional level in colleges and universities, which, for example, admit more White students per capita than they do students of any other race (National Center for Education Statistics, 2019a). This disparity in admission numbers is one of the most direct and visible examples of systemic White privilege in higher education. Educational attainment has a direct impact on individuals' overall quality of life, starting with their socioeconomic status (U.S. Bureau of Labor Statistics, 2019). By themselves the inequalities that result from underrepresentation in postsecondary education have a higher negative impact on people of color and their communities, but they also combine with other forms of injustice, like social or legal discrimination, to present people of color with more and more complex disadvantages. Another example is how learners of color have to overcome not only the academic challenges that come from academic work but also the stereotypes that society at large perpetuates, all while they cope with oppression on a societal scale and with microaggressions on an everyday basis.

Second, it can be difficult for people to become conscious of their own privilege and even more difficult to cast it off or to use it for the benefit of those less privileged than themselves. Checking one's privilege means questioning advantages that are unfair but are nonetheless beneficial to those who possess them or put them in the position of being right regardless of context. It also means resisting the urge to be fearful, selfish, and toxically competitive to move society forward. Examples of checking one's privilege as a learner can be as simple as not assuming that others don't know anything because they are not eager to speak up in class or mistaking one's beliefs or experiences for facts without considering that evidence is more important than beliefs or that others might have different experiences that can equally inform the truth. On a broader level, checking one's privilege means avoiding generalizations about who belongs in college or has what it takes to graduate and instead coming to understand, if not resolve, the inequalities that some learners face.

Third, when confronted with inequality and injustice, difference and inaction are only slightly less harmful than consciously perpetuating the status quo. Personally and professionally, instructors and designers are responsible for treating learners fairly and for helping them succeed. We are also responsible for ensuring that our institutions, disciplines, and professions do so as well. We do this with our advocacy and our agency as much as with our expertise—for example, by getting involved in social justice initiatives on our campuses as volunteers rather than employees or by modeling behaviors we would like others to take up, like challenging others in their assumptions, speaking up when confronted with microaggressions, or implementing inclusive practices during classes, meetings, and other activities and educating participants about their purpose and value. The way a college degree adds to one's privilege positions universities and faculty as gatekeepers because the sociocultural prevalence of Whiteness predisposes people and institutions to favor learners who conform to a fictitious ideal of the college-ready student.

These practices are unfair to not only people of color but also students who are White but otherwise do not match the fictitious norm society has constructed around White privilege (i.e., a learner who is middle class or higher, from an urban or suburban community, gender-conforming, fully abled, and so on). Finally, we should note that White privilege is harmful to White people at large because, if unquestioned, it can leave Whites with a false sense of entitlement and a skewed understanding of social realities, in denial of their own role in creating and perpetuating inequality, and resistant to social progress from anxiety or fear of not being granted the advantages they mistakenly believe they are due. This is why it is indispensable to pursue social justice and equity in higher education; it benefits all learners, and inaction makes us complicit in perpetuating injustice. As instructional designers, our roles as partners with faculty, leaders in our institutions, and advocates for students are therefore inseparable, and we are responsible for making higher education accessible, inclusive, and fair.

Promoting Critical Awareness Through Design

The design stage is a critical point in the development of educational activities and materials because it offers many opportunities to identify and address the challenges that lie ahead and not only create conditions that will facilitate learning but also compensate for the inequalities among students. This is especially true considering that the main benefit of a structured learning design process is as much a matter of time as of intent. Even if one understands inequality, it is much easier to address it in courses if one has prepared to do so ahead of time rather than waiting for issues to emerge. A well-structured design process provides continuous opportunities for instructors and designers to identify, examine, and deliberately address inequality.

Instructional designers can address racial inequality in university education in three fundamental ways. The first is to acknowledge and critically examine the biases in academic disciplines and institutions by creating safe spaces to discuss how inequalities affect our colleagues and to learn how to support them in their work, for example. The second is to situate that understanding in the context of our institutions and the communities they serve, such as creating connections between the campus and leaders or experts in the community that can help address local issues. The third and most crucial step is to act in pursuit of those goals and objectives, which we discuss in more detail later. If these steps seem familiar, it's not by coincidence. They correspond with the stages of the development of critical consciousness: awareness, critical reflection, and praxis or critical action (Freire, 2000, 2003; Freire & Macedo, 1987). This coincidence is important because it shows that promoting social justice is wholly compatible with teaching and learning. It also shows that social justice is not an additional burden or distraction for designers and educators. Instead, it is an essential aspect of quality in education regardless of the subject matter. As Barab et al. (2007) pointed out,

> Design-based researchers can instantiate a critical stance in different aspects of their design work and at different levels of its implementation, including transforming the curriculum, the student, the teacher, and the sociocultural contexts in which their designs are being realized. (p. 265)

As designers this allows us to reframe issues of inequality in the classroom as specific learning or institutional needs to be addressed directly through critical design and the transformation of teaching practice. This creates a process that has a double outcome. First, it produces learning experiences that will have more of an impact on learners' lives, and second, it can critically transform the culture of an institution and the community to make it more inclusive and fair. We can accomplish this by discussing accessibility, equity, and inclusivity as indispensable design elements as we work together with instructors during consultations and other development events. We have to acknowledge, of course, that challenging any of faculty's or colleagues' deeply ingrained beliefs, biases, or misconceptions might result in uncomfortable or otherwise difficult conversations. We must press forward, not only as a matter of ethics and principles but also for the sake of the learners in our classrooms. To achieve this, it's important for us to develop design practices to integrate educational innovation and social justice to show that accessibility, equity, and inclusivity are not an afterthought or a new requirement that's been added to quality education, but an essential part of it that has been neglected for too long.

The design process is likely to include the closest points of collaboration between educators and designers, contributing to a growing sense of community and collegiality that is a side benefit of the critical design process. When it comes to design, I propose three fundamental principles to follow to advance a critical design agenda: authenticity, responsiveness, and transparency. These principles can help promote learning outcomes that include empowerment, inclusiveness, accurate social and cultural representation, and more. This is not to say this is the only way to reach those outcomes but rather that critical outcomes become much less likely to emerge if these elements are absent from teaching and learning. How these principles apply in different settings and for different disciplines or curricula varies widely. In whatever form they take, they should align with the goals and objectives identified early in the process, following the backward design framework of goals, evidence, and experiences (Wiggins & McTighe, 2005). This is where established classroom materials and activities combine with emerging ones to promote critical transformation and innovation. These principles can also help designers and educators evaluate a design they have produced or encountered to assess its critical educational potential.

Authenticity

Authenticity applies to the rigor of disciplinary knowledge and the real-world relevance of learning activities. It also applies to the transformative characteristics of a design and to the critical intent of those who produce it. This level of authenticity can transform classrooms into communities of practice (Wenger, 1998) that support learning by situating learning in the context and the culture of an authentic setting and giving learners the opportunity to bring their identities and life experiences to bear during online course activities (Lave & Wenger, 1991). This creates alignment between the course and real-world issues or spaces. Of course, learning designs must promote the acquisition of disciplinary knowledge and skills. However, from a critical perspective, designs that seek to confront or overcome the influence of White privilege in the classroom must go beyond the minimum of authenticity represented by situated practice. Critical designs must be academically rigorous while at the same time addressing real-world issues and connecting directly to the identities and interests of learners who can bring the authenticity of their life experience to the process. Two conversations designers can have with instructors about approaches to authenticity are decolonizing the syllabus and learner-driven projects.

Decolonizing the syllabus (DeChavez, 2018) refers to a very specific and deliberate process that takes into account that as a symbol the syllabus upholds the privileged role of White culture in the college curriculum and seeks to decentralize it to make space to more accurately represent the diverse identities that exist in society. The process itself is practical rather than symbolic and asks instructors to abandon dominant discourses and established canons in favor of underrepresented perspectives, marginalized voices, and alternative ways of knowing and of making meaning, but this only scratches the surface. This process also asks instructors and designers to become deeply invested in understanding the experiences of the learners in their classrooms to better support their learning in multiple ways, as discussed in this chapter, not only for their benefit as learners but also to add to a collective transformative process that counteracts the negative effects of colonialism and White privilege in society at large.

Another design strategy to increase authenticity is implementation of learner-driven projects of different kinds. These projects can be individual or group based, creative or inquiry based, and iterative or not, as long as they align with the learning goals and objectives of a course and represent a proportional amount of work for all learners, in spite of differences in topic or structure. Examples of this include assignments that prompt students to use a critical perspective to respond to current events or address unanswered questions in a discipline and projects that involve students working with a particular community or organization that promotes social justice.

Responsiveness

Responsiveness in design refers to the ability to adapt activities and materials to connect with learners' identities and lives and to changing social conditions. Whether they (or we) are conscious of it or not, learners' mental or emotional state is invariably connected to or conditioned by identity and how learners see themselves among their peers and in their surroundings, such as in the classroom, at an institution, in different communities, and ultimately in the world. This state affects how learners perceive new knowledge and how they perform during learning activities or assessments. Things like trauma, microaggressions, discrimination, and the many forms of inequality can have an impact on learners' affect. Critical designs should respond to these issues as well as to the more visible aspects of identity, like race, class, gender, and cultural or ethnic background (Steele, 2011).

One example of a responsive design is assignment menus. Assignment menus are groups of assignments that accomplish similar goals and are similar in scope but allow learners to select assessments that let them put their best foot forward and better show their understanding of course material while providing them with the opportunity to engage with knowledge and practices they are not well versed in. These groupings also have lower overall stakes, such as giving greater weight to assessments learners do best in so they can focus on learning rather than performance. Other possibilities include working with learners and instructors to design learner-driven projects that give learners ownership over their learning and developing assessment frameworks that help instructors provide more individualized learning options and give better quality feedback. The overall goal of responsive design is to develop strategies for adapting courses, activities, and materials, sometimes in real time, to respond to the needs and identities of different students in ways that are sustainable in the long term.

Transparency

The third guiding principle for designing learning experiences that decentralize White privilege is transparency, which provides clarity to all learners but can also help them connect with classroom knowledge and engage in activities they might find unfamiliar, inauthentic, or awkward. The most prominent articulation of transparency in higher education can be found in the transparent design framework (Winkelmes et al., 2019), which is perfectly suited to this task (see chapter 10). Another approach to transparency involves explicitly acknowledging the biases and other forms of exclusion learners encounter in higher education and in the workplace and devoting time in the classroom to addressing these issues through learner-driven projects and by including learners in course development and in academic inquiry.

Transparency operates in connection with authenticity and responsiveness to address the issue that classrooms are not authentic settings in the same way that a community or a workplace can be (Lave & Wenger, 1991). This can disproportionately alienate learners of color, especially considering that the discourses, cultural norms, and class values they encounter in those classrooms are predominantly centered around White culture. Transparency makes explicit the fact that the critical outcomes that students are expected to achieve are important to learners' development and should be a central part of the learning experience. In other words, transparency helps advance social justice in connection with disciplinary knowledge, not in addition to it. Transparency can also make teaching more authentic and responsive by mapping the connections among the classroom, learners' lives, and the world at large from a perspective of assessment as well as design. This in turn contributes to the process of identifying different types of evidence of learning in accordance with the second step in the backward design framework (Wiggins & McTighe, 2005).

Conclusion

Throughout this discussion, we have seen that tackling White privilege in education is a necessary and complex task that requires us to commit to an iterative, multilayered, and collaborative approach. This is especially so considering that decentralizing Whiteness is only one aspect of inclusivity and social justice, which must integrate with other forms of inclusivity. Thinking about injustice is a step in the right direction, but without additional effort and attention, it doesn't necessarily address issues of ableism, digital inclusion, ageism, trauma, and so on. The need for transformation isn't limited only to the classroom either. Another key step in addressing White privilege in education is actively recruiting people of color as faculty and academic support personnel. Instructional designers can work with their supervisors and with other university administrators in human resources, for example, to approach candidates of color and support them in their work once they're hired.

The number of possible adjustments that could be made to accommodate all learners can seem daunting, which is why educators, designers, and other academic staff must work together to ease each other's load and to lend their expertise to bear on the issues we have identified. Making a profound difference in the learning experiences and outcomes of cohort after cohort of learners can affect more than those learners' lives and the culture of an institution. It will also have an impact on the community at large and, over time, at a systemic level. As instructional designers, we have the most impact when we advocate for each and every learner in the classrooms that we serve.

References

Barab, S., Dodge, T., Thomas, M. K., Jackson, C., & Tuzun, H. (2007). Our designs and the social agendas they carry. *Journal of the Learning Sciences, 16*(2), 263–305. https://doi.org/10.1080/10508400701193713

DeChavez, Y. (2018, October 8). It's time to decolonize that syllabus. *Los Angeles Times*. https://www.latimes.com/books/la-et-jc-decolonize-syllabus-20181008-story.html

Donnor, J. K. (2013). Education as the property of Whites: African American's continued quest for good schools. In M. Lynn & A. Dixson (Eds.), *Handbook of critical race theory in education* (pp. 195–203). Routledge.

Freire, P. (2000). *Pedagogy of the oppressed* (M. B. Ramos, Trans.) Seabury Press.

Freire, P. (2003). *Education for critical consciousness*. Continuum.

Freire, P., & Macedo, D. (1987). *Literacy: Reading the word and the world*. Bergin & Harvey.

Lave, J., & Wenger, E. (1991). *Situated learning: Legitimate peripheral participation* (Learning in doing: Social, cognitive and computational perspectives). Cambridge University Press.

Lopez, I. H. (2006). *White by law: The legal construction of race*. NYU Press.

National Center for Education Statistics. (2019a). *College enrollment rates*. https://nces.ed.gov/programs/coe/indicator_cpb.asp and https://nces.ed.gov/programs/coe/pdf/coe_cpb.pdf

National Center for Education Statistics. (2019b). *Indicator 23: Postsecondary graduation rates*. https://nces.ed.gov/programs/raceindicators/indicator_red.asp

Steele, C. (2011). *Whistling Vivaldi: And other clues to how stereotypes affect us*. Norton.

U.S. Bureau of Labor Statistics. (2019). *Unemployment rates and earnings by educational attainment*. https://www.bls.gov/emp/chart-unemployment-earnings-education.htm

Wenger, E. (1998). *Communities of practice: Learning, meaning, and identity*. Cambridge University Press.

Wiggins, G., & McTighe, J. (2005). *Understanding by design*. Association for Supervision and Curriculum Development.

Winkelmes, M. A., Boyle, A., & Tapp, S. (Eds.). (2019). *Transparent design in higher education teaching and leadership*. Stylus.

Instructors are looking for motivation strategies because their teaching goals extend beyond just getting learners to pass the course.

10

MOTIVATION FOR LEARNING

If We Build It, Will They Come?

Traci Stromie

It's the middle of October, you're sitting at your desk trying to attain inbox zero, and the phone rings. You pick up the receiver and hear a frantic voice on the line. It's Professor Cameron, an instructor you met recently, who needs a consultation as soon as possible because she is frustrated with her online course. Cameron comes to your office and says that one of her online courses feels like what happens in the movie *Groundhog Day*: The same thing is happening over and over, semester after semester. The course meets the enrollment cap soon after the registration period opens, and the learners are participating in the first few weeks but slowly disappear from the course without dropping the class. Some learners are engaged, dutifully completing assignments and chugging along, but it seems like they are making the minimum effort required to complete each task. Cameron tries sending emails to remind learners of the deadlines, but it does not seem to help. She is sure the assignments are meaningful because they are connected to her learning objectives, but she is at a loss on how to proceed.

This scenario is not uncommon. Instructors may come to you, the instructional designer, with a challenge, but they are not sure what the root cause is or what research-based strategies should be implemented to improve the course. At this point, you are likely taking on multiple roles: listener, investigator, and consultant. It is a balancing act between the skills you have and the perceived needs of the instructor. As mentioned earlier in this volume (see chapter 6), one of our main goals as instructional designers is to provide research-based suggestions to help the instructor be in the best position to make decisions for their course.

This chapter focuses on how you can support instructors in making choices during the course design process and when facilitating the course during the semester to help increase student motivation for learning. Motivation is personal, and what is motivating for some learners might not be motivating for others. However, we can borrow some theories from the learning sciences to look at what we know will influence learners' eagerness to engage with course material, complete activities at a high level, and stoke the fire of learning.

How Are You Motivated?

When most people hear the word *motivation*, often the first things that come to mind are intrinsic and extrinsic. Intrinsic motivation drives us to do things because we are interested, curious, want to learn more, or have a genuine desire to know or do something. Extrinsic motivation pushes us into action because we are looking to impress someone, make money, earn a reward, or get recognition from someone else (Deci & Ryan, 1985). Being aware of types of motivation is important because as learners come into a course, they might approach different assignments with different motivations, which will affect their behavior. For example, a business major who is required to take a general education science class might not be intrinsically motivated to complete lab assignments because the student does not see the relevance. However, the learner might complete the task because of external motivation to get a good grade and keep a high grade point average.

Expectancy-value theory provides a helpful framework for thinking about how to motivate learners (Wigfield & Eccles, 2000). Ambrose et al. (2010) added a third component that contributes to improving motivation in the classroom. All three components are value, self-efficacy, and a supportive environment.

Value is the relative importance a learner ascribes to a course, task, or assignment. Value can be subjective based on internal and external motivations. Learners are more motivated to complete tasks with a perceived high value.

Learners are motivated to complete tasks they think they will be successful with; no one likes to feel incompetent. Having high self-efficacy, the belief you can complete a task, is a critical component of motivation. It might be a challenge to get that same business major to write an analysis of contemporary British authors in an English course because the student does not expect to be successful on the assignment. Self-efficacy can be tied to the stories learners tell themselves, such as they are not a writer or not a math person or that they have performed poorly on a similar task in the past.

The supportive environment component reminds instructors how they can directly affect the motivation of the learners. Instructors should structure the course so learners see the value in what they are being asked to do and understand that the instructor cares about their success. Occasionally a supportive environment might happen by chance, but more often than not instructors need to be intentional about this in a course. Creating a supportive environment includes incorporating a positive tone, opening lines of interpersonal communication, and establishing trust and rapport (Ambrose et al., 2010; Chew, 2018; Kale, 2013).

The rest of this chapter explores the relationship between learner motivation and course design and delivery. Although instructors cannot affect all aspects of motivation in one semester, there are some considerations to keep in mind as they develop learning environments.

Motivation and Course Design

Designing a course with learners' motivation in mind can help alleviate challenges during the semester. If learners start out on the right foot, the instructor can create opportunities to increase value, self-efficacy, and autonomy, and students may be less likely to drop off during the semester, preventing the exact scenario described at the start of the chapter. The bottom line is that instructors will not have to chase down checked-out learners; they can review assignments that reflect learners' excitement to complete them and see their learners' skills shine. Your role as an instructional designer can be vital during this phase. You have the opportunity to guide the instructor toward making decisions that support motivation or build these components yourself.

Authentic Assessments

Authentic assessments "aim to be realistic, which means the task reproduces the ways and the contexts in which a person's knowledge and abilities are 'tested' in real-world situations" (Barkley, 2010, p. 29). They might be structured in a way that allows students "to create artifacts that have life and an audience beyond the course" (Linder & Hayes, 2018, p. 82) and provide an opportunity to encourage students to achieve objectives at higher levels of cognition (Linder & Hayes, 2018). Authentic assessments will vary based on the discipline and the course. It is likely that because learners are engaging in assessments that are more complex, relevant, and interesting than a multiple-choice test, for example, they "are often more motivated to do them than they are to do conventional assessment activities" (Barkley, 2010, p. 30).

Authentic tasks can improve motivation because they increase the value learners place on the task and allow learners to shift from the study of abstract theory to an engagement with relevant problems and projects (Ambrose et al., 2010). Learners go beyond recalling or identifying knowledge to a concrete task with products that could be used in a portfolio and maybe help them get a job or internship in the future. For example, learners in Marketing 101 might work with local nonprofits to create a social media marketing strategy, including plans, images, and sample posts. They can be designed within the constraints provided by the company, and the final products may be posted online by the client. Learners who want to pursue a career in marketing would likely find this assignment worthwhile compared to an essay in which they identify the components of a marketing plan.

Guiding instructors in designing authentic assessments can be a challenge because it is hard to precisely define what an authentic assessment looks like for each course. Wiggins and McTighe (2005) identified common components of authentic assessments. Authentic assessments should

- situate a problem in a genuine context,
- require active learning and being present by doing,
- align with course objectives while being innovative, and
- emulate a real-world challenge.

It is critical for learners to not be left on their own when completing authentic assessments. Encourage instructors to set up opportunities for practice, provide feedback, and allow revisions as the emphasis is on the process and real-world learning, not a one-time assessment event.

If an instructor is open to transforming some course assessments to be more authentic, you can spend time brainstorming possible tasks. Questions to ask the instructor might include the following:

- How might the facts students need to know be used in industry?
- What projects would entry-level employees in their field be assigned to?
- What could students create, based on the content, that could be included in a portfolio?

- Are there groups on campus or in the community that would be willing to donate time to help with this or would benefit from working with students?

Transparency Framework

The Transparency in Learning and Teaching (TILT) project, originally produced at the University of Illinois at Urbana-Champaign in 2009 and now hosted at Brandeis University, provides instructors with a transparency framework that can increase learners' academic confidence, sense of belonging, and skills valued by most learners (TILT in Higher Education, n.d.a). This approach connects to motivation through establishing a supportive environment by making the expectations of the instructor clear. The transparency framework asks instructors to reformat the assignments to be problem centered, or more authentic. Restructuring assignments in this way allows learners to operate at higher levels of cognition and connect complex skills that might otherwise only be practiced in isolation. Additionally, transparency allows learners to see explicit connections among assignments and the how and why of course design decisions that are typically invisible (Winkelmes et al., 2016).

To make assignments more transparent, designers and instructors create an assignment description sheet with three main areas: purpose, task, and criteria. In the purpose area, instructors or designers describe goals for the activity and why students are completing this assignment. The purpose section should focus on the skills and knowledge reflected in the assignment and ideally be framed around a problem. The skills area explains how the assignment is connected to long-term relevance and workplace abilities. The knowledge area communicates the connection to the course or module learning objectives. Basically, consider the purpose as a way for learners to clearly see what is in it for them.

The task section sequentially lists the steps students will take to finish the assignment. Instructions should keep the focus on the skills learners will be achieving and list any tasks that should be avoided. If there are pedagogical reasons to withhold specific steps in the task area so learners can struggle with a process, explain that in the purpose area to maintain trust, student confidence, and high self-efficacy throughout the task.

The criteria section describes the characteristics the instructor is looking for in a completed assignment and explains to learners how they will be graded. Grading criteria might be communicated as a checklist or a rubric. The transparency framework also puts an emphasis on helping learners analyze examples of final products (Winkelmes et al., 2016). This can increase confidence and self-efficacy because students realize they can complete tasks that meet the high expectations of instructors.

The TILT Higher Ed (n.d.b) website is an excellent resource containing slides and articles about the framework, templates, and checklists. If you create and facilitate any professional development for online course design, consider transparently framing your assignments to show instructors who participate what TILT looks like in action. This will clarify your expectations and allows instructors see how vital transparency is.

Assignment Format Options

One way a learner can have autonomy, or some control over their learning, is to allow them to make decisions on the format for completing assignments (Weimer, 2013). This might sound ridiculous, but stay with me. If an instructor's assignment asks learners to synthesize information or analyze data, the emphasis here might shift to the cognitive skill rather than the format of the completed assignment. Based on learners' skills and interests, instructors may give them the option to write a paper, create a presentation, record a video, or design a website. This allows learners to fulfill the goal of the assignment, synthesizing information in a format that is meaningful to them. Being flexible in how learners complete tasks "lends a sense of control, which can contribute to a student's expectation of success" (Ambrose et al., 2010, p. 89). This can have an impact on motivation by increasing learners' self-efficacy because they are completing tasks in a way that draws on their personal strengths.

Providing multiple assignment options requires a little more work for the instructor and designer, but it can be worth it. The TILT framework (Winkelmes et al., 2016) is beneficial if using various assignment options because the instructor can emphasize the purpose of the assignment by clarifying the skills and knowledge where learners should direct their efforts. For some learners, creating a video requires many skills they would have to teach themselves, which sounds like a nightmare, and they would prefer to write a paper. For other learners, video skills are second nature and allow them to use their creativity while also showcasing the knowledge they gained.

Clarifying grading components is also important here. Encourage instructors to use a rubric or checklist that describes the components that contribute to the final assignment grade. Rubrics are helpful because they streamline the grading and feedback process, saving instructors time during the grading process and keeping things consistent.

Instructors may be resistant to using rubrics as they have the perceived drawbacks of feeling restricting and possibly reducing student creativity.

Providing examples of different types of rubrics can show instructors they do not have to get boxed into one thing. Exploring analytic, holistic, and single-point rubrics can be helpful, and an internet search of rubrics for a specific discipline can give the instructor a good starting point.

Motivation and Facilitation

In the scenario at the start of the chapter, the instructor came to you halfway through the semester. Some of the course design approaches mentioned in this chapter could be implemented for the remainder of the semester, but depending on the class and university policies, the design of a course might not be able to change. Helping instructors implement some of the following facilitation strategies can increase motivation when a course design is fixed.

Video Announcements

Being intentional about the interactions in a course, specifically between instructor and content, instructor and learners, and learners and learners, can "help students feel part of a community, which sustains their persistence in online courses" (Nilson & Goodson, 2018, p. 132). This goes back to the supportive environment motivation factor. One strategy for community building and continued instructor presence throughout the semester is using videos for course announcements.

Videos can grab learners' attention because they are out of the ordinary compared to the text announcements they may expect. Video announcements can be quickly created using a cell phone or webcam and do not need to be polished to eliminate every flaw. Instructors can use videos as an opportunity to show their personality and passion for a course, and you can help them do this. Recording videos in unexpected places like the dining hall, gym, outdoors, or other locations that fit the context of the course can help learners connect with the person on the other side of the screen. If an instructor feels uncomfortable being in front of the camera, there are other approaches. A geography professor could film nature scenes while only recording their voice as a way to provide course updates and not get in front of the camera. As a part-time instructor myself, I love finding new ways to keep my announcements interesting. In the past, I have recorded myself near interesting landmarks while traveling to a conference, and on Halloween I recorded myself in costume. What innovative environments are available near your campus where you can help an instructor record a video?

Video announcements might include reminders about deadlines, updates about changes to the course, or brief introductions to content. They do not need to follow a script or be rerecorded until every last "um," "like," and "you know" is gone. Keep announcement videos short, fewer than 3 minutes, and be sure they are captioned (Mayer, 2008). Captioning makes the videos accessible, which is essential for learners who might need accommodations and for other learners who like to use them (Tobin & Behling, 2018). There is a bonus with this strategy: If you facilitate online professional development for instructors, create your own videos to showcase how fun and informative they can be.

Midsemester Evaluations

In the scenario at the beginning of this chapter, the instructor did not know what exactly was causing learners to disengage or only attempt to do the minimum in the course. Spending some time reviewing the course up to that point in the semester might provide a better idea about what has happened and what types of interventions to suggest. However, research shows that soliciting feedback back often and early in the semester "allows the instructor to improve even very challenging classes, strengthen student learning, enhance student motivation, and positively alter student attitudes toward the instructor and the course" (Davis, 2009, p. 461). These formative, midsemester evaluations are great to suggest to instructors to incorporate in a course, or they can be facilitated by the instructional designer. They are different from what happens at the end of the course because they give the instructor the opportunity to make adjustments for this group of learners. The midsemester evaluation fosters a supportive environment because the learners feel that their voices matter and are valued.

An online midsemester evaluation can be accomplished quickly using any survey tool. Most learning management systems have a built-in survey tool, but some learners might not believe that it is truly anonymous. In that case, the instructional designer or instructor can use Google Forms or a different free survey tool to check in with learners. Encourage instructors to avoid asking what students prefer. Instead, suggest focusing the questions on what contributes to learning. Sample questions include the following:

- What activities in the course contribute to your learning?
- What specific suggestions do you have to improve the course?
- What might improve your learning experience?

- What assignments have not helped you achieve the course learning objectives?

Similar to a midsemester evaluation, you can offer to facilitate a small-group instructional diagnosis (SGID) for an instructor at any point in the semester. This involves you setting up a survey asking for feedback from the learners. SGIDs take a little more coordination because the instructor needs to introduce you to the class, by email or announcement, explain who you are, and state the purpose of the SGID before you can send the survey link to learners. You collect the data, look for themes, and assist the instructor in identifying areas to make changes in the course. The instructor can share the feedback with learners "indicating what changes will be made or why certain things cannot be changed" (Svinicki & McKeachie, 2011, p. 338).

Whether you assist an instructor with an evaluation or facilitate a SGID yourself, it is essential to review the feedback and have the instructor address what the learners have said. If something cannot be altered in the course but is being communicated as a needed change, it is an excellent opportunity for the instructor to explain why the course is designed the way it is. Encourage instructors to find one or two things in the course that can be updated to show learners their voices are being heard and valued. This demonstrates to learners that the course is supportive and committed to their learning. Svinicki (2001) said that "we must remember that none of us is so good that we cannot be better" (p. 24).

Conclusion

Learners' attention is continually being pulled from online course environments each time they open a web browser to log in to a class. Course assignments and readings are competing with Instagram, Reddit, YouTube, and other popular social media sites. It is easy for learners to do the minimum to get their grade so they can go back to what they think really matters. Strategically planning a course and having ideas about how to engage learners during the semester can help instructors communicate why their course matters too.

It is likely that instructors coming to you for support have bought into the idea that their job is more than covering content. These instructors are looking for motivation strategies because their teaching goals extend beyond just getting learners to pass the course. They want to inspire learners to make connections between the content and their own lives, build relationships among the learners and their peers, and provide an opportunity for learners to demonstrate the knowledge and skills they gained in a meaningful and authentic way. They are truly looking to create a learner-centered course.

References

Ambrose, S., Lovett, M., Bridges, M., DiPietro, M., & Norman, M. (2010). *How learning works: Seven research-based principles for smart teaching*. Jossey-Bass.

Barkley, E. F. (2010). *Student engagement techniques: A handbook for college faculty*. Jossey-Bass.

Chew, S. (October 2018). *The importance of building student trust* [Keynote presentation]. Research on Teaching and Learning Summit Conference. Kennesaw, GA, United States.

Davis, B. G. (2009). *Tools for teaching* (2nd ed.). Jossey-Bass.

Deci, E., & Ryan, R. (1985). *Intrinsic motivation and self-determination in human behavior*. Plenum Press.

Kale, M. (2013). Perceptions of college of education students in Turkey towards organizational justice, trust in administrators, and instructors. *Higher Education*, *66*(5), 521–533. https://doi.org/10.1007/s10734-013-9619-7

Linder, K., & Hayes, C. (2018). *High-impact practices in online education: Research and best practices*. Stylus.

Mayer, R. E. (2008). Applying the science of learning: Evidence-based principles for the design of multimedia instruction. *American Psychologist*, *63*(8), 760–769. https://doi.org/10.1037/0003-066x.63.8.760

Nilson, L. & Goodson, L. (2018). *Online teaching at its best: Merging instructional design with teaching and learning research*. Jossey-Bass.

Svinicki, M. (2001). Encouraging your students to give feedback. *New Directions for Teaching and Learning*, 87, 17–24. https://doi.org/10.1002/tl.24

Svinicki, M., & McKeachie, W. (2011) *McKeachie's teaching tips: Strategies, research, and theory for college and university teachers* (13th ed.). Wadsworth, Cengage Learning.

TILT Higher Ed. (n.d.a). *Transparency in learning and teaching*. https://tilthighered.com

TILT Higher Ed. (n.d.b). *About Transparency in Learning and Teaching in Higher Education*. https://tilthighered.com/abouttilt

Tobin, T. J., & Behling, K. (2018). *Reach everyone, teach everyone: Universal design for learning in higher education*. West Virginia University Press.

Weimer, M. (2013). *Learner-centered teaching: Five key changes to practice*. Jossey-Bass.

Wigfield, A., & Eccles, J. (2000). Expectancy-value theory of achievement motivation. *Contemporary Educational Psychology*, *25*(1), 68–81. https://doi.org/10.1006/ceps.1999.1015

Wiggins, G., & McTighe, J. (2005). *Understanding by design.* Association for Supervision of Curriculum Development.

Winkelmes, M., Bernacki, M., Butler, J., Zochowski, M., Golanics, J., & Weavil, K. H. (2016). A teaching intervention that increases underserved college students' success. *Peer Review, 18*(1/2), 31–36. https://www.aacu.org/peerreview/2016/winter-spring/Winkelmes

As important as it is for our learners to learn and practice the skills of metacognition, it is equally important for us to also practice these skills in our own work as designers and instructors.

II

METACOGNITION AND REFLECTION

How We Know What We Know and Don't Know

Kathryn E. Linder

Designing opportunities to encourage metacognition, or thinking about how learning works, is an important component of instructional design. When learners reflect on their choices and performance on a regular basis, they begin to develop an accurate perception of not only what they have learned but also what they have left to learn. This chapter helps you identify the places where a reflective pause can help solidify learning and how best to build in those moments for reflection based on disciplinary constructs, the level of the learner, and the instructor's pedagogical preferences.

A basic definition of *metacognition* is "thinking about your own thinking" (McGuire, 2015, p. 16). Often accomplished through reflective activities, such as keeping a journal, discussions, peer and self-assessment, and a range of other tasks, the development of metacognitive skills ensures that learners will have the ability to "evaluate the demands of the tasks that they [are] given and . . . adjust their approaches to learning accordingly" (Ambrose et al., 2010, pp. 191–192). According to McGuire (2015), metacognition also allows learners to "become consciously aware of themselves as problem solvers" and "gives students the ability to accurately judge how deeply they have learned something" (p. 16). It is important to note that many learners may complete some or all of these tasks without overtly thinking about them. As Doyle (2011) has noted, reflection is "the lost art of college learning" (p. 145). When learners are not asked directly to reflect on their own experiences, they probably will not take the steps to do metacognitive thinking on their own. This can mean they may not consciously see the impacts of their choices on their future learning. It is important that the ability to reflect on learning is not assumed, which is one reason to overtly build metacognitive activities into a course and to explicitly explain these activities and their importance for a learner's growth and development.

Ambrose et al. (2015) have described the following five steps of metacognitive activities for learners, which offer a helpful framework when describing metacognition to learners or when designing metacognitive learning activities.

Assess the Task, Considering Goals and Constraints

This step is when the learners consider the various steps of the task that will need to be accomplished so that the task is completed successfully. They might also review any obstacles in their way of accomplishing the goals of a task or project. During this step, instructors can ask learners to reflect on what is involved in a particular assignment either through individual journals or in a discussion forum with peers; including peer discussion at this stage may help learners identify additional goals or constraints based on ideas from fellow learners.

Evaluate Knowledge and Skills, Including Strengths and Weaknesses

In this step, the learners consider what they already know about how to accomplish the task and what skills they might need to practice or learn more about before they can complete the task. They will catalog their strengths and weaknesses to better understand which components of the task may be easy or hard for them or where they may need to ask for additional assistance. One way to help learners complete this step is to ask them to identify areas of a task or assignment they feel confident about as well as elements of the task or assignment they still have questions about. By asking learners to share their areas of confidence and their questions with the instructor and their peers, you can help learners connect with others in their peer group who might help them along the way. Discussing this stage with a group of learners can also help an instructor identify patterns among learner strengths and weaknesses.

Plan an Approach

At this stage, learners will take what they know and decide how they want to approach the task. They will outline their plan for completing the task, including action steps, a time line, support structures, and any other components that will help them complete the task. To help learners with this step in a more explicit way, instructors can assign them to document their plan as a formal part of an assignment or project. Alternatively, ask learners to describe their plan to the instructor or another student in the course to gather feedback on their approach.

Apply Strategies and Monitor Performance and Progress

Once a plan is in place, the next step is for the learners to execute the plan and then to take note of what worked well, or what did not work so well, in helping them to accomplish the task. Depending on the scale of an assignment or project, students might apply several different strategies and need to monitor their performance and progress at different stages of completing their task or goal. Instructors can offer examples of the kinds of data or metrics that might be useful to learners as they are monitoring their progress. For instance, are students able to stay on target with their original project time line? Or have the students encountered any unexpected obstacles that have affected their work thus far?

Reflect on Results and Adjust Strategies as Needed

Finally, the learners will want to reflect on the overall plan they completed to see if they want to make adjustments for future tasks similar to the one they just finished. This is the stage of metacognitive work that is often forgotten or ignored because most learners have already moved on to future work or projects as they are wrapping up the previous task or goal. Offering learners concentrated time for reflection on the results of their work, particularly after that work has been evaluated by the instructor, is an important step. One way of doing this is by asking learners to read and respond to the instructor's feedback on their project or assignment, noting one thing they might want to improve or change for a future project or assignment based on what they have learned.

Including a focus on metacognitive activities in the course is important because reflection "causes an increase in the number of connections our students can make between the new information they are learning and their prior knowledge" (Doyle, 2011, p. 145). Through metacognitive activities, learners can better understand the knowledge they have gained over time, the specific learning experiences that have been most useful in that knowledge acquisition, and the knowledge they still have to gain in a particular discipline of study.

Learning New Study Skills: A Short Case Study

Let's take a first-year math course as one example of the power of teaching metacognitive strategies. In this course, learners have come with a range of educational backgrounds; some feel very confident about their math skills, and some feel less confident about their math skills. Perhaps most important, some of these learners never had to study for math tests they took in high school, and other learners studied with varying degrees of success. After the first set of practice problems in the course, many students express confusion and uncertainty, saying they had thought they understood the material being covered on the course lecture videos, but they struggled to complete the practice problems on their own.

This kind of scenario is a common one in many first-year courses, and it offers an excellent opportunity to engage in discussion on metacognition. For example, an instructor might ask learners in the course to document the ways they watched the lecture videos. They might ask learners to describe how they watched the video, whether they watched it more than once, and if they were multitasking while watching. They might also ask learners if they took notes while watching the videos. By asking learners to reflect on their strategies, and the effectiveness of these strategies, an instructor can help learners gauge what worked or didn't work for them.

Strategies for Embedding Metacognitive Activities

In a broader context of active learning, metacognition offers learners an opportunity to further process their experiences in the course. Indeed, if "one goal in teaching is to help learners to become more adept at meaning making . . . that means they need to spend time reflecting on the meaning of the experiences and new ideas they acquire" (Fink, 2003, p. 106). As described by Fink (2003), active learning involves experiences such as doing and observing, followed by reflection on those experiences and "*what* one is learning and *how* one is learning" (p. 104, emphasis in original) through those experiences. Although one way to embed metacognitive modes of inquiry into a course is through explicit learning objectives (see Box 11.1 for some examples), Doyle (2011) also offers the strategy of asking *metacognitive questions*, which he defines as questions "designed to help students construct their own meaning through self-questioning," as a possible way to help learners to reflect on their learning and the meaning it has in broader contexts.

Doyle (2011) offers four kinds of inquiries as a model:

- "What is your comprehension of the problem?" (p. 98).
  In short, can the learners describe the problem in their own words? By asking learners to describe or frame the problem in a larger context, they may become more aware of the areas of the problem they feel more confident in or where they have additional questions.

- "Are there connections between former and current problems?" (p. 98). This question helps learners reflect on when they may have encountered a similar problem in the past that might be connected to their current situation to see if they can transfer some of that previous knowledge to frame solutions to the problem at hand.
- "What strategies would you use to solve the current problem?" (p. 98). For this question, learners can think about what might have worked with similar problems in the past or brainstorm a range of solutions they think might be useful in solving the current problem. By asking about multiple strategies, this question encourages learners to be creative in considering how to approach the problem in front of them.
- "Reflect on the process used and the results of using that process." (p. 98). Similar to the fifth step Ambrose et al. (2015) described earlier in this chapter (see p. 131, this volume), this final mode of inquiry asks learners to evaluate how effective their solution was in solving the problem.

BOX 11.1
Sample Learning Objectives to Measure Metacognitive Skills

- Learners will be able to articulate a disciplinary problem in their own words.
- Learners will be able to make connections between course materials and previous learning experiences.
- Learners will be able to articulate a plan for completing a multistage project or assignment.
- Learners will be able to monitor their progress, including accomplishments and setbacks, while completing a multistage project or assignment.
- Learners will be able to effectively self-assess their approach to solving a disciplinary problem.
- Learners will be able to evaluate their strengths and weaknesses.

Fink (2003) and Doyle (2011), among others, state that metacognitive reflection can occur alone or through interactions with the instructor or other learners. In the following two sections, I offer some strategies for incorporating solitary and community-based metacognitive activities into a course.

Ideas for Solitary Metacognitive Reflection

The following are a few examples of ways for learners to engage in solitary metacognitive activities.

Short assessment techniques such as 1-minute papers or muddiest point responses help learners reflect on a learning experience they have just completed by answering one or two questions about the most important thing they have learned and how they might apply what they have learned in a different context, or noting anything that was confusing about what they just learned. In the online classroom, this can occur using a short quiz or survey that learners complete at the end of a module or activity. To ensure that the learner response is metacognitive, each question can include a follow-up asking learners to explain why they answered in the way they did.

Reflection journals have long been used to stoke metacognitive practices for learner internships, practicums, and other apprenticing experiences that do not lend themselves to traditional assessments but can be used in just about any course environment. Stevens and Cooper (2009) describe a journal as "concrete evidence of one's evolving thought processes, documenting valuable, often fleeting glimpses of understanding" (p. 3). By using reflective models like Rolfe et al.'s (2001) What? So What? Now What? approach, learners have an opportunity to place their learning in a broader context and personalize what they have learned according to their own lives and experiences. Learners can also pause and reflect on the present and future impacts of what they have learned.

Assignment wrappers, which ask learners to reflect on the process they used to complete a particular assignment and to include their own self-assessment of how successful this process was for them, are another strategy for asking learners to reflect on their learning. Assignment wrappers often include a series of reflective prompts for learners to respond to in a discussion forum or through a document they attach to an assignment that is submitted through the learning management system. These responses might be placed at the beginning of an assignment as a kind of introduction. They may also appear at the end of an assignment, offering a reflective conclusion, or in the beginning and the end when appropriate. Assignment wrappers can also easily be combined with a learner self-assessment rubric for a more structured reflection opportunity. (See Box 11.2 for some sample questions that encourage learner reflection.)

Ideas for Community-Based Metacognitive Reflection

In addition to solitary metacognitive reflective activities, there are also several strategies for learners to reflect with an instructor or with their peers as a larger community of learners. The following are a few examples.

With peer assessments learners are asked to evaluate each other's work and offer feedback as a method of helping learners look at learning from a

> **BOX 11.2**
> **Sample Reflective Questions for 1-Minute Papers,
> Reflective Journals, and Assignment Wrappers**
>
> - What was the most important takeaway from what we covered in this module? Why?
> - How will you apply what you learned about in this lesson to a future situation?
> - What was the easiest part of this assignment for you? Why?
> - What was the most difficult part of this assignment for you? Why?
> - What strategies did you use to complete this assignment? Did they work? Why or why not?
> - What study skills did you use to prepare for this test? What worked? What do you wish you had done differently?

new angle. Learners can discuss with one another why they took a particular approach with an assignment, for example, and receive feedback about the effectiveness of that approach from a peer. Moreover, asking learners to apply evaluative criteria to another's work can also help them to think about what it would mean to apply that criteria to their own process or assignment. Peer assessment is a valuable tool but needs to be scaffolded appropriately to ensure that it is helpful to the learners' learning. Instructors should consider offering some training, or a rubric, as guidance to how learners should offer feedback to their peers, such as a demonstration video that walks learners through using the rubric and applying it to an assignment.

Bean (2001) offers the technique of asking learners to compare expert and novice strategies of learning to reflect on how experts and novices approach problems differently as a way to "deepen students' understanding of how knowledge is created" and to "consider an answer not only [as a] product but also [as] the result of a process of disciplinary conversation" (p. 159). This approach can include modeling or demonstrations by the instructor (the expert) or dissections of expert approaches that are included in course readings or other materials. Through analyzing the process and systems of learning, learners can be made more aware of the steps involved in learning a new idea or concept.

A more formalized version of comparing expert and novice strategies, and more generally dissecting how learning works from a disciplinary perspective, can occur through what Pace (2017) and Middendorf and Shopkow (2017) have called *decoding* the disciplines. Through this method, instructors and learners work together to determine the bottlenecks that hinder learning in particular disciplines. This method of decoding asks learners to articulate specific steps involved in learning a particular task or strategy, and naturally this includes metacognitive processing between experts and novices.

In end-of-module or end-of-course reviews, as learners close out a particular segment of the course or as they prepare to end the course and move on to the next component of their program of study, metacognitive activities can help learners with long-term retention of the content they have just covered. These reviews of the material can happen in various forms, such as review discussions, games, study groups, or small-group journaling, but the goal is to ask learners to connect the material to what they have learned in the past as well as where they may be able to integrate what they have learned into their future studies. By asking learners to project or forecast how they might use what they have learned in the future, an instructor can help learners see the real-world applicability of the course materials and skills.

Going Meta: Using Metacognition as Designers and Instructors

I hope this chapter provides you with some ideas and frameworks for how to embed metacognitive strategies and learning objectives in a higher education course. However, our discussion doesn't end here. As important as it is for our learners to learn and practice the skills of metacognition, it is equally important for us to also practice these skills in our own work as designers and instructors. The following are some ways to include metacognitive activities in your own day-to-day work.

Keep a teaching or design journal. It can be hard to fit reflection time into an already busy teaching schedule, but keeping a journal that answers the simple questions of what went well, or didn't go well, in each course period is a simple and time-effective way to be metacognitive about our pedagogical choices. (Quick tip: Some instructors import their syllabus into Google Docs and use the commenting feature to make notes about what they plan to change for future terms.) This kind of journal keeping works well for instructional designers as well, particularly if you are recommending similar pedagogical strategies across disciplines and course types. By checking in with instructors to see what is working and not working for their learners, patterns will start to emerge that can inform future recommendations.

Form a pedagogy reading group. Making explicit connections between pedagogical theories and our own practice is one of the best metacognitive practices that we can engage in, but first we need to know the theory behind our choices. A reading group to help keep you up to date with the latest scholarship of teaching and learning articles or books on pedagogical innovations is one method that allows you to not only read something but also think about what it would mean to apply it with the helpful feedback of a group of colleagues. (See the reference list at the end of this chapter for some suggested readings.)

Read and process learner feedback. Each term, we receive helpful data from our learners about what is helping and hindering their learning through either informal midterm feedback from checking-in sessions or end-of-term formal feedback mechanisms. When using learner feedback as a prompt for metacognitive reflection, I recommend starting by writing down in your journal what you think went well during a particular term. Then consider the things you might want to change in the future. Once you have your own ideas written down, read through the learner feedback to see what it tells you in comparison to what you thought you already knew. This activity can be affirming or eye opening, depending on the alignment between your reflection and the learners' feedback. Most important, once the data have been reviewed, an action plan should be created to implement useful changes based on what you have learned.

References

Ambrose, S. A., Bridges, M. W., DiPietro, M., Lovett, M. C., & Norman, M. K. (2010). *How learning works: 7 research-based principles for smart teaching.* Jossey-Bass.

Bean, J. C. (2001). *Engaging ideas: The professor's guide to integrating writing, critical thinking, and active learning in the classroom.* Jossey-Bass.

Doyle, T. (2011). *Learning-centered teaching: Putting the research on learning into practice.* Stylus.

Fink, L. D. (2003). *Creating significant learning experiences: An integrated approach to designing college courses.* Jossey-Bass.

McGuire, S. Y. (2015). *Teach students how to learn: Strategies you can incorporate into any course to improve student metacognition, study skills, and motivation.* Stylus.

Middendorf, J., & Shopkow, L. (2017). *Overcoming student learning bottlenecks.* Stylus.

Pace, D. (2017). *The decoding the disciplines paradigm.* Indiana University Press.

Rolfe, G., Freshwater, D., & Jasper, M. (2001). *Critical reflection for nursing and the helping professions: A user's guide.* Palgrave.

Stevens, D. D., & Cooper, J. E. (2009). *Journal keeping: How to use reflective writing for learning, teaching, professional insight, and positive change.* Stylus.

When learners are not overloaded with a bunch of unfamiliar tools, they can draw their attention to getting the most value out of the technologies being introduced.

12

INTEGRATING TECHNOLOGY

It's New and Shiny, So It Must Be Good for Learning

Bonni Stachowiak

For some instructors, the idea of incorporating technology into their classes is an inviting concept. Others prefer to limit the use of digital tools and stick with the basics. In this chapter, we examine practical ways to work with online instructors to integrate educational technology without overwhelming learners in the process and hindering their learning. Learning management systems (LMSs) can be used as a compass for individuals, helping them navigate their learning in a familiar environment. However, opportunities to explore beyond the boundaries of an LMS can be fruitful as well.

Ultimately, we want to form partnerships with online instructors to scaffold students' learning to help them acquire new skills and to increase their confidence in the process. Having a shared perspective that digital skills are diverse and are accessible to us all is paramount. To accomplish that, we must not fall into the temptation of introducing a number of different educational technologies to our learners all at once.

In selecting which tools to use in a class, have your online instructors consider ease of use, the overall number of platforms being integrated, and whether the service is in alignment with the instructor's ethics. Evaluating that last criterion can be the most challenging. What has become known as the Audrey test presents a set of questions to ask when evaluating the ethics of an educational technology company (Watters, 2012). I encourage you to take a look at Watters's criteria and come up with your own method of analyzing tools prior to recommending them to online instructors.

Avoid Overloading Learners With Too Many Tools

It can be tempting to introduce a myriad of technologies in a class, especially given how many of them can closely fit the outcomes. However, it is essential to help online instructors focus not on the tool but rather on the learning outcomes they are seeking to teach. After a brief learning curve, the applications should mostly get out of our way and allow us to shift our attention to the broader objectives.

When considering which educational technologies to integrate into online classes, remember that students may be familiarizing themselves with other applications during that same time. Will they be using library databases that are new to them to support their work? Does the class require new learning about a statistics application or more in-depth spreadsheet features than students have previously used? Do longer writing assignments in the class demand the need to develop students' knowledge about using section breaks, styles, and auto table of contents features in a word processor?

If your class uses some type of simulation to help learners master the course outcomes, and you also plan on delivering content using the LMS, it may not be the best time to also require the use of an external messaging system. Support instructors in limiting their tool set to only those applications that will directly benefit students as they pursue their development goals. In particular, watch for the number of separate log-ins or apps that individuals will need to access to keep up with the course assignments and communication.

When learners are not overloaded with a bunch of unfamiliar tools, they can draw their attention to getting the most value out of the technologies being introduced. This gives them an opportunity to scaffold their learning and helps them use the takeaways from the course in other courses down the road. Having one central hub for a course can also be helpful in bridging any gaps in knowledge, which in most cases will wind up being the LMS, discussed in the next section. There are also ways to use educational technology without needing to exit the LMS, and this offers the best of both worlds.

Use the LMS to Reduce Friction

There are two primary ways to reduce the complications inherent in bringing separate apps and services into classes and expecting people to take on an additional learning curve. One way is to use a set of standards that allows an external service to communicate with an LMS so that the application shows up inside the LMS, where students can use it in an already familiar environment.

The second way is that the outside website can be viewed and interacted with inside the LMS through a simple process known as embedding.

Many of these websites offer ways to bring their tools into an LMS without a student ever needing to visit a site outside the LMS. The technology that makes this possible is called learning tools interoperability. Being a programmer is not a necessary prerequisite to bring a service into the LMS that you know will benefit your students and is made available in a seamless process.

Another way to make the integration of outside services into the central hub of the LMS is through embedding. When we embed content on the web, we make it viewable in a place other than where the original is located. The most often used case of embedding involves videos. Instead of asking learners to visit YouTube to watch a video, we can embed the video in a page on the LMS and limit complications of students leaving the LMS and hoping they actually make it back into the system. Videos may be embedded in the context where they are being discussed.

The opportunities with embedding extend well beyond videos, however. Take a look at any site where you build content or engage in some way with learners to see what sharing options are provided. Most often you will be presented with a way to copy the embed code and then paste it into the LMS. The advantage of embedding is that learners are not required to set up additional log-ins outside the LMS or to navigate in an unfamiliar interface.

Get Outside the LMS for Greater Freedom and Longevity of Learning Evidence

The first portion of this chapter focuses on making use of the LMS. However, some find this an unwise, and even unethical, strategy. Their criticisms are that people come into an institution, regularly depositing evidence of their learning into the LMS. Then when they leave, these artifacts are no longer accessible to them. Also, the skills they built up in using the LMS are not as transferable as other literacies can be, such as working more extensively with website creation and blogging tools.

In the early years of the first decade of the 21st century, the University of Mary Washington began early experimentations with faculty and staff building their own web presence through domains that would eventually lead to their Domain of One's Own initiative (Reingold, 2016). Since 2013, all new students at this university have received a domain to use throughout their years at the university and to take with them when they leave. A domain is a name given to a website, such as https://teachinginhighered.com or https://coachingforleaders.com. Students receive their website and begin creating evidence of their learning across multiple classes and assignments. When learners graduate, they take the domain with them, having learned how to maintain a web presence over the course of their time at the university.

Burtis (2016) lists the following four objectives in creating a Domain of One's Own:

1. Provide students with the tools and technologies to build out a digital space of their own.
2. Help students appreciate how digital identity is formed.
3. Provide students with curricular opportunities to use the Web in meaningful ways.
4. Push students to understand how the technologies that underpin the Web work, and how that impacts their lives. (para. 64)

Not all of us teach at institutions that support an overarching program like Domain of One's Own. There are free web platforms that can support similar aims but without requiring the same institutional infrastructure in place. WordPress is one such platform. It is an open source technology, which means there is no cost to using it, unlike other software applications. Paid options are available, but the free version allows learners to experiment with creating their own space on the web.

In a doctoral class I teach, learners create their own website on WordPress.com and begin blogging about a topic that is of interest to them. I used to ask them to write a blog about the course content (technology and leadership) but found that it caused many of the learners to feel apathetic about the exercise and not find it relevant. However, when I gave them the autonomy to choose their own focus for their website, it ignited their interest and engagement. Since then, I have had people create websites for their professional presence online and develop content related to a topic of interest, and even one person made one for her rescue dog, Dr. Lizzie. Although they can pay for a personalized domain, I encourage them to use the free platform from WordPress until they have spent enough time playfully experimenting and getting to know the basics.

Blogging and website creation are not the only ways students can work outside the LMS. Another tool that is frequently used is social annotation. Annotation in the analog world means highlighting articles and making notes in the margins. Digital annotation platforms allow annotation of web pages and PDFs in the same way. However, the technology offers us the possibility of sharing these marks with others. Hypothesis (https://web.hypothes.is/) is a popular digital annotation platform in which I can pull up an article online that I want to make notes on and save those marks for the next time I visit that site. My annotations can be private (viewable only by me), visible for a group of people I am collaborating with, or transparent to anyone who visits that page and is logged into Hypothesis.

Working outside the LMS gives learners a sense of knowing that what they are working on matters. The assignments can be seen as contributing to some larger effort well beyond the arbitrary boundaries of a given class. People who are not enrolled in the class can contribute to and comment on what the learners are working on, and the collaboration can extend past the formal end date of the term.

The Dangers Beyond the LMS

Although the benefits of moving our work out of the LMS are substantial, so are the risks and downsides. There are some logistical challenges, such as the lack of or the limited ability to track students' contributions. Additionally, if the external tool requires accounts to be set up, it can be confusing or overwhelming to students who are less comfortable establishing new log-ins and passwords for websites.

The largest challenge for me in working with learners is the justified reluctance to have one's identify in the online public sphere. Individuals may be concerned for personal reasons (e.g., someone in the process of escaping from a domestic abuse situation or someone caring for a child in the foster care system, which is protective of the child's identity ever being revealed online). There are also plenty of reasons related to the marginalized group the learner may be a part of as, unfortunately, trolling and harassment are still ever present in online spaces. For this reason, I am always sure to have an option for those who do not want to divulge their identity online. Learners are always welcome to use pseudonyms or to work with me to have their content password protected or submitted in another way.

A Middle Ground

Fortunately, technology companies have figured out a way to offer us a middle ground. Those of us ready to move out into the open may use their tools to facilitate learning. However, these platforms are often integrated into our LMSs, allowing us to have the best of both worlds. For example, the social annotation tool Hypothesis has now made its set of tools available to use within the LMS. It takes less time to set up group members using this option because the LMS has already identified who is enrolled in a particular class and can make the necessary adjustments to that Hypothesis group without the instructor having to do that manually.

Scaffold the Use of Technology

Whether you bring tools into the LMS or encourage students to make their way outside the LMS, it is essential to help learners become familiar with the new tools and gain confidence using them. In education, this is known as scaffolding the learning. Instead of expecting mastery of every aspect of the technology from the beginning, online instructors can start with a foundation and then add additional pieces as students progress.

When I teach WordPress to my doctoral students, the first week they are given a series of websites to visit and are asked to reflect on their own identity and what they want to express in an online space. The second week they set up a WordPress account and create a site on the platform. After this point, they take a WordPress class to discover more. During the third week, they create an About page and make any customizations they would like on the prebuilt contact page. Later in the third week they write their first blog post. The first post assignment description helps them discern how writing for the web is different from the kind of academic writing they may be accustomed to. Each subsequent post adds a new skill into the mix.

Scaffolding is particularly important when developing online classes. As we invite learners into an often unfamiliar environment, we can help instructors avoid the sense of being overwhelmed that people can have when entering this new space. Scaffolding also gives instructors the opportunity to provide feedback along the way and help students avoid going too far down a path that will ultimately not get them where they want to be. Another essential consideration is to avoid subscribing to unhelpful perspectives about technology competencies, discussed in the next section.

Negate Limiting Beliefs About Technology

The myth surrounding the supposed collective generational capacities for using technology is pervasive and consists of assertions regarding the binary way to view the digital capacity of the young and old—for example, "Younger people are born with iPads in their hands. They already know how to use technology, so we can remove those portions of our curriculum." These youthful people are often referred to as *digital natives*. This belief also depicts older people as having a harder time learning technology and being reluctant to change—for example, "I'm just not a technology person. I'm a digital immigrant." The theory of the existence of digital natives and digital immigrants was first offered by Prensky in 2001.

These mind-sets are problematic for multiple reasons. Although younger people do tend to be more comfortable with telling people about themselves in online platforms, it by no means translates to mastery of digital literacies. Generalizations are made about the younger generations that do not take into consideration how widely technological competence varies in this demographic. As Bennett et al. (2008) remind us, "It may be that there is as much variation within the digital native generation as between the generations" (p. 777).

Members of older generations do not do themselves any favors by perceiving themselves as having a fixed mind-set when it comes to technology. Digital literacy should not be viewed as something we either possess or will forever be lacking in. Even Prensky (2009) found some fault with his own description of natives and immigrants and proposed a look to digital wisdom for a better paradigm.

Fortunately, another model describes these differences and how people engage with technology. White and Cornu (2011) proposed a paradigm that does not focus on fixed characteristics but rather on a way of describing how people connect online as *visitors* or *residents*. These two descriptors exist on a spectrum, allowing greater granularity in depicting people's online practices.

Visitors see the web as a way of accomplishing tasks. They may use the internet to look up information or to make a bank deposit. They prefer to be anonymous in whatever few online interactions they may have and are concerned about issues of privacy and security. Email is a tool they make use of for connecting with others, although you are unlikely to see them becoming excited about setting up an Instagram account to share pictures of their kids' latest antics. White and Cornu (2001) stated,

> The internet is not a "place" to think or to develop ideas and to put it crudely, and at its most extreme, Visitors do their thinking off-line. So Visitors are users, not members, of the Web and place little value in belonging online. (para. 31)

Residents take a different perspective on the value proposition of the web. They also leave artifacts of their self-expression behind after they log off and are more comfortable with shaping a digital identify. They have set up accounts on multiple social media sites, and sharing their opinions and articulating their ideas in these places feel comfortable to them. Residents appreciate the relationships their existence in these online places provides, often forming friendships with people they have never met in person.

The distinctions between visitors and residents should not be viewed as binary; instead, they sit on each end of a spectrum. These two types also are not intended to depict individuals' technological capability. In fact, digital capacity is diverse and cannot be effectively assessed in a dualistic way.

As I work with instructors who perceive themselves in a binary way when it comes to technology, I encourage a change of language. Instead of "I'm just not a technical person," I encourage something like "I am working on becoming . . . ." The end descriptor to that statement is whatever instructors have arrived at in adopting some aspect of technology to enhance their teaching. Establishing this as a norm has been useful in being able to continually develop and to work together toward the instructors' goals.

Another aspect of dualistic thinking is having an on-off switch for technical skills. When we believe that we either have it or we don't, we limit a more precise way of thinking of the types of digital literacies we might pursue. The All Aboard! (2015) digital skills project defines these competencies by identifying six primary stops using a subway metaphor:

1. Tools and technologies (word processing, databases, browsers, maps, etc.)
2. Find and use (search, keywords, referencing and citation, digital copyright, etc.)
3. Identity and well-being (online identity, security, privacy, data protection, password management, digital footprint, etc.)
4. Teach and learn (course design, producing content, response systems, online and blended learning, presentation skills, etc.)
5. Communicate and collaborate (video conferencing, online communication, journals, messaging, wiki, etc.)
6. Create and innovate (graphic design, Web content, screencasts, design thinking, remixing content, digital video, etc.)

The All Aboard! digital skills map is useful in extinguishing the temptation to think of digital literacy as consisting of a single set of skills. It also provides an opportunity for more productive conversations with online instructors about what they are hoping to achieve with their use of a particular application or web service. Resources that assess one's digital literacies can be useful to bring into our dialogue with online instructors to help increase their capacity over time.

This chapter provides a set of practical ways to develop students' digital literacies and incorporate technology into our classes. It also argues that the theory that we all fall into the category of being either digital natives or immigrants is not conducive to recognizing the growth that is still needed in the case of digital natives or to building the confidence that it is absolutely possible to grow into being a more technically literate person in the case of digital immigrants.

References

All Aboard! (2015). *Towards a national digital skills framework for Irish higher education: Review and comparison of existing frameworks and models.* https://www.teachingandlearning.ie/wp-content/uploads/NF-2016-Towards-a-National-Digital-Skills-Framework-for-Irish-Higher-Education.pdf

Bennett, S., Maton, K., & Kervin, L. (2008). The "digital natives" debate: A critical review of the evidence. *British Journal of Educational Technology, 39*(5), 775–786. https://doi.org/10.1111/j.1467-8535.2007.00793.x

Burtis, M. (2016, August 19). Making and breaking Domain of One's Own. *Hybrid Pedagogy.* http://hybridpedagogy.org/making-breaking-rethinking-web-higher-ed/

Prensky, M. (2001). Digital natives, digital immigrants part 1. *On the Horizon, 9*(5), 1–6. https://doi.org/10.1108/10748120110424816

Prensky, M. (2009). H. Sapiens Digital: From digital immigrants and digital natives to digital wisdom. *Innovate: Journal of Online Education, 5*(3), Article 1. https://nsuworks.nova.edu/innovate/vol5/iss3/1

Reingold, J. (2016, September 21). *A brief history of Domain of One's Own, part 1.* UMW Division of Teaching and Learning Technologies. http://umwdtlt.com/a-brief-history-of-domain-of-ones-own-part-1/

Watters, A. (2012). *"The Audrey test": Or, what should every techie know about education?* Hack Education. http://hackeducation.com/2012/03/17/what-every-techie-should-know-about-education

White, D. S., & Cornu, A. L. (2011). Visitors and residents: A new typology for online engagement. *First Monday, 16*(9). https://doi.org/10.5210/fm.v16i9.3171

PART FOUR

COMPONENTS OF ONLINE CLASSES: PRACTICAL EVERGREENS

It means that learning interactions are always unavoidably and unequivocally designed.

13

COURSE STRUCTURE

Spend Time Engaging With Course Materials, Not Hunting for Them

German E. Vargas Ramos

Generally speaking, when we think about course design the first thing that comes to mind is the process used to develop a course. Of course, the nature of that process varies wildly across different contexts. Courses can be custom developed from scratch, or they can be built based on preexisting templates, an inherited syllabus, or a long-standing traditional model that may be institutional or disciplinary. They can be built intentionally, with precise attention to certain details, prescribed or otherwise, or they can develop organically, with elements that emerge or evolve through holistic means. Their design can be guided unilaterally by an individual instructor or designer, or they can be developed by teams of varying sizes with participants, sometimes even the learners, playing different roles in the process. The possibilities seem endless and daunting, so much so that instructors and designers struggle to find ways of enhancing teaching and learning while at the same time producing more engaging and sustainable designs.

One thing holds true regardless: To create more successful online learning experiences, designers and educators should resist the urge to do things the way they've always been done, which might lead us to rely on simplistic, outdated, or insufficient course development models. With a small to moderate effort, we can adjust existing workflows or strategies and develop new design practices that can go a long way toward facilitating the teaching and learning process, which instructors value, such as promoting closer collaborations among instructors and other academic support personnel, like instructional designers, learning media developers, librarians, and the like (Collay, 2017).

To begin, we must consider a number of high-level constants that apply in every possible learning design case. We then move on to a discussion of how to create course structures that are flexible and sustainable, support more effective instruction, and are more responsive to learners' needs. The first constant to consider in the context of this chapter is the fact that learning experiences, like all human activity, are mediated (Bakhtin, 1986). This has always been the case as teaching evolved from being primarily mediated by speech to incorporating printed text and other media, digital or otherwise. It means that learning interactions are always unavoidably and unequivocally designed. In other words, teaching interactions are constructed through an intentional scripting process that precedes the actual interaction. This intentional pre-scripting is a fundamental, ever-present aspect of any design process, including instructional design. Being more conscious of this process and conducting it more deliberately offer more opportunities to produce responsive rather than prescriptive designs. The difference between the two is qualitative. More successful designs anticipate learners' differences and needs and provide contingencies to respond to them as they come into play. Less successful designs force learners to conform to rigid or narrowly defined notions of how knowledge is to be acquired and employed.

The second overarching constant that connects all teaching interactions is that they create experiences (Fink, 2013). That is, whenever someone teaches something, there are learners who perceive (i.e., feel), participate in, and will remember that teaching interaction as part of their life experience (Wenger, 1998); how, or even if, learning happens during the course of that experience is a different topic. The point here is that teaching interactions do not produce learning directly; instead, they influence the conditions in a given space or context in a way that is intended to be conducive to learning. It is important to keep this in mind during course development because educators' intentions and their teaching practices may not necessarily result in the expected outcomes in the same way that even high-quality teaching practices cannot always guarantee learning. In other words, how teaching is perceived or experienced is just as important as how it is intended (again, designed). This means that educators and designers are responsible for not only creating learning experiences that are effective in principle but also managing those experiences to remove structural or instructional elements that may present learners with obstacles, injustices, or harm.

Finally, we should note that more than ever before, we can now think about a course as a concrete object, a bounded collection of materials and experiences that have structural or quantifiable features (e.g., internet bandwidth, digital file formats and sizes, web-based and desktop software) that have an impact on its qualitative characteristics (e.g., participant identities and presence, teaching practices, student learning, participant interaction).

The widespread presence of computers and online learning in U.S. higher education may not have significantly changed the nature of college at a fundamental level, but it has made course design and its impact on teaching and learning more explicit and prominent, particularly where online learning is concerned. Online courses can be seen and reviewed in their entirety before they can be personally experienced thanks to learning management systems (LMSs) and other web-based tools that can show participants a preview of what a course will look like from beginning to end. Before online courses, the closest approximation of a course prototype was either its course catalog description or its syllabus, both of which are limited in their size and scope as well as in their capacity for representation. As a document that outlines a course functionally as well as philosophically, the syllabus is a logical entry point into a discussion of how the structure of a course contributes to its success as a learning experience and is especially a way to open this conversation during consultations with instructors.

The LMS as a Container: Why Bother? Model

We are all familiar with this model of LMS usage and the resulting course structures. It describes the barest and most basic implementation of an LMS. A syllabus is posted on the course space as a downloadable document and accompanied by a series of folders or pages that contain course documents and other media organized by type or by some other simple framework. These are usually complemented by prompts involving the use of asynchronous discussion tools and the occasional online assessment. There is nothing inherently wrong with this kind of design, especially when an online course space is meant to supplement face-to-face class activities rather than to host a class entirely. However, from a user experience perspective, this kind of design leaves much to be desired. Visually, it's simple, which may be beneficial in certain contexts, but it isn't necessarily appealing. More important, without additional scaffolding, this design fails to provide learners with cues to help them navigate and revisit the material. In other words, it does little to help them learn. Figure 13.1 illustrates this concept.

Experientially, this approach to course structure obscures the interconnected nature of knowledge by presenting it to learners in a disembodied, inert, and superficial format; it's the equivalent of handing students a mishmash stack of photocopies and calling it a textbook. Worse yet, it gives students the impression that a course (and knowledge) is just a pile of documents. This course structure is unresponsive to learners' needs in that it almost ignores the fact that teaching and learning are happening online, which means that most online learners are on their own as they make their way through course

Figure 13.1. The LMS as a container.

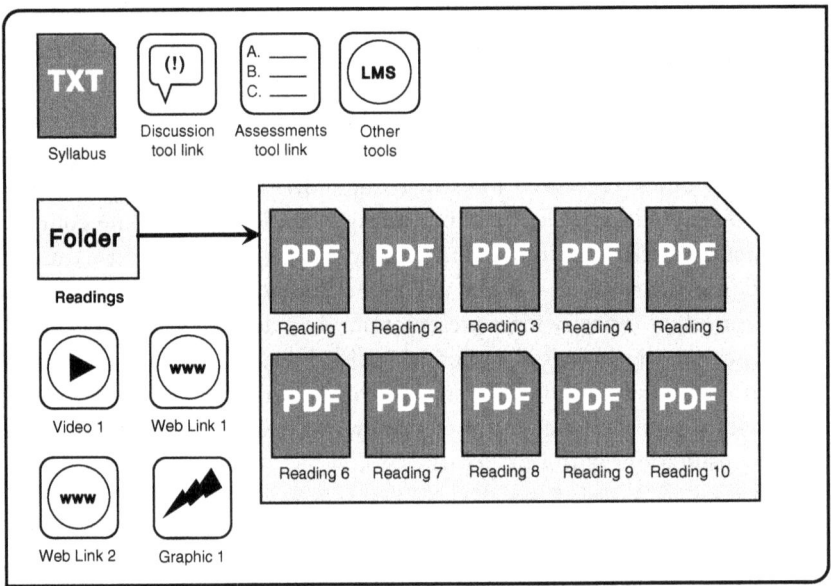

materials and don't have the benefit of a physical classroom to provide context and a sense of presence (Garrison et al., 2000) or to receive clarification or feedback from instructors in the moment, which is important to learning (Annand, 2011). An unstructured or ill-structured online course fails to provide cues that could compensate for this lack of context to some degree. It also takes valuable engagement time away from learners, who have to constantly wade through course materials to find the information they need (Shea et al., 2006). Poor course structure also presents an obstacle to instructors, who may find themselves spending too much time guiding learners through the material and fielding nonacademic issues and questions.

The LMS as a Schedule: Basic Model

This approach to course structure arranges course materials chronologically and is a slight improvement over the container approach. This popular approach is seen most often in an online course that uses a framework of folders or documents to arrange course materials on a day-by-day, week-by-week, or similar basis (Figure 13.2). Using the LMS as a course schedule connects course knowledge to a particular point in time and may signify a sequence or order in which that knowledge is to be approached. Often the sequence behind this structure is hierarchical rather than chronological;

Figure 13.2. The LMS as a schedule.

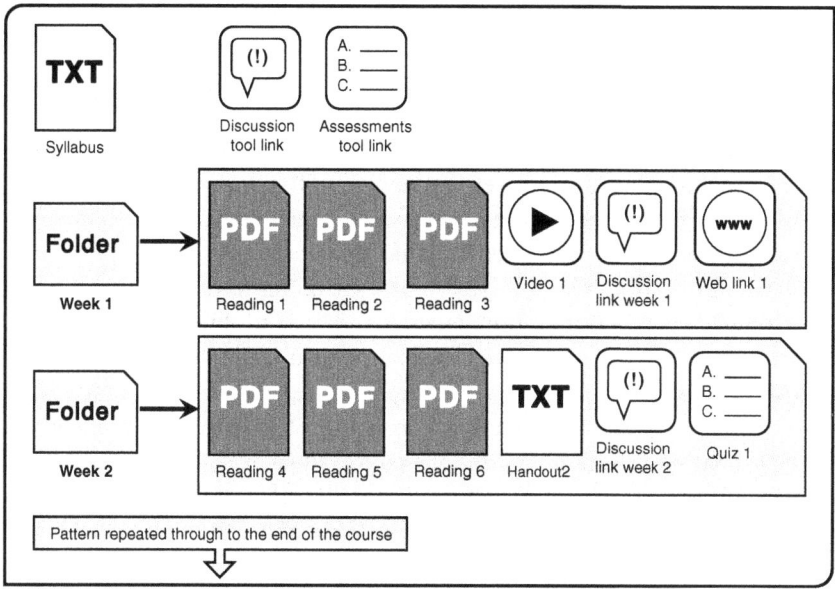

that is, it is favorable or necessary to master one aspect of knowledge or skill before moving on to a more complex or difficult one. This course structure suggests to learners that knowledge possesses a linearity that may or may not actually exist. There are cases in which a chronologically arranged course is meaningful or necessary. Examples include courses that connect disciplinary knowledge with real-world events as they occur or courses involving the completion of a large project from beginning to end. On a functional level, this kind of approach presents learners and instructors with a familiar framework for teaching and learning, but it should not be used simply out of habit. There are other more flexible and responsive structures that can do more than just organize content when linearity is not an integral part of course activities.

The LMS as a Tool Kit: Bells and Whistles Model

This approach takes better advantage of the different tools inside and outside an LMS. The course structure can vary under this approach, but it is distributed among any number of tools beyond the staples of the LMS. These tools are meant to mediate different learning activities directly online. Examples include course blogs and wikis, online office suites and similar collaborative tools, virtual classrooms or online conferencing services, and even activities or demonstrations that use interactive media like virtual or augmented reality. These activities are often, but not necessarily, conducted asynchronously. Aside from how learners interact with each other, their use is unchanged regardless of whether a course meets face-to-face, online, or somewhere in between. This approach to course structuring is multilayered in a way that the previous two cannot be. It requires a fundamental layer that collects course materials and outlines a course's schedule, but these are not the focus of the learning experience; they are only a foundational layer that helps manage course logistics and organize course content. As the bones of a course, this foundation can often look like one of the two models previously discussed or a combination of the two. It contributes to the learning process by helping learners access course materials and by scaffolding their use of the more advanced, more interactive learning tools online learning has to offer.

Above this foundation, however, there is a second, more advanced and more dynamic layer of interaction consisting of activities that make use of the synchronous and asynchronous course tools available in an LMS to mediate communication and capture student work individually or collaboratively. Basic examples include graded discussion forums, journals, and other reflection activities as well as assignments and assessments that are fully contained in the LMS. More advanced examples include metrics to measure student engagement with course materials and with peers, rubrics and support materials to guide learners with richer feedback, and low-stakes automatically graded quizzes or mini challenges to gauge understanding on the fly. This model relies on not only static materials but also course tools like discussion forums and online quizzes or synchronous virtual classrooms and online conferencing systems. These activities make up the core of the learning experience under this model and are intended to not only present content to learners but also promote engagement (Lister, 2014), disciplinary thinking (Dumford & Miller, 2018), interaction with online peers (Nandi et al., 2015), reflection on learning (Johnson et al., 2017), and so forth in a way that can be recorded by the LMS and often assessed by the same. It's important to note, however, that this course model is the combination of rich, well-organized media collections combined with the use of interactive tools to facilitate learning activities. These elements do not function as well in isolation. They must be closely integrated and informed by robust, impactful educational goals and objectives to create enhanced spaces that promote high-quality learning. Figure 13.3 illustrates this model.

From a learning experience standpoint, this design approach can produce richer, more active learning experiences (Lister, 2014). It also introduces complexities to a course design that should not be allowed to become obstacles to learning so that learners are always clear on what they should be doing and how. If the fundamental layer of course structure is too sparse, or

COURSE STRUCTURE   *157*

Figure 13.3. The LMS as a tool kit.

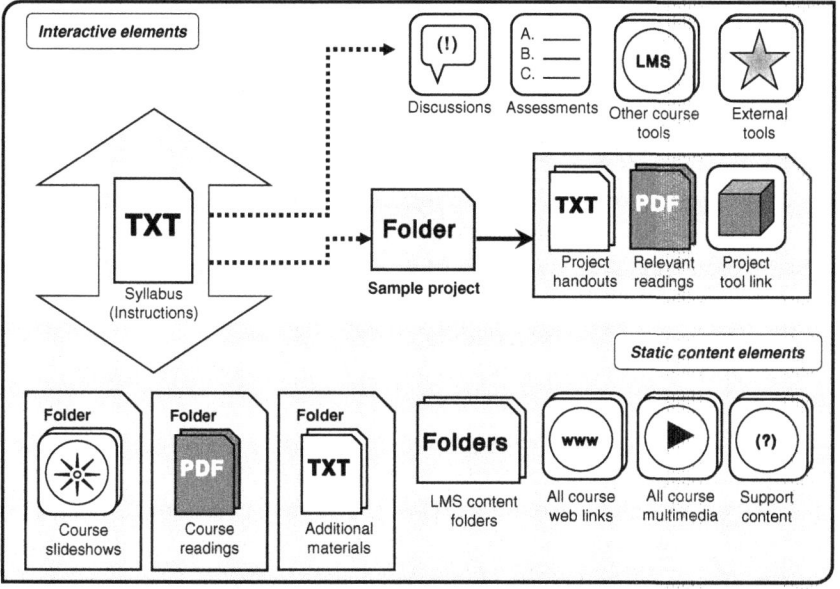

if it is disconnected or misaligned from the rest of the course, it can interfere with the learning process (Shea et al., 2006). For example, students may have a hard time using course tools or focusing on course activities if the materials they need to access to complete a task, like readings, handouts, and other resources, are not available in the LMS; if they are difficult to find among other content; or if course tools are used disproportionately to their relevance or learning curve. This can compound whatever learning curve the course's tools or the LMS itself might pose to students. This is important because this approach to online courses requires more than just access to technology; it assumes a higher-than-average level of digital proficiency from learners and instructors. Designers and instructors should work together to provide learners with the support and resources they need, or they may invalidate the advantages this type of course provides. This may require working with other academic support professionals, like librarians, instructional technologists, disciplinary tutors, and so on, who can help learners with the specific challenges they may face. However, in the course itself, instructors and designers should provide clear instructions, reminders, examples, and supporting materials on how to use these tools in general as well as in relation to specific course activities. These can include step-by-step tutorials, links to the help section of the LMS, custom instructions and guidelines, and samples of successful uses of course tools.

Opening Up Course Structures

Our discussion so far has illustrated how different course structures can not only present but also represent knowledge. They provide students with guidance on how to navigate their learning, as much as course material, and highlight key connections between the concepts and skills within a course, as well as how each can contribute to or hinder teaching and learning. But we are not even close to exhausting the possibilities when it comes to the potential structures that could be developed under different conditions. Regardless of whether it's more unconventional or traditional, the structure of a course should increase the alignment between the instructors' educational intent, the nature of the knowledge to be covered, the corresponding methods of assessment, and the needs and identities of learners. Therefore, it's important to realize that the structure of a course as learners experience it should not be centered on the media in a course (readings, videos, handouts) or the course tools (discussion forums, quizzes, assignments, etc.). Rather, it should be created from the instructor's educational intent and the arrangement of course media and tools. It should be represented in two layers, an experiential dynamic layer that uses the content elements of an LMS (modules, multimedia pages, embedded videos, links to course tools, etc.) and an underlying static layer consisting of course media and other functional elements (folders, document files, LMS tools, links to external tools and resources, etc.). Figure 13.4 illustrates this arrangement.

Figure 13.4. Open course structures: Static media layer.

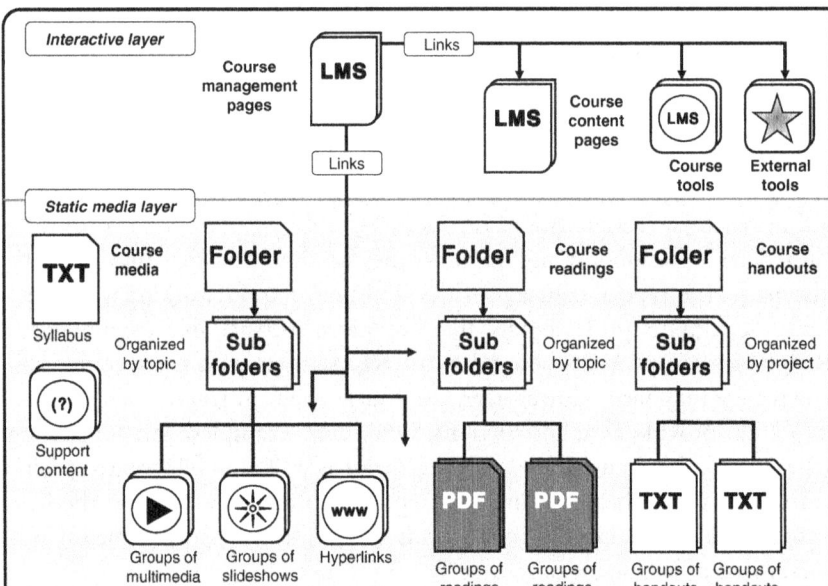

COURSE STRUCTURE   *159*

Using the content creation tools provided by an LMS to create the dynamic layer of a course lets instructors and designers creatively articulate and rearrange different elements of its design (timing, goals, materials, activities, assessments, etc.) without the need to modify its underlying media structure (folders, documents, multimedia files, web links, course tools, etc.). This is the case regardless of whether the changes have to be made between one instance of a course and the next as the course shell is copied for new groups of learners over time or during a course as it is taught. In either case, this allows instructors to focus on teaching and on learners' experiences while making courses easier to manage from a technical standpoint. It also allows learners to access media and resources directly as they review course materials, complete projects, or prepare for assessments. As can be expected with online courses, most of the course-building work happens before the start of a course. Proper preparation may also require regular conversations and check-ins between instructors and designers to address issues before or during the course. This extra development time is an investment that pays off in the long run by making future instances of a course easier to configure and teach. The following examples show how creating a static media layer and a dynamic interactive layer in a course creates a flexible framework that can support different learning experiences with minimal modifications. Figure 13.5 also illustrates this concept.

Figure 13.5. Open course structures: Interactive layer.

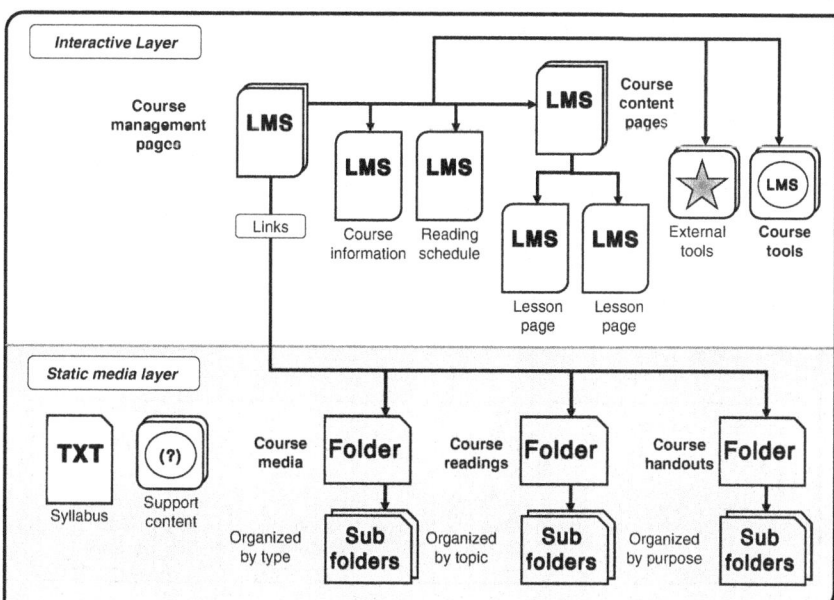

Example 1: Linear and Nonlinear Activities in the Same Course

These courses combine whole-group activities conducted at the same pace by all learners with other activities learners complete at their own pace in any order, partially or selectively. This is suitable for traditional courses as much as for courses that are highly individualized or driven by learner projects. In traditional courses, this approach can provide opportunities for individualized practice or for brushing up on prerequisite skills, like in mathematics or language learning. It can also allow learners to take on different topics and processes in their projects while still presenting them overall with similar learning experiences and requirements. When it comes to practice or remedial work, this kind of course structure can help manage the process of giving credit to learners who need to do additional work to fully meet a course's academic requirements because of any obstacles that may make it difficult for them to perform at the same level as their peers. Figure 13.6 illustrates this concept.

Example 2: Project-Based, Event-Based, and Blended Courses

Although the activities in these types of courses follow a set sequence (e.g., week by week or lesson by lesson), this is more because of convenience or convention rather than explicit educational intent. Although these courses

Figure 13.6. Combining linear and nonlinear course content.

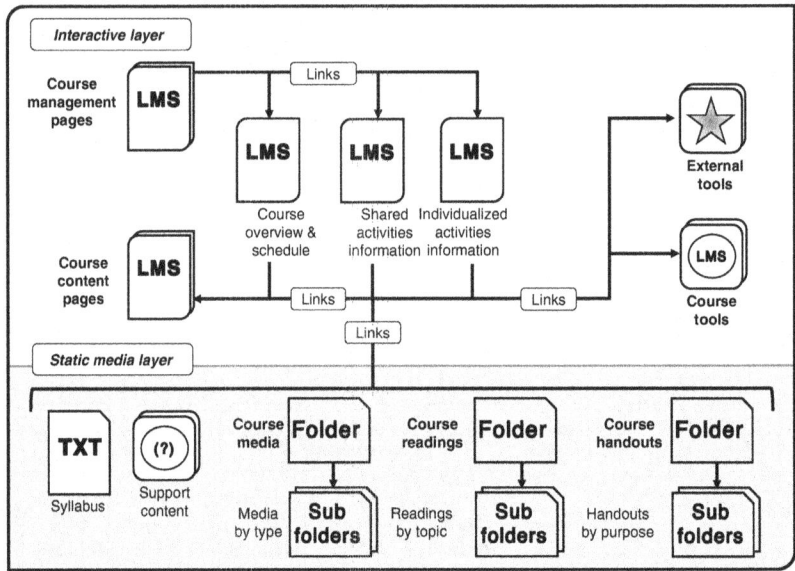

Figure 13.7. Project-based and blended courses.

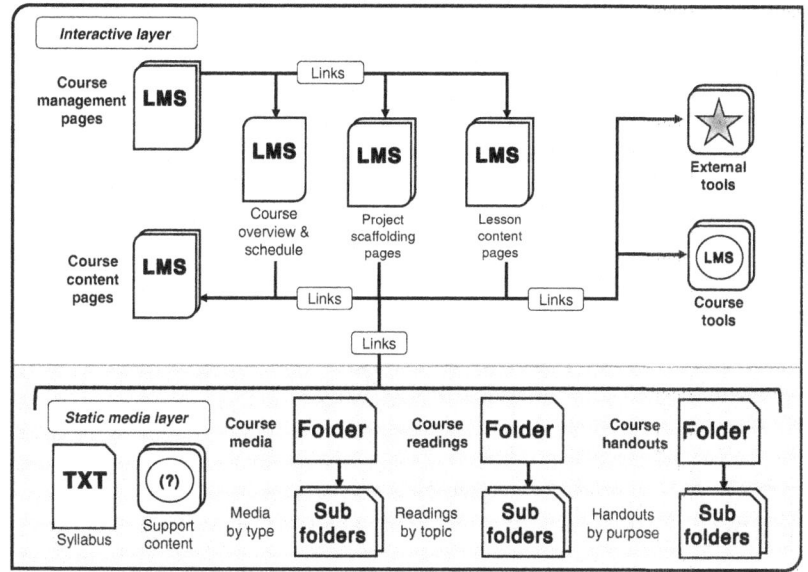

possess a similar underlying (static) layer as the ones in the previous example, their experiential (dynamic) layer may be very different depending on the kinds of activities. The emphasis of the dynamic layer of the course is meant to facilitate interaction and to support learners' exploration and collaboration rather than to present them with content or guide them through extensive collections of material. In project-based courses, this type of structure provides space for learners to develop their projects individually or in groups. It allows the creation of courses that are connected to real-life events as they happen outside the context of the class altogether. It can also help instructors and learners to document and examine the results of activities that happen outside the LMS, like student research, simulations, and other face-to-face interactions. Finally, this type of course structure makes it easier to present learners with material and activities in an iterative or selective format as they complete certain activities or master certain knowledge or skills. Figure 13.7 illustrates this structure.

Conclusion

These strategies combined with the appropriate learning designs place the LMS at the center of learning rather than as a supplement to course activities, but they do so in a way that maintains the centrality of teaching and learning above the use of technology for its own sake. They turn the LMS into a hub for learning, a function that can be enhanced by connecting course activities to real-world knowledge and skills as well as to learners' lives. They also make it easier for designers and instructors to be more responsive to learners' needs and identities regardless of the course type and to provide learners with individualized and differentiated opportunities for learning that integrate into the overall learning context. This positioning is critical as we take steps to deliver on the promise of online courses and other digitally mediated educational experiences to make learning more meaningful by taking advantage of the wealth of media and information we can now bring to bear in a course and make education more accessible, personalized, and sustainable by providing multiple pathways for learner engagement and development.

References

Annand, D. (2011). Social presence within the community of inquiry framework. *The International Review of Research in Open and Distributed Learning, 12*(5), 40–56. https://doi.org/10.19173/irrodl.v12i5.924

Bakhtin, M. M. (1986). The problem of speech genres. In C. Emerson & M. Holquist (Eds.), V. W. Mcgee (Trans.), *Speech genres and other essays* (pp. 60–102). University of Texas Press.

Collay, M. (2017). Transformative learning and teaching: How experienced faculty learned to teach in the on-line environment. *Journal of Transformative Learning, 4*(2), 21–42.

Dumford, A. D., & Miller, A. L. (2018). Online learning in higher education: Exploring advantages and disadvantages for engagement. *Journal of Computing in Higher Education, 30*, 452–465. https://doi.org/10.1007/s12528-018-9179-z

Fink, L. D. (2013). *Creating significant learning experiences: An integrated approach to designing college courses*. Jossey-Bass.

Garrison, D. R., Anderson, T., & Archer, W. (2000). Critical inquiry in a text-based environment: Computer conferencing in higher education. *The Internet and Higher Education, 2*(2–3), 87–105. http://dx.doi.org/10.1016/S1096-7516(00)00016-6

Johnson, C., Hill, L., Lock, J., Altowairiki, N., Ostrowski, C., da Rosa dos Santos, L., & Liu, Y. (2017). Using design-based research to develop meaningful online discussions in undergraduate field experience courses. *The International Review of Research in Open and Distributed Learning, 18*(6). https://doi.org/10.19173/irrodl.v18i6.2901

Lister, M. (2014). Design of e-learning and online courses: A literature analysis. *MERLOT Journal of Online Learning and Teaching, 10*(4), 671–679.

Nandi, D., Hamilton, M., & Harland, J. (2015). What factors impact student-content interaction in fully online courses. *International Journal of Modern Education and Computer Science, 7*(7), 28–35. http://dx.doi.org/10.5815/ijmecs.2015.07.04

Shea, P., Li, C. S., & Pickett, A. (2006). A study of teaching presence and student sense of learning community in fully online and Web-enhanced college courses. *Internet and Higher Education, 9*(3), 175–190. https://doi.org/10.1016/j.iheduc.2006.06.005

Wenger, E. (1998). *Communities of practice: Learning, meaning, and identity.* Cambridge University Press.

When creating an instructional video, keep in mind what the learner can do before, during, and after engaging with the video.

14

MULTIMEDIA

Moving Beyond Passive to Active Learner Engagement

Danilo M. Baylen, Jonathan Gratch, and Linda Haynes

How many movies or TV shows can you remember that made you laugh or cry? Most likely you can recall a specific scene you could not wait to share with others. Videos or video clips are forms of digital resources an educator can use to support the teaching and learning processes (Brown, 2019; National Teacher Training Institute, 2006). Videos have the capabilities to make the impossible possible, such as exploring inside the human body, stars in distant galaxies, or caverns deep inside the earth. Videos can provide experiences of traveling back in time and seeing history unfold or managing dangerous experiments from the safety of the classroom.

More than 1,000 tools are available to create multimedia artifacts using videos. This chapter is not concerned with the specific tools in multimedia development, because the technology is constantly changing. Instead, this chapter focuses on how multimedia artifacts can use and integrate videos as instructional tools. For consistency of the language used across sections of this chapter, a *multimedia artifact* as a term means a video or video clip. The chapter explains why the length of a multimedia artifact matters and how various development and production practices are guided by principles to improve the quality of the multimedia artifact and contribute to reducing the workload for those who create videos. Several principles are identified and addressed in creating multimedia artifacts that engage learners, mitigate cognitive overload, and support specific types of instruction (Clark & Mayer, 2008; Mayer, 2009).

How Can Videos Best Support Teaching and Learning?

The National Teacher Training Institute (2006) reported that the use of instructional videos contributed to better retention of information, improved understanding of concepts taught, and increased motivation of students. Videos can connect with diverse populations, especially those acquiring information and learning differently. As an instructional tool, videos can provide a common experience for students to discuss, examine, and engage in problem-solving activities.

Brown (2019) identified and discussed the benefits of using videos to support learning. Students tend to accept videos easily as a tool for learning. They provide students with multisensory experiences that facilitate increased understanding of the content. Videos deliver more information that can require fewer words, and visuals make concepts easier to understand. Videos allow educators to integrate the world beyond the classroom and eventually provide learners with engaging experiences involving the activation of multiple senses in processing information. Finally, video making as a learning experience, involving pre- to postproduction work, can create immersive, stimulating activities for the students.

Principles of Multimedia Development

What makes a video an engaging experience for students? Visual media can support the learning process, so videos need to be designed to have an effective impact on student learning. Mayer (2009) identified and discussed principles that guide the creation of videos to becoming useful instructional tools: multimedia, contiguity, modality, redundancy, coherence, personalization, segmenting, and pretraining.

The application of the multimedia principle means that words and graphics are used to communicate content or elicit comprehension of concepts or processes. Words alone may not be as useful. A good example would be pairing an image of an apple with the word *apple*, either as a spoken word or as on-screen text.

The contiguity principle addresses the importance of aligning words to corresponding graphics. Printed texts should be near corresponding graphics. Spoken words should be synchronized with the appearance of an image. One way of visualizing this principle in action is hearing the word *apple* spoken while seeing a graphic of an apple on the screen.

The modality principle focuses on hearing the words spoken rather than seeing them written out. The use of audio narration instead of on-screen text is helpful because the learner is able to use two senses, seeing the image and hearing the audio narration.

The redundancy principle advocates for the use of audio or texts to explain visuals but not both. Adding on-screen text to the narration is acceptable in particular situations, such as identifying parts of an object like the human body.

The coherence principle serves as a warning to all multimedia creators to pay attention to extraneous audio, graphics, and texts. For example, background music can be distracting and interfere with learning and retention.

Who wants to listen to a grumpy or monotone voice? Nobody. The personalization principle is vital in the delivery of a multimedia artifact. Mayer (2009) states that a voiceover narration should be conversational rather than formal. As a principle, personalization can be enacted through voice quality and polite speech.

For videos created with the instructor on camera, hearing the instructor's voice and seeing the instructor's face may not be sufficient for maintaining student attention and ensuring retention of learning. Specific strategies related to dynamic drawings and eye contact can influence student engagement and retention of learning more than the instructor being visible in the video (Fiorella et al., 2018). If the instructor is visible in the video, eye contact with the camera is more effective for supporting student engagement and learning than an instructor looking toward a whiteboard. In videos where the instructor is not visible, student learning can still be supported with the use of dynamic drawings—that is, drawn on screen from beginning to end during the video—more than the use of static images, which are already completely drawn and in place on the video screen.

The principles of segmenting and pretraining focus on multimedia artifacts that lend themselves to a demonstration of procedures or step-by-step processes. Some of the best examples demonstrating these principles are those involving how-to activities, such as building or making something, such as assembling a birdhouse or baking muffins. Segmenting refers to identifying each step in the process and sequentially demonstrating all of the steps. Segmenting the delivery of selected content provides an opportunity for the viewer to revisit, rewind, and reproduce the process at any point.

Pretraining provides an opportunity for the viewer to learn specific names and labels or characteristics of relevant concepts in advance. If one will be demonstrating a cooking segment, then the pretraining component of the multimedia would consist of identifying the ingredients as well as cooking tools and utensils. Also, to help the viewer create a schema of what the process involves, a presentation of all the steps to be demonstrated would be useful as this helps the viewer anticipate what comes next and removes any mystery about how the demonstration will end.

Multimedia Concepts

Two important concepts and principles relevant to multimedia production are dual coding or visual and verbal channels (Paivio, 1971) and chunking (Miller, 1956). Graphics and printed texts are processed by the viewer's cognitive processing system through the eyes, and the audio translation enters through the ears. This psychological principle states that separate channels people use for processing visual and pictorial material and auditory and verbal material are referred to as dual channels. According to Paivio (1971), the act of processing information in the two channels is called *dual coding* and can lead to deeper understanding.

Chunking is an effective strategy for managing an overwhelming amount of information, either text, graphics, or audio (Miller, 1956). Chunking is a process in which individual pieces of an information set are broken down and then grouped. Bower (2000) described chunking as "a familiar collection of more elementary units that have been inter-associated and stored in memory repeatedly and act as a coherent, integrated group when retrieved" (p. 12). In creating a multimedia product, chunking can be achieved by grouping relevant information into meaningful clusters or chunks. Small or short chunks of information are easier to remember than one long continuous set of information. Chunking is especially helpful for showing relationships and hierarchies.

What Are the Uses of Videos for Instruction?

For most of the latter half of the 20th century, video was the realm of film and video production professionals and required the use of high-cost equipment to produce and distribute a video product. With the onset of the smartphone and YouTube era, people have greater access to high-quality video than ever before and a means to distribute the video to a global audience. The availability of high-quality video cameras of various sizes, shapes, and specializations has enabled video to be captured almost anywhere at any time.

The near ubiquity of video-capable smartphones and other video cameras, plus the means to distribute the video instantly across the globe, has enabled video to enter the educational environment in a manner once only reserved for professionals. However, this high availability of content and access does result in varied approaches and quality of instructional videos.

Video can be used to support learning in many ways. Spannaus (2012) offers a list of six means to include video in support of teaching and learning: demonstrate a procedure, expert presentation, present a case study, dramatic reproduction, show a process, and virtual tours. In addition to the types of videos discussed by Spannaus, Halls (2012) describes videos as a way to manipulate images to enrich learning and enable educators to maintain a consistent standard in information delivery as multimedia products become even more accessible and easier to produce.

What Are Readily Available Instructional Videos?

One of the most well-known sources for finding videos available on the internet is YouTube. Type a single word related to a content topic in the search box, and a long list of videos becomes readily available to access. Try searching using some common words for the following:

- mathematics, such as fractions, algebra, or parallel lines;
- social studies, such as government, continents, or cultural traditions;
- science, such as an atom, a cell, or a motion; or
- language arts, such as adjectives, metaphors, or literature.

Any of those simple searches will result in an almost endless list of possibilities. A YouTube search can be filtered by upload date, type (e.g., video, playlist), duration, and features (e.g., live, subtitles or closed captioning, Creative Commons), and the search can be sorted by upload date, view count, and rating. Students are likely to search YouTube, Google, and class web pages for educational videos (Leonard, 2015). Of course, with a tremendous number of videos available, the knowledge and expertise to decide which videos are best are necessary. Finding existing videos can reduce time needed for course development while taking advantage of recognized sources of expert knowledge.

A strategy for sorting through the large volume is to access websites that are targeted to higher education with online video resources, such as MIT Open Courseware (Massachusetts Institute of Technology, 2019) or the Carnegie Mellon Open Learning Initiative (Carnegie Mellon University, 2019). Another strategy from Sherer and Shea (2011) is to filter YouTube by accessing YouTube.com/edu and subscribing to specific YouTube channels, such as those associated with organizations like National Public Radio (https://www.youtube.com/npr) or the Public Broadcasting System (http://www.youtube.com/PBS).

How Can Videos Be Created on a Shoestring Budget?

Videos created by instructional designers or instructors frequently use one of two designs: talking head videos or presentation videos.

Talking Head Videos

The talking head video is precisely what the name suggests: a close-up of the instructor lecturing directly to the learners for an unspecified length of time, generally up to an hour or more. Talking head videos are typically designed to replace the traditional lecture and are often used in online courses to provide content in classes designed on instructor-centered lectures. These videos are easy to produce, require minimal equipment and personnel, and need minimal (if any) postproduction.

An instructor can produce a video by using the camera built into a computer. The videos are quick to create and distribute to the class. However, these videos tend to run long, virtually mimicking the lecture environment, whereas a class could run from 50 minutes to nearly 3 hours. Using eye tracking to determine where a viewer was focusing while watching videos, Nielsen (2005) found that even a talking head video of only 24 seconds in length resulted in a lack of engagement as the viewers' eyes began to roam across the screen and attempt to focus on other on-screen and off-screen elements. Talking head videos are still common today and are used in a variety of fields including education and marketing. These videos may be more helpful if they are combined with other video elements, such as diagrams or images to add interest and enrich learning.

Presentation Videos

Another common educational video, the presentation video, shares some design cues with the talking head video but replaces the constant single-camera view of the speaker with a single perspective of a presentation (e.g., PowerPoint). The visual component can be more engaging to the viewer as the images presented on the screen directly connect with the auditory presentation of the speaker. This combination of narration and images enables dual coding for making stronger cognitive connections and improving learning retention (Paivio, 1971; Mayer, 2009, 2014). However, as in the talking head videos, the duration of the presentation can run much longer than the viewer's attention and frequently results in disengagement. In the case of presentation videos, the video producer, though, can produce a slide design that is engaging to the viewer by including images and audio along with personalizing the narration.

Design Principles for Instructional Videos

As talking head and presentation videos are still the most common videos for instruction, the question that remains is how instructors, focused on learning outcomes, can select or produce quality videos for learning. From the design perspective suggested by Sweller's (1988) theory of cognitive load and reinforced by Nielsen's (2005) findings in viewer attention using eye tracking, instructional videos should be short in duration. Chunking a long video into multiple shorter videos helps maintain learners' focus and engagement. Thus, an hour-long lecture video may be chunked into smaller videos each running about 3 to 5 minutes. Although no consensus has been found about the total running time for an instructional video, each segment should have a clear beginning, middle, and end.

Keep in mind the multimedia principle (Mayer, 2014) and dual coding (Paivio, 1971) to reinforce learning with audio and visuals. The opportunity to provide narration and imagery facilitates enhanced learner engagement. Also, remember the personalization principle (Mayer, 2014). Pairing the audio and visual components with an emotional sentiment will provide additional reinforcement for retention of content by adding another dimension to the viewing.

The presenter's or narrator's personality can assist in the connection between emotion and displayed content through tone; inflection; and, if on screen, body language and facial expression. Likewise, a rapport can be developed between students and the instructor if the instructor is the narrator or is on screen in the video. Narrate using first person rather than third person, and do not be afraid of close-ups.

When selecting images and audio, remember the coherence principle (Mayer, 2014). Do not include irrelevant or extraneous graphics, words, or sounds. Including irrelevant elements will produce the opposite effect on the student—disengagement and distraction.

An adage in filmmaking is "show, don't tell," which means that the video producer should show the audience the action rather than tell the audience what is happening. For example, a student seeing a chemical reaction occurring on the screen will be more inclined to stay engaged than a student just being told about the reaction by a talking head.

Accessibility

Learners with disabilities should be considered in the production of videos through the selection of colors used, font size and style, and visual framing to produce content that effectively conveys the information in the video. Finally, make sure to include captions, audio descriptions, and transcripts for those hard of hearing or for any who wish to have the visual text to reinforce or clarify audio content in the video.

How Do Students Engage With Instructional Videos?

Although viewing a video is considered a passive activity, strategies have been developed to encourage students to interact with the video content, such as interactive controls to allow self-pacing, assignments directly related to the video, and interactive quizzes embedded in the video.

Interactive Controls for Self-Pacing

This may seem unimportant in today's world of streaming video, but providing the viewer with interactive controls over the playback of the video will assist learners by enabling them to rewind, fast-forward, search, and replay the video at will (Zhang, 2006). These simple controls, which are embedded and can be disabled in most video playback systems, provide the viewer with a semblance of control over their learning and the speed of their learning.

Student Assignments Connected to the Video

The following four types of assignments can be easily integrated into the learning experience with videos (Sherer & Shea, 2011):

1. Listening and writing an assignment: After watching a video, students respond to question prompts on an online discussion board or possibly generate and submit discussion questions.

2. Short production assignment: The students create an instructional video and upload it to a website or learning management system where others can comment or respond to questions generated by the students. For example, students can create a science-related video to explain the parts of a cell or a literature-related video to explain the roles of characters in a play.
3. Collecting and archiving assignment: Students collect and archive online videos from multiple sources to expand a course website with a relevant video collection.
4. Short presentation assignment: After locating relevant videos, students write an analysis of the video content and collaborate with others in a discussion board for commenting or responding to questions.

These types of assignments allow students to go beyond passive viewing. Students can be actively engaged in collaborating with others, contributing to knowledge, and appreciating opportunities for learner choices. When creating an instructional video, keep in mind what the learner can do before, during, and after engaging with the video.

Interactive Video Quizzes

Other strategies for active engagement with video content include quizzes or surveys embedded in videos. Instructors can use video tools embedded in learning management systems or websites to insert questions at certain points in a video time line. When students play the video, a question appears at the point in the time line set by the instructor. The video pauses automatically to show the question. Students click on their chosen response, and then the video continues to play until it pauses for the next question. An important consideration is the timing of the questions. Questions that appear too early or too late show low rates of correct student responses. The first question should appear after 25% of the video has played (Wachtler et al., 2016). The interactive video quiz allows student engagement with the learning content and allows instructors to collect data related to learning outcomes.

Conclusion

Videos have supported instruction for many years. However, we need to remember a video is only one of many tools available to us. Videos should be selected when they are the best or most efficient means to support the educational process. Effective design and the strategies for learning are important considerations in the use of video for supporting teaching and fostering learning.

References

Bower, G. H. (2000). A brief history of memory research. In E. Tulving & F. I. M. Craik, (Eds.), *The Oxford handbook of memory* (pp. 3–32). Oxford University Press.

Brown, L. (2019). *Benefits for teacher using video in the classroom.* Wondershare. https://filmora.wondershare.com/video-editing-tips/benefits-for-using-video-in-classroom.html

Carnegie Mellon University. (2019). *Open learning initiative: Teach with OLI's proven courses.* https://oli.cmu.edu/

Clark, R. C., & Mayer, R. E. (2008). *E-learning and the science of instruction: Proven guidelines for consumers and designers of multimedia learning* (2nd ed.). Pfeiffer.

Fiorella, L., Stull, A. T., Kuhlmann, S., & Mayer, R. E. (2018). Instructor presence in video lectures: The role of dynamic drawings, eye contact, and instructor visibility. *Journal of Educational Psychology.* Advance online publication. http://dx.doi.org/10.1037/edu0000325

Halls, J. (2012). *Rapid video development for trainers: How to create learning videos fast and affordably.* American Society for Training and Development.

Leonard, E. (2015). *Great expectations: Students and video in higher education.* SAGE. https://studysites.sagepub.com/repository/binaries/pdfs/StudentsandVideo.pdf

Massachusetts Institute of Technology. (2019). *OCW Course Index.* MIT Open Courseware. https://ocw.mit.edu/courses/

Mayer, R. E. (2009). *Multi-media learning* (2nd ed.). Cambridge University Press.

Mayer, R. E. (2014). *The Cambridge handbook of multimedia learning* (2nd ed.). Cambridge University Press.

Miller, G. A. (1956). The magical number seven, plus or minus two: Some limits on our capacity to process information. *Psychological Review, 63*(2), 81–97. https://doi.org/10.1037/h0043158

National Teacher Training Institute. (2006). *Video strategies: Why use video in the classroom.* Thirteen Ed Online. https://www.thirteen.org/edonline/ntti/resources/video1.html

Nielsen, J. (2005). *Talking-head video is boring online.* Nielsen Norman Group. https://www.nngroup.com/articles/talking-head-video-is-boring-online/

Paivio, A. (1971). *Imagery and verbal processes.* Holt, Rinehart, and Winston.

Sherer, P., & Shea, T. (2011). Using online video to support student learning and engagement. *College Teaching, 59,* 56–59. https://doi.org/10.1080/87567555.2010.511313

Spannaus, T. W. (2012). *Creating video for teachers and trainers: Producing professional video with amateur equipment.* Pfeiffer.

Sweller, J. (1988). Cognitive load during problem solving: Effects on learning. *Cognitive Science, 12*(2), 257–285. https://doi.org/10.1207/s15516709cog1202_4

Wachtler, J., Hubmann, M., Zöhrer, H., & Ebner, M. (2016). An analysis of the use and effect of questions in interactive learning-videos. *Smart Learning Environments*, *3*(1). https://doi.org/10.1186/s40561-016-0033-3

Zhang, D., Zhou, L., Briggs, R. O., & Nunamaker, J. F. (2006). Instructional video in e-learning: Assessing the impact of interactive video on learning effectiveness. *Information and Management*, *43*(1), 15–27. https://doi.org/10.1016/j.im.2005.01.004

Collaboration doesn't just magically happen.

15

GROUP WORK

Online Collaboration Isn't Always Horrible

Emily Goldstein

Collaborate, verb: to work jointly with others or together especially in an intellectual endeavor (Merriam-Webster, n.d.)

Look around. The workplace, educational institutions, and nearly every interaction that takes place in our lives require collaboration every day. According to Michaelson and Sweet (2008), "When group members bring many different perspectives to a task, their process of collaborative knowledge-building in pursuit of consensus is powerful to watch" (p. 10).

Ensuring that our learners are prepared for careers is on the mind of every instructor, so how can instructional designers convince faculty that group work isn't horrible? Consider the core values or skills of graduates at an institution. At the University of Missouri–St. Louis, we expect our graduates to have skills that include critical thinking, creative thinking, communication, diversity, information literacy, integrative thinking, and qualitative thinking.

These skills require learners to collaborate with their colleagues, faculty, and the community to be successful. Collaboration early in entry-level courses allows students to master the skill by the time they reach the upper-level courses. The outcome is that a student will bring "individual responsibility and accountability for independent, out-of-class learning" and that the group will take "group responsibility for collaborative, in-class learning through application of content in the context of real-world problems" (Hunt et al., 2003, p. 132).

Collaborative projects are valuable because they not only increase the critical thinking skills of the learners but also expose learners to the diversity of ideas and backgrounds of their group members, and they become more inclusive thinkers. With countless ways to structure group projects and collaboration experiences for learners, this chapter provides a framework that leads to positive feelings about group projects and sets them up to be more beneficial than frustrating. Group work created with the following characteristics in mind will more likely lead to successful implementation of group projects.

Collaboration as a Course Goal

Collaboration doesn't just magically happen. In online courses, an initial barrier learners encounter is distance. Collaboration appears even more difficult because learners don't have the physical proximity to encourage in-person collaboration with each other. Treating collaboration with the same level of importance as a course goal can help guide instructional designers and instructors in designing and scaffolding such a project to make it successful. But what do we mean by collaborative learning?

Collaborative learning is a way to have learners working together to solve authentic problems with other learners. They participate in the mutual sharing of ideas to create a multidimensional project. In collaborative learning, learners shouldn't be able to complete the project individually. Cooperative learning uses a divide and conquer approach but doesn't have the same educational value. "Because collaborative learning requires negotiation, argumentation, and continually making implicit knowledge explicit, it demands a greater cognitive load" (Linder et al., 2018, p. 73). Therefore, including collaboration as a course goal is essential to give learners authentic, real-world experiences in the classroom.

When working with faculty to create course goals, ask them, What do you want your learners to remember about this course 2 years from now? It is important for their expectations to be front and center. This simple question might leave them questioning their end goal. Was their answer that they read the textbook and took a quiz? Probably not. Remind them that course goals, or objectives, must be actionable and measurable. If they aren't, reevaluate and ask the faculty members what they want their learners to remember 2 years from now.

For example, an instructor recently shared with me,

> I want my learners to develop a collaborative working relationship with their classmates. To help them hone that skill, in my syllabus, I included information about my expectations for them and how each project helps them meet that objective. Being transparent and letting them know what the course entailed from the beginning was *[sic]* crucial.

The overall course goal she needed learners to meet was for them to use modern technologies to research, retrieve, synthesize, construct, and present information for academic disciplines in an entry-level educational literacy course. The following unit-level objective set forth how they would master that skill: Apply the research you have identified and evaluated in a collaborative social media campaign.

The objective is layered and complex. Bloom's taxonomy is one of the frameworks instructional designers use to develop learning objectives. The learners have to identify and evaluate research, apply (third level of Bloom's taxonomy) that research, and create a social media campaign, all in a collaborative group (Krathwohl, 2002). This process doesn't happen in a week; it occurs over the course of the semester.

As the designer, you can help the instructor evaluate if collaboration is central to course goals or if it is merely a nice idea. If the goals of the course do not align with collaborative work, then forcing collaborative approaches on the learners isn't likely to be successful. If the goals do not connect with collaboration, try to steer the instructor toward course designs that will complement the learning objectives without complicating the design by injecting interaction where it doesn't benefit the learners.

Interaction Early in the Course

The instructional designer can help prepare the learners for collaborative work by helping the instructors design their course in a way that gets learners interacting from day one. Normalizing communication and connection with classmates from the very beginning can demonstrate to the learners that their online experience will not be in isolation. Ensuring that the online course cultivates a feeling of community to combat isolation allows learners to build trust through these conversations that connect them to each other. One method of connecting learners is through an introductory discussion.

Starting on the first day of the course, learners should have the opportunity to get to know their classmates in a nonthreatening, low-stakes way. The designer can recommend doing this through a discussion board or another similar tool. According to Du and Xu (2010), "Using technology can result in students becoming bored, inattentive, or even frustrated with the online discussion experience" (p. 13). In addition, "Distance learners have indicated experiencing a sense of social isolation" (p. 14). To counteract that isolation, acclimating them to the course and their classmates is essential.

Having learners contribute to an introductory discussion board is twofold. First, learners get to know each other in a light, low-stakes way, and second, learners notice the similarities and differences among them. Consider providing learners with the opportunity to post their introductions in video format to the discussion forum to expand the group's connections and personalization.

However you design the course, provide opportunities for connection at the very beginning of the course to begin to lay a foundation of connection and trust to later build on with more cognitively demanding collaborative activities. Learners are more successful when they have the opportunity to get to know their classmates and when they see real-world value in what they are doing and how it fits into the context of their learning.

Designing the Project

The design of the collaborative project can make or break the activity. Two aspects of peer learning work toward cognitive gains in learners: positive interdependence and individual accountability (Wentzel et al., 2017). Positive interdependence means that the learners need each other to complete the task at hand. If the project can be completed by just one person who is anxious about grades and needs total control by commandeering the assignment, then the project is not structured well enough to be collaborative. Examples of positive interdependence include providing guidelines on roles and structuring guidelines to positively enhance participant interaction in the collaborative experience (Brewer & Klein, 2006).

Slackers quiver in fear at the idea of individual accountability, a strategy group members can wield to help encourage everyone's involvement in the project. Ask instructors how they envision individual accountability. Will there be peer assessments or self-assessments? Will they happen at the end of the project or at various points during the project to provide opportunities for course correction? I've heard many instructors talk about dismissing approaches for individual accountability because they believe there are slackers in the working world and learners need to figure out how to work with them. To me, that sounds like an excuse because the instructor doesn't want to help learners navigate the frustrations of collaboration. If instructors are not willing to help learners figure out how to work together, then designers may want to suggest more individualized approaches to course design for the sake of the learners and the instructor. Collaboration is more successful when it's thoroughly integrated into all aspects of the course, even in the instructor's role.

Constructing and Scaffolding

When constructing an assignment, list the steps learners will be required to take for the project to be considered complete. Ask the instructor to write out all the steps practitioners in the professional world go through to solve the same kinds of problems, and then discuss how those steps could be authentically replicated for the assignment. Projects or assignments that are authentic are better received by learners because they will feel like the messy, somewhat ambiguous, real-world problems they will be solving in their professional lives. Considering what learners are able to do at the current moment and what you want them to do will help you set up the project. "Without scaffolding [learners] will have a difficult time navigating coursework and developing mastery" (Sardo & Sindelar, 2019, para. 5).

When building the assignment with the instructor, consider the following components: The assignment aligns with the objectives, it has milestones (or checkpoints) for completion, and the instructor includes the criteria for assessment in the form of a bulleted list or a more detailed rubric. Will the project be graded on how it came along as a whole, each step of the way, as a group, or individually? Those are all important for the learners to know.

Liu and Tsai's (2008) study found that group development was an aspect of collaborative learning that faculty need to pay close attention to. Furthermore, Linder et al.'s (2018) research found the following:

> Group assignments and projects require increased time on task; require that students interact with peers and faculty about substantive matters over extended periods of time; provide opportunities to give, receive, and consider more feedback than independent assignments and projects; and provide skill-building opportunities valued in many places of employment where collaboration is necessary to conduct business successfully. (p. 71)

Problem-Based Learning

So far in this chapter, we have talked about collaborative projects inside the course. What if the instructor wants the whole course to be collaborative? Collaborative problem-based learning (PBL) is an active or experiential form of learning in which learners are exposed to complex, real-world project-based tasks with no correct answer (Hmelo-Silver, 2004). In PBL, learners collaborate in small groups to identify key issues pertaining to the problem and engage in self-directed learning to gather resources and information to assist with the development of strategies to solve the problem. PBL "is designed to facilitate, among other things, the development of critical analysis and problem-solving skills" (Karantzas et al., 2013, p. 39).

The practice of PBL, begun at McMaster University in 1969, "is used to help students identify their own learning needs as they attempt to understand the problem, to pull together, synthesize and apply information to the problem, and to begin to work effectively to learn from group members" (McMaster University, 2015, para. 1).

Our campus has several departments that have chosen to use PBL to enhance instruction; it challenges learners by asking them to think through authentic learning simulations.

Group Logistics

At this point, you and the instructor have connected collaboration to the objectives of the course and decided on a few projects that will be good candidates for learners to coconstruct knowledge. About this time the instructor will inevitably ask, "So how do I actually form the groups? Does it matter who is grouped with whom?" Most learning management systems have the ability to create randomized groups from the class roster, which is a very tempting approach. But do randomized groups work well, or should the instructor try to manually create more intentional groups? Is it okay for groups to form based on previous established relationships? And in keeping with the theme of this book, what is the learner-centered approach?

According to Chen and Kuo (2019), "The most frequently used methods for group formation include random grouping (Chan et al., 2010; Huxland & Land, 2000), selection by teacher (Hilton & Phillips, 2010), and selection by students (Hilton & Phillips, 2010)" (p. 95). The ideal number of students in each group is three or four (Lou et al., 1996). Smaller groups will not have enough diversity to generate ideas, and larger groups give students an opportunity to hide. If given a choice, learners self-select homogenous groups, but great value comes from working with other learners with diverse backgrounds and beliefs. There are countless ways to form groups, and the instructor will need to examine the context to make the best call.

These groups can stay the same for the duration of the semester, or they can change. Chen and Kuo (2019) found that most of the students in the study needed time to get to know the others in their group before starting the PBL activity. It was indicated that a period of students getting to know their classmates preceded the productive work on the task, but there was no difference in learning performance between groups that remained consistent or changed throughout the term.

As you work with the instructor, ask the following:

- Question 1: Will you assign students to groups? If you are assigning them to groups, what is your purpose? If you aren't assigning them to groups, why?

- Question 2: Will the learners organically form groups? If not, why? If they don't form groups organically, how are you structuring group formation so students can get to know more students?

Crafting Roles

Although the projects can be created with levels of individual accountability, one practical way of communicating individual responsibilities is through various project roles. Roles can be used for almost anything. In our Center for Teaching and Learning, we use roles when working with faculty in orientations and workshops, which helps each member contribute to the learning experience. Using groups of three to four members, select the number of roles and customize them for your own purposes. The three roles we use the most often are manager, note taker, and reporter.

The manager provides leadership and direction for the group, leads discussions, suggests solutions to team problems, and helps give each team member an opportunity to share to ensure each member is heard. The note taker keeps a public record of the team's ideas and progress and checks to ensure that what is being said is clear and accurate. The reporter provides a verbal summary of the discussion based on the notes from the note taker, collaborates with the note taker to be sure the notes are accurate, listens to what others say, and repeats it in the individual's own words. In the online arena, those in this role report to the whole class.

Learners can always work together to create and define their roles in the project and collectively agree to each individual's responsibilities. This can also help build in authenticity by defining the scope of work and delegating responsibilities fairly.

Evaluating and Grading

The last major hurdle in designing online collaborative projects is figuring out how to assess the process and the product. The pressing need is to evaluate the process of collaboration because that's the real learning objective, actual collaboration, not just the creation of a deliverable, which learners can create on their own.

Have Learners Design Their Group Contracts

Now that you have set the tone, and learners know the expectations of the course, have them create a document that describes their expectations for each other. Another faculty member shared that she puts the responsibility of setting expectations and communication guidelines on them by providing structured questions to help them shape their group norms. If they return at the end with complaints (and not much time to manage them), she is able to point them back to their original commitment and use their own words and standards to shape the appropriate response. It has also shifted the vast amount of group work points to individual points, which also relieves some frustration (Anonymous, personal communication, July 30, 2019).

Those questions about guidelines for the group include the following:

- How will the group communicate?
- What is a reasonable time frame or deadline for communication?
- What constitutes an excused delay in participation?
- What are the policies for work assignments—that is, how will the work be divided, what are the group roles and deadlines, how do we edit one another's work, and so on?
- Will the groups follow the three-strikes rule? If not, explain the process for determining the instructor's involvement.

Self-Evaluation and Peer Evaluation

After the project is complete, but before it is submitted, the group members should evaluate their work. Did they all contribute their fair share? Did they glide along without contributing? Self-evaluations and peer evaluations are common ways to evaluate the contributions and collaboration of group members. A peer evaluation doesn't have to be a written memo; instead, you can gauge the performance of learners and their work using a form. Peer evaluations should take place at the end of a project but can also happen at any point in the group project, and the instructor should communicate how evaluations will happen. The following is an example of evaluation questions for individuals and team members:

- Self-Evaluation
  - I responded to team members' efforts to coordinate work through email, meetings, and so on in a timely manner.
  - I contributed my fair share to the group's assignment. The work I contributed included _____.
  - How I contributed work that met the quality expectations of the group.
  - How I met the expectation of myself. Was I a team member I would want to work with again? Why, why not?

- Team Member Evaluation
  - Member responded to team members' efforts to coordinate work through email, meetings, and so on in a timely manner.
  - Member contributed a fair share to the group's assignment.
  - How the team member's contributed work met the quality expectations of the group.
  - If given the opportunity, would I want to work with this person again?
  - Additional comments about the group member

In these evaluations, students identify themselves. The instructor can then choose whether to share the results of the evaluation with students who disagree with it.

Grading the Process

Intentionality is key when creating a collaborative experience for learners. "Forthright directions and explanations of why particular activities are evaluated the way they are can avoid unnecessary problems in the collaborative activity and can help students negotiate conflict in constructive ways" (Linder et al., 2018, p. 81). These directions could be in the form of a rubric with specific criteria laid out for learners. Remember, how well learners collaborated with their peers is just as important as the deliverable.

Asking for Feedback

Teaching is an iterative process. Ensuring that instructors ask for feedback from their learners to improve the rubric or project in the future is an easy way to ensure learners' positive feelings toward collaborative group projects. Asking for formative feedback along the way can help restore projects that are in the process of going off the rails. The request can be formal, as part of an assignment or a rubric, or informal, through an assignment or in conversations with students.

Contract or not, what happens when everything goes downhill in a group project and chaos ensues? You ride it out and learn from it, find the tension if there is one, and change accordingly.

Interaction, engagement, and a sense of community are essential components to ensure successful collaboration in online courses and contribute to a learning environment that leads to learner success. True collaboration is hard and messy, but it's valuable too. Instructional designers can work with faculty to help them create meaningful and thoughtfully designed collaborative experiences for learners. Who knows—after experiencing intentionally designed collaborative projects, learners and instructors may not dread the next online group project.

References

Brewer, S., & Klein, J. D. (2006). Type of positive interdependence and affiliation motive in an asynchronous, collaborative learning environment. *Educational Technology Research and Development, 54*(4), 331–354. https://doi.org/10.1007/s11423-006-9603-3

Chen, C., & Kuo, C.-H. (2019). An optimized group formation scheme to promote collaborative problem-based learning. *Computers & Education, 133*, 94–115. https://doi.org/10.1016/j.compedu.2019.01.011

Du, J., & Xu, J. (2010). The quality of online discussion reported by graduate students. *The Quarterly Review of Distance Education, 11*, 13–24.

Hmelo-Silver, C. E. (2004). Problem-based learning: What and how do students learn?" *Educational Psychology Review, 16*(3), 235–266. https://doi.org/10.1023/b:edpr.0000034022.16470.f3

Hunt, D. P., Haidet, P., Coverdale, J. H., & Richards, B. (2003). The effect of using team learning in an evidence-based medicine course for medical students. *Teaching and Learning in Medicine, 15*(2), 131–139. https://doi.org/10.1207/s15328015tlm1502_11

Karantzas, G. C., Avery, M. R., Macfarlane, S., Mussap, A., Tooley, G., Hazelwood, Z., & Fitness, J. (2013). Enhancing critical analysis and problem-solving skills in undergraduate psychology: An evaluation of a collaborative learning and problem-based learning approach. *Australian Journal of Psychology, 65*(1), 38–45. https://doi.org/10.1111/ajpy.12009

Krathwohl, D. R. (2002). A revision of Bloom's taxonomy: An overview. *Theory Into Practice, 41*(4), 212–218. https://doi.org/10.1207/s15430421tip4104_2

Linder, K. E., Hayes, C. M., & Thompson, K. (2018). *High-impact practices in online education: Research and best practices*. Stylus.

Liu, C., & Tsai, C. (2008). An analysis of peer interaction patterns as discoursed by on-line small group problem-solving activity. *Computers & Education, 50*(3), 627–639. https://doi.org/10.1016/j.compedu.2006.07.002

Lou, Y., Abrami, P. C., Spence, J. C., Poulsen, C., Chambers, B., & d'Apollonia, S. (1996). Within-class grouping: A meta-analysis. *Review of Educational Research, 66*(4), 423–458. https://doi.org/10.2307/1170650

McMaster University. (2015). *Education methods: Problem based learning (PBL)*. https://mdprogram.mcmaster.ca/mcmaster-md-program/overview/pbl---problem-based-learning

Michaelsen, L., & Sweet, M. (2008) Team-based learning: Small group learning's next big step. *New Directions in Teaching and Learning*, no. 116, 7–27. https://doi.org/10.1002/tl.467

Sardo, C., & Sindelar, A. (2019, March 27). Scaffolding online student success. *Faculty Focus*. https://www.facultyfocus.com/articles/online-education/scaffolding-online-student-success/

Wentzel, K. R., & Edelman, D. W. (2017). Instruction based on peer interactions. In R. Mayer & P. A. Alexander (Eds.), *Handbook of research on learning and instruction* (pp. 365–387). Routledge.

If the goal is to facilitate robust, interactive, student-centered discussions, synchronous learning is a compelling solution.

16

SYNCHRONOUS LEARNING

Good to See You Again

David Wicks and Annie Tremonte

Between the two of us, we have been incorporating synchronous learning into our online instruction for more than 8 years, most notably as part of the Seattle Pacific University Digital Education Leadership graduate program, designed for educators specializing in the exploration of how digital technology can be used to enhance learning and teaching. Many people assume that synchronous online learning is a live lecture, where a large group of learners watch and listen to their instructor online rather than in a lecture hall. We have been wondering how we disrupt this assumption. As proponents of synchronous learning that is student centered and focused on highlighting learner voices, the class conversations we facilitate must have fewer participants. Although the option of synchronous learning in larger classes exists, the focus of this chapter is on learning environments with less instructor talk and more learner voices. Our courses always include asynchronous components as well as learners sharing their research and engaging in peer teaching and assessment through discussion board comments (Park & Kim, 2015).

Synchronous web meetings provide opportunities for learners to make themselves known to their instructors and their fellow learners alike. The act of making oneself known in an online course is called *social presence* (Richardson & Swan, 2003). Social presence supports the process of critical thinking in an educational experience (Garrison et al., 2000). In asynchronous text-based courses, learners make themselves and their views known by what and how they write. In synchronous courses, learners use their web cameras to give other learners and instructors a glimpse into their world and ideas. In a web meeting, participants are able to establish social presence through their facial expressions and voices and occasionally by including a pet or a small child who joins them on screen. The use of audio and video in synchronous learning creates an exchange rich with nuanced, nonverbal cues. For example, a learner provided nonverbal cues indicating the mispronunciation of her name each time the instructor said it. The learner's nonverbal cues resulted in the instructor's consultation with the student that resolved the issue. This important check-in, which increased the social presence, was possible because of the visible nonverbal cues. As this example indicates, it is always our goal to make all learners feel welcome in the course and cared about as individuals.

The Why: Why Online Learning and Why Is Synchronous a Good Choice?

Why do students take online courses? Why does synchronous learning provide powerful learning opportunities?

Inclusivity

Web-based coursework creates an inclusive educational experience for a wider diversity of students. Learners might work full-time, live beyond commuting distance of the university, or have family commitments that prevent physical attendance. When seat time is a required expectation in a course, we not only limit educational opportunities for all learners but also miss out on the diverse academic contributions of those who are unable to participate. This is where online learning can be quite powerful. We recently taught a class in which one of the learners participated from a time zone 15 hours different from ours. Online learning allowed this student to seek the education she wanted without quitting her job or disrupting her family's life. Our learning community benefited from the opportunity to have rich discussions about the similarities and differences between cultures. Although the time difference made scheduling web meetings challenging, it was a powerful chance to incorporate cultural similarities and differences into real-time discussions. Facilitating an inclusive synchronous space also means being responsive to universal design principles (Rose et al., 2005). All students bring different strengths, and, subsequently, all students benefit from support. Providing access to agendas and presentation slides in advance, and recording meetings for transcription are how we increase access to learning. Live captioning, which is available on a variety of platforms, and transcriptions of direct instruction created in advance are additional ways to increase accessibility.

Synchronous Learning

For many, online learning connotes independent readings, asynchronous discussion boards, and interactions with faceless instructors or peers at incongruous times of the day. Currently, most online courses are based on asynchronous interactions to maximize flexibility. Although this format works well for many, time flexibility should not be the singular driver of online learning opportunities in higher education.

Synchronous learning provides opportunities for real-time feedback and interaction. Platforms such as Zoom, Google Meet, and Skype are examples of current technologies educational institutions use to host web meetings. Many other platforms exist, and of course all will continue to converge and evolve so we avoid comparing platforms here. In this chapter, we explore features of synchronous learning that are ubiquitous to all platforms and can support engaging interactions. Of course, web meetings can have technical problems, such as learners signing on and not being able to access their microphone or video camera, so we also discuss logistical considerations and instructional practices that are necessary for a successful synchronous learning environment.

The How: How Is Synchronous Learning Integrated to Support Online Instruction?

As an instructional designer, you may work with instructors who are initially focused on replacing the physical classroom with the online space. For example, an instructor most familiar with the lecturing environment may be interested in recording their teaching for learners to view online. One of the challenges with the online approach is that it is often a one-to-many environment. You can have thousands of learners watching a live online lecture without any interaction with the instructor or other students. What are the instructional goals of such a course? What is the purpose of using a synchronous learning environment if there is no teacher-to-student or student-to-student interaction? If this course is a survey or introductory course, with content delivery the primary focus, a prerecorded video or podcast might work better for direct instruction because it would allow students to pause and rewatch content they did not understand. If the goal is to facilitate robust, interactive, student-centered discussions, synchronous learning is a compelling solution.

A handful of basic questions can help to establish a vision for the course design. What do you want your learning environment to look like? What are your goals for your learners? Common goals of a synchronous learners-centered environment might include increasing collaboration, highlighting learner voices, or providing an authentic audience of peers. Instructional strategies to support these goals might include breakout groups or breakout calls for think-pair-share and other small-group activities. The use of collaborative online tools, such as mind maps and word clouds, can be useful for formative assessment activities and prompting students' prior knowledge.

We find that synchronous web meetings are most powerful when learners arrive ready to engage and discuss. Because we expect this of learners, instructors should also arrive ready to facilitate. With our approach, we have the ability to be responsive, to interact with learners more directly, and to build trust and community. Students care about their learning when they feel cared about (Teven & McCroskey, 1997).

Consider Class Size

Class size is a significant consideration for a synchronous online class. Who is speaking and when are somewhat of a dance in a live online space, especially if participation is assessed. Learner participation through synchronous discussion works fairly well with a class size of 10 learners or fewer. Through practice, learners develop the skill to sense openings to speak and are pretty good about sharing the stage, especially when communication norms have been established. As the number of participants increases, synchronous learner participation through voice becomes more challenging to accommodate as raising hands and taking turns become increasingly necessary. However, at some point, time becomes a determining factor of how many people get a chance to speak. Large class sizes can also dramatically affect the ability to build relationships and community. In a larger online course, breakout groups might be used in conjunction with content delivery to engage students at a deeper and more interactive level.

Build Relationships and Community

We know that relationship building is an important component of academic development (Hattie, 2009). Learners engaged in healthy relationships in which their social and emotional needs are met feel a sense of belonging. This sense of belonging not only influences engagement but also is a motivating force for contributing to the larger learning community.

Online learning allows students to engage in learning directly from their homes, potentially with a child sleeping in another room, a dog underfoot, or a doorbell that can ring at any time. This understanding is actually an asset, not a drawback, as it values learners as individuals with lives. We have discovered that this understanding alone sets the stage for community building to take place. Learners and instructors in our online program occasionally show their pets or children during class (sometimes humorously unintentionally) and it serves to let us all know we are human and we care. In some cases, we find out who really likes dogs and small children as we see people's faces light up when a sleepy child plops down on the lap of an unsuspecting synchronous learner or instructor or an inquisitive dog nose pokes into the frame.

Taking the time in class to greet everyone by name or ask about everyone's week is a powerful way to build connections. Little by little, this builds bridges across time zones and geographical locations, connecting the real humans sitting behind screens to one another as collaborative learners. In fact, the very awareness of how disconnected it can feel to interact online serves to inspire an intentional focus on community building. It has been our experience that after working online for a number of weeks, we have the chance to meet learners in person. At that first meeting, sometimes we danced around the words "Good to see you again" and "Good to meet you." Having never physically met before, social convention dictates for us to use the word *meet*. However, we laugh, recognizing how well bonded we already are. Sometimes we may even question whether we have already met in person. This familiarity is possible only if we have done a good job of limiting instructor talk and promoting learner voices.

When graduation time comes, students in Seattle Pacific University's online digital education leadership graduate program are often chatting like they are close friends who see each other every week. Well, in fact, they do see each other every week, they just aren't in the same physical location. The first cohort to enter the program in 2014 continues to schedule video calls on an intermittent basis to reconnect and catch up on happenings in their careers and lives. In a recent course, one learner emphasized the importance of the weekly web meetings by saying that the synchronous time was critical for her personal experience and application.

Establish Logistical and Technical Norms

Facilitating a functioning synchronous learning environment also means being cognizant of some logistical and technical considerations. As an instructional designer, it is useful to make recommendations to ensure these considerations support rather than distract from the learning.

Location

As an instructional designer, you might need to consider recommendations for the physical location of instructors and learners engaging in the synchronous web meeting. A quiet space devoid of too much distracting background noise is preferred. Coffee shops, while often a sought-after telecommuting workspace, are not ideal for this reason. Similarly, sharing a space with a family member or calling in while driving a car (yes, it has happened) is also not ideal. In our teaching, we proactively have a conversation about ideal workspaces with instructors and learners. Although choices might be different for faculty and students, establishing these norms is the first step to ensure a focused learning environment for what are often short opportunities for synchronicity.

Camera Enabled
As an instructional designer, you may also need to provide guidance about cameras and headphones. We ask instructors and learners to enable their cameras during live calls. This not only provides some accountability for attendance and participation but it also continues to deepen the development of community and connectedness among instructors and learners. There is a line between accountability and privacy, however. Compliments about a pet or small child who appears on screen are appropriate. Probing questions about specific titles of books on shelves or who is shown in pictures in the background are not.

Simultaneously, a bit of trust goes a long way. If a camera is disabled, we might establish a shared understanding as a class about what this means. Perhaps learners have something personal to attend to that cannot wait until after class. In this case, disabling a camera is a thoughtful move to avoid distraction. But what if it is always off? In one such case, a disabled camera meant that a learner was actually having technical problems and never asked for help. In these situations, it is important to have a conversation in private to avoid putting a student on the spot. We must remember that in any online course, we are accepting the challenges of spaces that are personal and, sometimes, unpredictable. Meeting these challenges is an art, not a science.

Headphones, Earbuds, and Microphones
More often than not, learners will use different audio technologies to participate. Headphones are important because they help eliminate feedback when more than one person is speaking and echoing when a person's microphone is too loud. Some learners are soft-spoken, and others are loud. The use of headphones or earbuds gives the listener control over the volume level and minimizes interruptions. A good microphone that is not rubbing against a shirt collar or scratchy beard will benefit all listeners and help the speakers get their point across without distractions.

Muted When Not Speaking
We have already established that each learner brings a different physical environment into the course. Our aim is to accept and respect this. However, there are ways to balance acceptance and respect and still facilitate an engaging digital learning environment. One way is to ask participants to mute themselves when they are not speaking. Microphones pick up background noise and static that can be distracting to everyone else in the meeting. A norm around muting can help mitigate this distraction. Also, learners should not be offended if the professor mutes them. Participants are often unaware that their microphone is buzzing or that others can hear their keyboard tapping. A private message during or after class can eliminate minor distractions that become major frustrations as the course moves forward.

Lighting
To engage fully and see everyone clearly, recommendations from an instructional designer about lighting are useful. Instructors and learners can avoid shadows on the face by using a small light or lamp with a shade beside the computer screen as well as minimal light in the background.

Access Advocation
As an instructional designer, you should prepare your instructors to look for signs of learners with inadequate access to technology. We must remember that if a university is not providing devices and infrastructure, all learners are bringing their own unique technology with them. What happens when a learner has bandwidth issues or technical difficulties? It is important to support learners and let them know to not panic because the meeting is being recorded. In our experience, these types of problems typically come up more frequently at the beginning of the term and wane as the course progresses. It can, of course, be distracting for participants to troubleshoot by logging on and off during a web meeting. Some learners find it helpful to work through some of the potential technical challenges with a peer on their own time early in the course. For those who cannot resolve an issue quickly during a synchronous web meeting we recommend logging off and using the recording instead. Working with information technology staff to support students is an important way to ensure that all students have proper access to learning.

Chat Features
Chat features can be either a valuable asset or an annoying distraction. Chat works well to brainstorm ideas, share resources, and ask questions without

interrupting a speaker. However, it may be problematic if some learners prioritize sharing text comments over participating by voice. When used appropriately, the chat can be filled with valuable commentary and resources by the end of a meeting. Capturing transcripts of the chats is an important component of maintaining accessibility, and we recommend devising a strategy for capture. We share a link to the chat transcript with the meeting recording in the announcements area of the online course.

Advanced Preparation

Synchronous course meetings should not be too long as we do not want students sitting in front of their computers for excessive periods of time. To ensure a concise meeting, prepare and share an agenda prior to the web meeting. Without an agenda, the web meeting might be chaotic. The more organized the instruction, the better. Using agendas is a way to structure the learning, provide transparency to learners, and honor everyone's time. It is the preparation that supports intentional sharing of resources and the discussions that follow. Opening tabs that will be shared or used during screen sharing, having formative assessment data ready to share, and collaborating on a document in advance all serve as more than just preparation. They maximize the possibility of meaningful dynamic interactions during the meeting. Without this, time may be wasted delivering content by teacher talk when prerecorded podcasts can present content more efficiently, allowing students to rewatch autonomously.

Practice 21st-Century Skills

Learners need nuanced communication skills to determine how to engage in synchronous discussions, specifically when reading someone's body language is limited by seeing only a face in a box. Online courses can provide opportunities to develop many new, useful skills not always present in a traditional classroom. Twenty-first-century skills, such as communication, collaboration, critical thinking, and creativity, are crucial skills for working with others across cultures and time zones. Through this work, we see learners gain the confidence to elevate their voices, and as instructors we develop a sense of wait time and methods of invitational questioning.

With screen sharing capabilities, there may be more opportunities for students to take on the roles of facilitators and leaders. Learners have opportunities to demonstrate in real time the creative solutions they have developed to demonstrate mastery of a course's authentic assessment activities. In our case, students share the instructional lessons they've redesigned to better integrate technology to solicit feedback from their peers. If we see a web meeting only as a substitution for the missing physical classroom, we might overlook the transformative learning opportunities this medium provides. It is a chance to practice critical thinking skills on the fly, negotiate digital communication and collaboration skills, navigate presentation tools, and share resources with remote participants, sometimes all while facilitating peer discussions simultaneously (Office of Educational Technology, 2014). Learners even gain a better understanding of the technical components involved in this work by using better lighting techniques, improving their audio, and regulating their learning through planning, monitoring, and reflection (Shea et al., 2012; Wicks et al., 2015).

Define Participation

Should participation in a web meeting be a requirement or an option? What is acceptable for participants to do while in a synchronous meeting? Learners may think it's acceptable to fold laundry or cook dinner, especially if the class is lecture based. When multiple students appear on the screen wearing aprons and holding cooking utensils, you should realize that there may have been too much instructor talk in the first class meeting. By designing the synchronous events to hinge on interaction, the temptation or even ability to engage in other activities while on a call is diminished, and the time spent is more valuable to the overall learning of the course objectives. We might consider how students are being asked to engage. Is the learning experience relevant to all students? Is the environment inclusive? Are there opportunities for learner voices?

As the size of the class grows, an instructor may need more help with determining how to support student participation. Some digital platforms include a hand-raising feature. Although such a feature may be distracting, it may be the only equitable way to share the stage in a larger class. As always, establishing communication norms at the beginning of a program or course will set expectations and make sure all voices are heard.

Record

As an instructional designer, it is important to consider the learners who are unable to attend a class meeting. A key advantage of a web meeting is that it is easy to record. Making recordings of class meetings available to learners is sound universal design (Rose et al., 2005). Recordings are helpful to students who missed class, but they also benefit students with disabilities, those who speak a different first language, and for any learner who wants to review a key point in the meeting. We then ask how we might hold students who missed class accountable for interacting with the learning. We choose to use discussion forums in the learning management system to facilitate an asynchronous discussion of the real-time interaction. We ask learners to interact with the video recording by asking and answering questions using separate posts and including a time stamp with each post so others know where to look in the recording. However, we avoid an inauthentic prescription of requiring a specific number of comments or questions. We found that learners who miss a class also miss the class. Learners who are not present during a class want to be part of the community, obtain social connection, and of course provide comments. This engagement is the true connection, not necessarily the actual comments that may or may not develop into a text-based discussion thread, although it certainly still sometimes does. We also know learners who were in original attendance still go back and rewatch parts of the recordings even if they didn't miss the class to reinforce their comprehension of the contents of the session. We are thoughtful in how we post recordings for learners to view, consciously using unlisted settings to make sure that only those with a link can gain access. At the same time, we realize that anything on the internet can be hacked or accidentally transmitted, so we remind participants to avoid using identifying information and use only information they would be willing to share publicly. Instructional designers need to help instructors understand that some topics may not be appropriate for synchronous web meetings.

Conclusion

As a learner-centered instructional designer, you are an important link for those who need to cast aside assumptions of what online learning looks like in favor of practices that support community, student voices, and the acquisition of real-world skills. This chapter provides a lens into how synchronous learning opportunities can powerfully shift an online course from being merely a place to access information to a space for dynamic real-time interaction. Synchronous learning provides opportunities for immediate feedback and interaction, as well as the opportunity to facilitate robust, interactive, student-centered discussions.

Although responsiveness is desirable, intentionality of design and preparation are equally important. Establishing norms, setting expectations, and preparing for the meeting are crucial because synchronous learning does not allow time autonomy for instructors and students.

As an instructional designer, it is important to consider who the learners are in the course. Learners are diverse people with real lives, real pursuits, real viewpoints, and real challenges. There is not a one-size-fits-all approach to designing a course with synchronous components. Rather, we must get to know our students and trade coverage of content for practices that build community and highlight student voices to truly drive autonomous thinking and learning. As an instructional designer, you might be the only one who can model how this is possible for those who may not have seen it in action before. When synchronous learning is done well, your instructors will be saying "Good to see you again" rather than wondering why no one comes to class.

References

Garrison, D. R., Anderson, T., & Archer, W. (2000). Critical inquiry in a text-based environment: Computer conferencing in higher education. *The Internet and Higher Education, 2*(2/3), 1–19.

Hattie, J. (2009). *Visible learning: A synthesis of over 800 meta-analyses relating to achievement*. Routledge.

Office of Educational Technology. (2014). *Learning technology effectiveness.* https://tech.ed.gov/wp-content/uploads/2014/11/Learning-Technology-Effectiveness-Brief.pdf

Park, S., & Kim, C. (2015). Boosting learning-by-teaching in virtual tutoring. *Computers & Education, 82*, 129–140. http://doi.org/10.1016/j.compedu.2014.11.006

Richardson, J. C., & Swan, K. (2003). Examining social presence in online courses in relation to students' perceived learning and satisfaction. *Journal of Asynchronous Learning Networks, 7*(1). http://dx.doi.org/10.24059/olj.v7i1.1864

Rose, D. H., Meyer, A., & Hitchcock, C. (2005). *The universally designed classroom: Accessible curriculum and digital technologies*. Harvard Education Press.

Shea, P., Hayes, S., Smith, S. U., Vickers, J., Bidjerano, T., Pickett, A., Gozza-Cohene, M., Wilde, J., Jiana, S. (2012). Learning presence: Additional research on a new conceptual element within the community of inquiry (CoI) framework. *The Internet and Higher Education, 15*(2), 89–95. https://doi.org/10.1016/j.iheduc.2011.08.002

Teven, J. J., & McCroskey, J. C. (1997) The relationship of perceived teacher caring with student learning and teacher evaluation. *Communication Education, 46*(1), 1–9. https://doi.org/10.1080/03634529709379069

Wicks, D., Craft, B. B., Lee, D. D., Lumpe, A., Henrikson, R., Baliram, N., Bian, X., Mehlberg, S., & Wicks, K. (2015). An evaluation of low versus high-collaboration in online learning. *Online Learning Journal, 19*(4). http://dx.doi.org/10.24059/olj.v19i4.552

There is no one formula for a good online discussion, just as there is no single formula for a good face-to-face discussion or class meeting.

17

DISCUSSION FORUMS

Our Love-Hate Relationship With Discussion Forums

Shannon Riggs

The online discussion forum is one of the simplest, most straightforward, and most flexible pieces of educational technology at an online educator's disposal. Paradoxically, it is also one of the most misused, underused, and challenging to master. When discussion forums are designed and used well, instructors and learners often love this part of an online course because the forums promote student engagement with the content, the instructor, and other learners. Real conversation, with all the interest, thoughtfulness, listening, and speaking it involves, can happen in online spaces, and when it does, the participants are meaningfully engaged just as they are when such conversations take place face-to-face. When designed and used poorly, online discussions can fill instructors and learners with dread. Poorly designed and facilitated discussions feel rote, mechanical, and downright inauthentic. Instructional designers who can guide faculty to better uses of this versatile tool can have a transformative impact on student learning experiences and can help make online teaching more satisfying for instructional faculty. Online discussions should be exciting, invigorating spaces where the learners and instructors feel motivated to participate as conversationalists—speakers and listeners all.

The Promise of Discussion Forums

All learning management systems offer online discussion forums, and for good reason. In one location, in one activity, online discussions provide an opportunity for learners to interact with the course content, the instructor, and each other. In asynchronous discussion forums, ideas can be shared; questions can be asked and answered; and concepts can be applied, analyzed, and discussed. Through a variety of intellectual, collaborative, and social interactions, learners can feel they are part of a learning community. Yuan and Kim (2014) identified a series of guidelines instructional faculty can follow to create learning communities, several using online discussions: assigning roles, encouraging task-oriented and social interaction, and designing discussion activities that require collaboration. In addition to strengthening the sense of belonging to a learning community, participation in discussions can lead learners to practice solitary activities that improve learning. Discussion forums, well designed and facilitated, can be the vehicle for several high-impact practices (Association of American Colleges & Universities, 2008). Although high-impact practices have typically been applied in traditional on-campus classes, efforts have been made to extend these well-established practices online (Linder & Hayes, 2018). For example, discussion boards can be important tools in writing-intensive courses when they are used for facilitating peer review and in collaborative assignments and projects where learners need to communicate and work together as a team.

Despite promising guidance from the research, in my work with faculty in online education, I have frequently encountered resistance on the value of discussion boards. One faculty member I worked with stated that we could use discussion boards in his class, but they would be for learners only. He would not read their posts or participate. I gently inquired whether such a scenario would ever work in one of his on-campus classes. Another wanted help in removing discussion boards from her class entirely because she did not want to provide learners with a way to share homework answers with each other. I reminded her that students could easily contact each other using the course roster and email and suggested that it might be beneficial for her to be able to monitor those interactions rather than force them into private spaces. More often, though, I have encountered faculty members who simply find discussion boards overwhelming because of the volume of communication. In my experience, discussion boards are frequently perceived as busywork for the learners to write and for faculty to read and grade.

Post Once, Reply Twice

For many faculty and their learners, there is a deep disconnect between the promise of discussions and their implementation. Examining what is perhaps the most commonly used discussion design of all, post once and reply to two peers, can help us understand why. In this question design, faculty pose a question to open the discussion and instruct learners to post an original response to the question, and then, throughout the week, return and reply to at least two peers' original responses. On its face, this discussion design seems to have merit. It requires each student to interact with the content and with each other, and the instructor can interact and ask follow-up questions or post guiding comments to indicate when learners are on track or are missing something. However, anyone who has participated in this type of discussion as either a student or facilitator knows that the conversations that take place adhering to the participation guidelines of this design framework rarely compare in rigor, depth, or authenticity with conversations that take place in the face-to-face classroom. Instead, these overly structured conversations feel like square dancing without the music. Everyone involved is so focused on the rules of engagement that they forget that the content and nature of the conversation are what matters.

Rethinking Post Once, Reply Twice

Post once, reply twice has several significant design flaws. First, it leads to repetitive answers. Simple knowledge-based questions, such as asking learners to answer a factual question, leave room for only the first respondent or two to contribute something meaningful. Even more complex knowledge-based questions, such as asking every student to summarize an assigned reading, limit the conversation as only the first couple of learners' posts contribute meaning. After the first few participants answer, responses to knowledge-based questions become repetitive. Even open-ended questions that call for students to share opinions and life experiences can feel redundant because learners are able to draw conclusions from the first few responses without taking part in the exercise of responding themselves. The scope of the post once, reply twice discussion format is limited from the start as it does not provide a structure for expanding or deepening the coverage of the topic the way a more natural conversation would.

This question framework also does not make the instructor's role clear. An experienced instructor adept with asynchronous communication skills can overcome this, but the design itself does not provide a role for the instructor other than assessment at its conclusion. Indeed, the implied purpose of this question design is more like a quiz than a class discussion. By asking every student to respond to the same question, the purpose seems to be to assess knowledge, skill in constructing the answer, or both. If the instructor is asking a question and everyone has the same answer, an individual quiz or assignment would be a more appropriate choice. Furthermore, the post once, reply twice model does not promote listening as authentic conversations do. In a real conversation, the parties involved listen in addition to speaking. Meaning is constructed, emotions are stirred, and minds are changed through discourse. There is trust and openness and a shared commitment to further the discussion for the benefit of the group. In real conversation, our purpose is not to assess our partner's knowledge but rather to engage in an exchange where the conclusions are not necessarily known. The value for learners is not gaining factual information but to be intrigued by the nuances of the topic and to participate in making meaning. This kind of conversation requires as much careful listening as speaking. Repetitive, rote responses to poorly designed questions are boring, do not build on each other, and do not motivate good listening behaviors. The post once, reply twice model therefore does not inherently promote the critical thinking required when listening and contributing to an authentic conversation. Finally, and perhaps most damaging to a class, this design invites peer responses that are not genuine and therefore break the social trust that learning communities depend on to thrive.

Certainly many online discussions begin with this kind of framework, and learners and instructors can work beyond the design to have more natural and authentic conversations in this space. Those richer, more productive discussions happen despite the design framework and run the risk of leaving behind learners who believe they have met the assignment criteria by posting once and replying twice. Consider how much more effective online discussions can be, though, if the design could clearly support effective discussions from the start.

Alternatives to Post Once, Reply Twice

How could online discussions be designed? One way is to model seminar-style face-to-face class discussions, where the instructor facilitates a conversation in which students in the class listen and participate. The goal in this familiar approach to teaching is for students to converse with the instructor and each other, not for every student in the class to participate in a predetermined pattern. One student or several might reply. Everyone in the class carefully listens to the initial responses, then the instructor or another student either proposes a differing view or asks a new question that expands or deepens the discussion. In the traditional face-to-face environment, the role of listening is apparent and does not typically require instruction. Online, however, listening in asynchronous class discussions may require direct instruction as listening behaviors are not as readily apparent. Wise et al. (2012) identified several behaviors that constitute good listening in online asynchronous discussions, including "students who open a broad array of messages, those who orient towards particular authors, and those who concentrate their participation in few, but intense sessions" (p. 463). To participate in an authentic online conversation, learners cannot simply enter and drop some text into a post. They must perform good online listening behaviors, absorb the nuances of the conversation, and formulate thoughtful contributions, which may be a response or may introduce a whole new thread.

Another effective approach is for the instructor or designated students to emphasize key takeaways or a summary of what has been discussed. However, although Wise and Chiu (2014) found that assigning summarizing roles to students on a rotating basis improved the summarizers' listening behaviors, those behaviors were not sustained when students rotated out of the summarizer role.

To use a seminar-style conversation model in an online, asynchronous format, expectations for participation should be communicated to learners in advance, because a lively, unfolding conversation is unfortunately likely not what they are expecting to happen in a discussion forum. Helpful design elements to include would be stating the expectation that the instructor and learners need to participate throughout the week, that everyone agrees to read all contributions, and that contributions that continue in a thread are as equally valuable as those that begin a new thread of the conversation. Learners accustomed to the post once, reply twice model may need to be directly instructed that every student does not need to reply to the opening question or prompt. Wise et al. (2012) advised that "encouraging students to create concise posts that build on existing threads was suggested as a way to support students in reading a greater portion of the discussion and thus being better prepared to engage in a coherent discussion" (pp. 475–476).

Other effective face-to-face class discussion models can be adapted for use in online asynchronous classes as well. In face-to-face classrooms, asking the class to break into small discussion groups offers several advantages. Small-group discussion creates more opportunity, along with the expectation that all individuals will participate. Using this approach even on an occasional basis makes it uncomfortable for students to be free riders—that is, unprepared for class and allowed to observe and absorb the hard work of better-prepared classmates without contributing an individual effort.

Using the small-group discussion approach also helps introverted students and those with a fear of public speaking by providing more comfortable spaces in which to engage. The small-group approach also invites more risk-taking and collaboration. Speakers work as a team. They brainstorm, discuss, deliberate, and form ideas together. This approach can help build critical thinking, communication, and collaboration skills in addition to knowledge acquisition. The small-group discussion approach can also be employed in online asynchronous discussions with the same benefits for learners. Most learning management systems allow the creation of separate discussion areas that specific groups of students can access. Groups can be formed randomly or manually if customizing group membership is desired. Labeling small-group discussion areas and ensuring that group members are identified in some way at the start of the discussion period help distinguish the small-group area from a whole-class discussion forum. Explicitly stating that the small-group area is not visible to the whole class may be helpful for some learners. Similarly, stating how the instructor will participate in the small-group discussions may also prove helpful. Wise et al. (2012) advised considering the total number of posts students must manage when deciding between whole-class and small-group discussions; "when a greater number of posts per participant are required, it may be prudent to reduce the group size to keep the total number of posts manageable for students" (p. 476).

Online discussions can also be used to introduce and initiate learners to the specific methods and patterns of discourse appropriate for the discipline of study. In a science course, learners might be asked to observe something in their environment and reflect on what they observed. Those reflections can be shared, and learners can then be asked to identify which aspects of the reports are truly based on measurable observation and which aspects of the writing might stray into the realm of drawing inferences or conclusions. In this way, a science instructor can help learners distinguish between what can be measured and proven from assumptions and hypotheses that are not yet proven. A class in rhetoric and composition might ask learners to reflect on a sample of persuasive writing. Initially, learners may be asked to state why they agree or disagree with the author. Later, setting aside personal opinions, learners can be asked to identify how the sample argument was constructed, which appeals were emphasized, and which audiences might be persuaded by the rhetorical approaches selected. Experienced instructional designers can obtain valuable information to inform discussion designs by asking the instructor which habits of mind and patterns of thinking are important for learners to practice. Layering topical conversations with metacognitive prompts specific to disciplinary approaches is a valuable strategy for enriching online discussions. When instructors notice posts in which learners have successfully exhibited a disciplinary-appropriate pattern of thinking, they can call attention to that post, ask learners to either identify the pattern or state it outright, commend the poster, and encourage others to do likewise.

Removing Discussion From the Forum

Interestingly, online discussions may be limited by more than poorly designed discussion questions. Another factor contributing to our love-hate relationship with online discussions could be our failure to use the online medium to its fullest advantage. By labeling these tools *discussion boards* or *forums*, we limit our thinking about the kinds of learning activities that can take place, and we limit our conception of the modes of expression possible within these spaces. If discussion boards were named *interaction spaces* or *engagement forums*, they might invite more variety in their use. By opening the space to other kinds of learning activities and to more than the written word, instructional designers can help faculty and learners realize the potential of the online medium.

Most learning management systems come equipped with multimedia capabilities, which are often conveniently integrated into the online discussion tool. Even in more rudimentary learning management systems, links to student-recorded multimedia can easily be shared. In the early days of online education, sharing multimedia, such as sound clips or video recordings, required expensive, specialized equipment and involved file formats and sizes that made sharing them challenging. Technology has advanced significantly, and most learners have access to smartphones or laptop web cameras that help make recording and sharing learner-created multimedia objects simple. The challenge for instructional designers and faculty, then, is to design meaningful learning activities that require learners to create, share, and discuss student-created media.

Video-based assignments are one obvious choice, but care should be taken to adhere to best practices and usability guidelines, such as keeping video content brief and ensuring sufficient lighting and sound quality. For courses that include learning outcomes related to effective and professional communication, providing guidance for the creation of effective videos in addition to content-related guidance can help learners meet communication-related outcomes. Video-based assignments can vary significantly by discipline and the level of the course, but could include the following:

- video introductions that help learners engage socially and form a learning community at the start of a new class;
- presentations on assigned research topics or explaining aspects of complex course readings;
- video of learners explaining key terms or responding to assigned readings in their own words, to prevent learners from copying and pasting responses to these kinds of questions from internet searches;
- recordings of learners practicing conversation and pronunciation skills when studying world languages;
- demonstrations of a physical technique or process; and
- video recordings sharing selected, curated observations from the student's environment, such as plant varieties from the student's geographical area.

Advantages of using discussion spaces for video-based assignments include the potential to improve learner interest and engagement and help learners and educators feel more connected personally and socially. Video-based assignments that require learners to step away from their computers into more authentic, real-world environments can help learners connect class activities with a stronger sense of the assignment's relevance in the real world. Additionally, in classes of geographically or culturally diverse learners, greater varieties and breadth of content can be covered, enriching the diversity of the learning experience for all.

Many possibilities exist for sharing student-created multimedia in online discussion spaces that can lead to learning activities, engagement, and interaction that cannot be adequately described as discussion per se. Instructional designers would be wise to caution faculty in using these activities when learners may have privacy or safety concerns that would prohibit them from appearing in videos, but accommodations and alternatives can be prepared and held in reserve for when they are needed. For example, survivors of domestic violence or victims of stalkers may have compelling safety-related reasons for keeping their identities and locations secure from view. Accommodating students—and informing students that accommodations are available—is responsible educational practice and may also be required by law.

Video-based assignments offer many educational advantages but may also make some learners and educators anxious or uncomfortable. Sometimes a video may also be too cumbersome or lengthy for the message being conveyed. Fortunately, online discussion forums also offer many opportunities for learners to share and discuss a variety of student-created still images, with discussions ensuing either in multimedia or simple text format. Learners can share photographs, scanned diagrams, or screenshots of spreadsheets, databases, or anything displayed on their computer screen. Using freely available editing tools, learners can annotate digital images by circling an item to focus on, using arrows to indicate movement or process, or adding labels.

Instructional designers and educators can help learners be inclusive of class members who may have visual impairments by providing direct instructions on how to provide alt-text descriptions for instructional images. (Alt-text descriptions are read aloud by assistive technologies for users with visual disabilities. They need to be added for any image that conveys information but not for images that are merely decorative. The text should convey the full meaning of the image for readers with disabilities.) As many students go on to professions that require online public communication, developing inclusive communication skills is advantageous.

Student-created visuals can also venture into more creative expressions, at least on occasion. Some faculty find that weaving a more creative learning activity into the course at key junctures can help engage learners and reinvigorate student motivation when it wanes. Learners can be asked to make, share, and discuss creative visuals, such as word clouds, infographics, data visualizations, memes, or GIFs. Assignments requiring creative expression can lead learners to explore and communicate more complex thinking and emotional aspects of the content being studied. Examples of this kind of learning activity might include the following:

- To prepare for a midterm exam, learners can be asked to share a word cloud indicating which key terms and concepts they have been studying. Then, learners can help each other identify and fill in gaps in preparation for the exam.
- Learners can create concept maps in lieu of or to accompany a presentation on a given topic.
- As a summary or metacognitive reflection activity for a unit or course, learners can create infographics advising an audience of future learners in the class.
- For critique or evaluative kinds of learning activities, learners can be asked to use a meme generator or GIF creator to create a meme or GIF about a concept from the course.

The combination of visuals and text involved in these kinds of assignments can help learners engage deeply and creatively with the subject. In designing learning activities that use discussion forums but go beyond simple text-based discussions, instructional designers and faculty can help learners develop content knowledge, critical thinking skills, and communication skills that will help learners communicate effectively in digital and electronic formats, which are career skills many professionals need.

Conclusion

Our love-hate relationship with the discussion board can be traced to design flaws and to a lack of appreciation for the broader design possibilities inherent in common discussion forum tools. Instructional designers must recognize that instructors and learners may come to discussion forums with a lack of familiarity of the potential of online discussions and possibly with outright reticence.

Instructional designers would be well advised to proactively state that discussion forms are complex, flexible tools that require skillful design and practice in facilitation. Openly identifying the tool as complex and flexible can help to create space and increased attention to development. There is no one formula for a good online discussion, just as there is no single formula for a good face-to-face discussion or class meeting. Instructional designers play an important role in helping faculty create discussion designs that promote authentic interactions and learning experiences by introducing faculty to the wide array of possibilities that the online medium allows. When we can construct a discussion activity that supports the kinds of interactions that help learners engage meaningfully with the content, the instructor, and each other, we achieve harmony of design and use, and the learning experience feels productive and meaningful for instructors and learners alike.

References

Association of American Colleges & Universities. (2008). *High-impact educational practices*. https://www.aacu.org/leap/hips

Linder, K., & Hayes, C. (2018). *High-impact practices in online education: Research and best practices*. Stylus.

Wise, A. F., & Chiu, M. M. (2014). The impact of rotating summarizing roles in online discussions: Effects on learners' listening behaviors during and subsequent to role assignment. *Computers in Human Behavior, 38*, 261–271. https://doi.org/10.1016/j.chb.2014.05.033

Wise, A. F., Marbouti, F., Hsiao, Y. & Hausknecht, S. (2012). A survey of factors contributing to learners' "listening" behaviors in asynchronous discussions. *Journal of Educational Computing Research, 47*(4), 461–480. https://doi.org/10.2190/EC.47.4.f

Yuan, J., & Kim, C. (2014). Guidelines for facilitating the development of learning communities in online courses. *Journal of Computer Assisted Learning, 30*(3), 220–232. https://doi.org/10.1111/jcal.12042

Careful and intentional course planning and design, as well as an instructor who is engaging, present, and offers feedback, can create a learner-centered environment

18

PRESENCE

Online Courses Still Have to Be Taught

Olena Zhadko

An organized structure, thoughtful objectives, and authentic assessments can create a meaningful learning experience and reaffirm for learners that an online instructor cares about their success. This chapter uncovers how to address teaching online when there's no front of the classroom. We use Chickering and Gamson's (1987) framework to examine best practices in teaching online.

When online education became more prevalent, many instructors were concerned that they would no longer be needed and that their jobs might be eliminated. Those who were open to experiment did not necessarily know what the long-term effect of technology would be. Online education as it is today is a relatively recent development. Even though experimentation with online courses started on college campuses in the early to mid-1990s (Kentnor, 2015), the rapid growth and development of online programs at traditional nonprofit institutions did not begin until 1998 (Arenson, 1998). While instructors are key to learners' success and are responsible for creating engaging learning experiences, this development faced major resistance from instructors because many were skeptical of the new modality (Mitchell et al., 2015). Shelton and Saltsman (2005) gave several reasons for instructor resistance to teaching online: understanding the online teaching practices (or lack thereof); institutional support, or lack thereof; and concerns about the rigor of teaching online because of assumptions that online instruction is of a lower quality than traditional face-to-face instruction. Since then, a number of studies have attempted to provide assurance that online education is equal to or even exceeds the quality of in-person instruction (Bailey et al., 2018; Cavanaugh & Jacquemin, 2015).

For online education to be effective, one needs a different approach to teaching and learning requiring a technical skill set and pedagogical competencies to carry out superior teaching practices (Bernard et al., 2004). Simply digitizing learning materials, uploading them to a learning management platform, or using video conferencing to conduct remote instruction will not suffice. A thoughtful and intentional course design is needed, and instructional designers are uniquely skilled and trained for this role. To create an effective learning environment, an instructor needs to develop and align measurable learning outcomes and deliberately create or choose assessment measures and instructional strategies. To design such a learning path, multiple forms of expertise are needed. Instructional designers can work in collaboration with instructors to assist with the course design process and empower and support instructors designing engaging and effective learning experiences online. Besides subject specific expertise, instructors also support and engage with learners as they follow the learning path created by the course design. Teaching online involves creating a learning road map and building opportunities for learners to engage with the instructor, peers, and course materials.

The Framework

Chickering and Gamson (1987) examined good teaching practices and developed seven principles of good practice to guide educators in the design and facilitation of learning. The principles of good teaching practice were first established for in-person instruction. Chickering and Ehrmann (1996) expanded on these principles to explain how technology could support them and offered an overview of the intersection of technology and pedagogy and their interdependency. In this chapter, we use the following seven principles as the framework to reflect on how online instructors can strengthen their teaching through intentional course design and how instructional designers can contribute to the process.

As instructional designers play a key role in supporting instructors with course development, it is hoped that instructional designers use this framework in their work with faculty. Although every one of these principles is important, instructional designers can introduce each element in different stages of course planning at the most appropriate time or place. When creating a faculty development program on preparing instructors to teach online, these principles can be used as the foundational structure for developing such a program.

Principle 1: Good Practice Encourages Contacts Between Learners and Instructor

An online classroom can be isolating and lonely. It is important to enable learners to engage in communicating with their instructor and peers. We don't learn in isolation, connection and reciprocity are necessary to support learning, and instructors' genuine interest can motivate and ensure learners' persistence. Choosing an effective communication tool is essential to learners' success (Conrad & Donaldson, 2011). An instructional designer should advise instructors to develop a course facilitation or communication plan to ensure that tools and structures are in place throughout the course. This plan might include a schedule of course announcements and built-in opportunities for learners to contribute to and comment on course activities. Remember that referring to learners' contributions and highlighting their work will ensure that they pay closer attention to the instructor's communication and will further engage them with the course. Instructional designers need to remember to plan for the instructor's engagement in a course discussion (not necessarily responding to every post) by addressing misconceptions, offering relevant examples, asking for clarification, or simply highlighting a particularly good contribution.

A learning management system (LMS) contains several tools that support communication, including announcements, discussion forums, emails, journals, blogs, wikis, and video conferencing. An instructor can engage learners at an individual or group level while creating opportunities for learners to engage with each other. First and foremost, an instructor can establish presence in the course from the very beginning by creating an icebreaker that engages learners socially and intellectually (Boettcher & Conrad, 2016). An icebreaker can prompt learners to share something personal about themselves and something related to the subject—for example, what they expect to learn or what they already know about the subject. This principle could be applied in the initial stages, throughout, and in the final stages of course planning.

Principle 2: Reciprocity and Cooperation Among Learners

Technology has enabled each learner to not only become more visible in an online classroom but also engage with peers in a more meaningful way. In a traditional classroom, when learners actively engage in a discussion, it might appear that everyone contributed. Howard (2015) discusses the idea of the "norm of consolidation of responsibility" (p. 48) in classroom discussions.

> [This norm] . . . means that in the typical college or university classroom, a small number of learners (five to eight) will account for 75 to 95 per-

cent of all learner verbal contributions to discussion regardless of class size. Research has consistently confirmed the existence of this norm. (p. 48)

An online instructor could be much more aware and better informed about each student's contributions as LMS tracking has enabled easy data collection of learners' activity and participation. When designing an online classroom, opportunities for learners to connect with each other, whether through weekly discussions, group projects, or other learning activities, need to be intentionally planned.

Instructional designers can remind instructors to set up a structure for reciprocity and opportunities for learners to cooperate. For example, when contributing to an online discussion, learners can be asked to create an original post first and then post responses to peers. Learners can make use of the notifications feature that many of the tools contain to know when someone responds to or comments on their post. See chapter 17 on the practicalities of using discussions for cooperation among learners.

Although setting up online group work is not an easy task, an instructional designer can assist an instructor with creating engaging group work online. A robust structure or road map with milestones (touchpoints that prompt learners to engage) and deliverables (an outline, a paper, a presentation, etc.) that make each and every individual accountable will facilitate the learning process. See chapter 15 for more on structuring group work online.

Online classes are not merely based on individual work; there is a wide range of educational technology tools enabling learners to collaborate and reciprocate. Tools by themselves are meaningless unless an instructor uses them to create engaging learning experiences. An instructional designer can assist instructors in the intentional selection of the most appropriate tool for the task and guide them in the process of structuring collaborative work online.

Principle 3: Good Practice Uses Active Learning Techniques

In an online classroom, mere presence and showing up are not enough because then each individual becomes an active learner by default. Data tracking and analytics are built in and could make learning more visible, capturing learners' participation and interactions. An instructional designer can assist an instructor in making the most of these tools and make data-informed course design modifications.

A wide range of instructional strategies can create active learning opportunities in an online class. For example, learners can watch a course lecture and reflect on it in a discussion or review, select current events pertaining to the topic, and offer their interpretation and commentary using social media. Learners can also engage in a brainstorming session by contributing to a virtual wall and posting images or commentary linking to the original source for reference. Learners can also respond to a prompt, summarizing key takeaways on a module's topic. Furthermore, learners can be asked to create a weekly journal entry reflecting on their learning while reexamining the subject from different perspectives (theoretical and practical), using a variety of sources.

Instructional designers should encourage instructors to send learners away from a computer screen to engage with the world and report back to the class. For example, learners can contribute a story of images capturing an element of public health in the neighborhood or film an example of fluid mechanics that connects theoretical learning to the practical application.

Although digital platforms and tools enable this type of active learning, intentional course design and instructors can ensure that learners are engaged. An instructor, with an instructional designer ready to assist, can carefully craft a learning path with instructions and prompts for learners to actively engage with instead of taking the back seat of a passive observer.

Principle 4: Good Practice Gives Prompt Feedback

It is a no-brainer that technology can make it easier to offer immediate, consistent, and effective feedback. Instructional designers can empower instructors and assist them in experimenting with the new technology and new ways to give feedback. First and foremost, low-stakes assessments, tests, and quizzes can check for understanding and offer immediate (automated) feedback to learners. Test options can be set up for learners to view feedback on each individual question and even retake a test after reviewing the feedback, especially if the purpose is to support learning. Online test generators can simplify and streamline test creation and make this usually time-consuming process more efficient.

The audio or video feedback tool, often available in an LMS, increases instructors' efficiency in offering prompt individualized feedback to learners for incorporation into future assignments. For example, an instructor can record an audio comment offering general feedback on a paper, complimenting the student on the good work and pointing out some areas for improvement, or record a screencast while grading a paper and offering more specific details on the areas for improvement.

Rubrics built into the LMS and associated with a learning activity (e.g., discussion or assignment) can also enhance the instructor feedback and provide specific streamlined commentary on student work.

Consider asking learners to add a paragraph to their next assignment explaining the elements of feedback they have incorporated or simply reflecting on what they learned from the feedback they received. An instructor may also create opportunities for peer feedback. To help learners provide meaningful feedback, modeling feedback could set a good example.

Offering detailed and meaningful feedback requires time and intentional planning. An instructional designer could assist an instructor in making the most of the educational technology tools and becoming more efficient by creating recurring opportunities throughout the course that allow students to reflect on and incorporate the feedback they receive in their future work.

Principle 5: Good Practice Emphasizes Time on Task

Time on task is a lot more apparent in face-to-face classes. In an in-person class, when you ask learners to work in groups for 10 minutes, you can see them engage in real time. In an online class, typically asynchronous, time on task is integrated into online activities. Intentional course design makes it easier for learners to really focus on learning activities while offering flexibility and enabling learners to learn on their own terms and pace.

Although it is not ideal for learners to write papers on their cell phones, it might be helpful for them to listen to audio or video lectures, work on a practice quiz, or read lecture notes and complete academic tasks when they can, no matter where they are, as long as they can focus on learning. Again, that can happen only when a course is designed to provide these opportunities for learners. Instructional designers can assist instructors with learning how to monitor learner progress and time on task by using LMS activity reporting to inform them of how each individual learner is performing, identify areas of struggle, and plan for interventions and course design modifications.

Because of the nature of online learning, the focus is on total time on task rather than on seat time, and learning activities need to be planned and structured to ensure consistency throughout a course. The New York State Education Department (2019) offers guidance on determining time on task in online education: "Time on task is the total learning time spent by a learner in a college course, including instructional time as well as time spent studying and completing course assignments (e.g., reading, research, writing, individual and group projects)" (para. 1). Typically, in a three-credit course, learners are expected to spend 45 hours per credit, totaling 135 hours on learning activities and assignments. A well-designed online course consists of learning modules, digestible learning units, that ideally inform learners about the amount of time to be spent on each activity. Instructional designers can be a valuable resource for instructors when moving from face-to-face teaching to teaching online. For example, instructional designers can introduce instructors to a course workload estimator created by Elizabeth Barre and Justin Esarey at the Center for Teaching Excellence at Rice University, which can help with planning a robust and manageable online learning path for students (Barre & Esarey, n.d.).

Principle 6: Good Practice Communicates High Expectations

Technology is a natural enabler for communicating high expectations (Chickering & Gamson, 1987). By communicating high expectations, learners who don't know where they should be heading are given a destination as well as a roadmap. Instructional designers can assist instructors in articulating and communicating high expectations. For example, including a section in the LMS titled *Tips for Success* can help learners understand what they need to do to be successful in an online class. These tips can include general expectations for the course, behavioral expectations, engagement expectations, and specific academic expectations. These expectations need to be referred to throughout the course, when appropriate, to ensure that students are well informed and remember to follow those guidelines.

Such expectations can be modified and reused by instructors in all online courses they teach. Instructors might note the formality of the language to be used in an online setting, or caution students on the use of humor because of possible misinterpretations. These instructions can also note the importance of being respectful when disagreeing with someone else's opinion and the need to express thoughts in a noncritical way. If teaching a synchronous course, when the class meets on video, instructors might remind learners to turn off any mobile devices or other computer applications and arrange to be in a quiet place to actively engage in a course discussion. For an asynchronous course, when requiring learners to contribute to an online discussion on specific days, reiterating the importance of posting on those days or by a specific date is essential when setting high expectations for students. Such instructions may also include a penalty or consequences when those expectations are not met (e.g., a grade point deduction). In instances when instructors are interested in having learners create shared engagement expectations for the course, instructional designers can also assist with that task.

When assisting with course design, instructional designers can prompt instructors to specify expectations and help with creating instructions for course activities and assignments. In some instances, scoring rubrics or checklists in conjunction with general guidelines or specific detailed instructions could help learners understand what is expected of them. For example, instructional designers can share sample rubrics, providing clear criteria and standards of achievement that could help with managing expectations and guiding learners' responsiveness. An instructional designer could also ensure that such instructions are used throughout the course; for example, they could be posted in one area with links in multiple locations. Instructional designers can also assist faculty in articulating their genuine respect and belief in learners' capabilities, encouraging learners to meet course expectations for every activity and assignment, and creating opportunities for recognizing learners' accomplishments.

Principle 7: Good Practice Respects Diverse Talents and Ways of Learning

Instructional designers can assist faculty in making the most of educational technology when designing an online course experience, enabling all learners to succeed. An LMS offers a menu of options allowing customization of a learning environment to meet all learners' needs. Instructional designers are uniquely skilled in helping instructors make the most of technology tools while considering individual needs for learning, and they are often knowledgeable about universal design for learning principles. Learning opportunities for all learners can be created with intentional course design and by enabling learners to take responsibility for their learning as well. For example, learners can submit a five-page paper or produce a 5-minute video or multimedia presentation to demonstrate their learning on a particular topic. At the same time, instructors can use a variety of tools to create or curate course content from text to multimedia and then offer several options to learners. Some learners may be inclined to read more, while others might prefer multimedia to a traditional text. Thus, a specific course unit may include a video lecture, a podcast, an article or a book chapter, or a website for students to review. Instructional designers can advise and assist instructors in creating an engaging online learning experience by offering course templates, examples or samples, or a mock-up of a course module.

Conclusion

Course planning and design are essential elements of teaching, and effective use of technology can lessen the burden for instructors. Careful and intentional course planning and design, as well as an instructor who is engaging, present, and offers feedback, can create a learner-centered environment. Instructional designers can work with instructors to design, plan, and implement courses for the most engaging online learning experiences.

References

Arenson, K. (1998, November 2). More colleges plunging into uncharted waters of on-line courses. *The New York Times*. https://www.nytimes.com/1998/11/02/us/more-colleges-plunging-into-uncharted-waters-of-on-line-courses.html

Bailey, A., Vaduganathan, N., Henry, T., Laverdiere, R., & Pugliese, L. (2018). *Making digital learning work: Success strategies from six leading universities and community colleges*. The Boston Consulting Group and Arizona State University. https://edplus.asu.edu/what-we-do/making-digital-learning-work

Barre, E., & Esarey, J. (n.d.). *Course workload estimator*. Rice University Center for Teaching Excellence. https://cte.rice.edu/workload#howcalculated

Bernard, R. M., Abrami, P. C., Lou, Y., Borokovski, E., Wade, A., Wozney, L., & Huang, B. (2004). How does distance education compare with classroom instruction? A meta-analysis of the empirical literature. *Review of Educational Research, 74*(3), 379–439. https://doi.org/10.3102/00346543074003379

Boettcher, J. V., & Conrad, R.-M. (2016). *The online teaching survival guide: Simple and practical pedagogical tips*. Jossey-Bass.

Cavanaugh, J. K., & Jacquemin, S. J. (2015). A large sample comparison of grade based student learning outcomes in online vs. face-to-face courses. *Online Learning, 19*(2). http://dx.doi.org/10.24059/olj.v19i2.454

Chickering, A., & Ehrmann, S. (1996), Implementing the seven principles: Technology as lever. *AAHE Bulletin, 49*, 3–6.

Chickering, A., & Gamson, Z. (1987). Seven principles of good practice in undergraduate education. *AAHE Bulletin, 39*(2), 3–7.

Conrad, R.-M., & Donaldson, J. A. (2011). *Engaging the online learner: Activities and resources for creative instruction*. Jossey-Bass.

Howard, J. R. (2015). *Discussion in the college classroom: Getting your students engaged and participating in person and online*. Jossey-Bass.

Kentnor, H. (2015). Distance education and the evolution of online learning in the United States. *Curriculum and Teaching Dialogue, 17*(1, 2), 21–34.

Mitchell, L. D., Parlamis, J. D., & Claiborne, S. A. (2015). Overcoming faculty avoidance of online education: From resistance to support to active participation. *Journal of Management Education, 39*(3), 350–371. https://doi.org/10.1177/1052562914547964

New York State Education Department. (2019). *Distance education program policies: Determining time on task in online education*. http://www.nyscd.gov/college-university-evaluation/distance-education-program-policies

Shelton, K., & Saltsman, G. (2005). *An administrator's guide to online education*. Information Age.

Nothing about emergency pivoting online is easy—not for instructors, learners, or instructional designers.

19

REMOTE INSTRUCTIONAL DESIGN

The Best We Can

Tammy M. McCoy and Jerod Quinn

The global pandemic of COVID-19 is shaking the world and has glaringly displayed the many cracks in the foundation of American education in general and of higher education, specifically precarious funding models, ineffective pedagogies, and a very real digital divide. Caught off guard and in most cases unprepared, universities across the nation floundered to figure out the next steps. Faced with the reality that "normal" was never going to be the same again, institutions had to adopt a make-it-work attitude. Instructional designers found themselves answering the call of duty and reporting to the front lines to guide battle-weary faculty through the unfamiliar remote learning space with a learner-centered approach. During these interactions, it became clear that there are no easy answers and that it is necessary for the overtaxed instructional designers to allow ourselves a measure of grace, knowing that all we can do in these precarious circumstances is the "best we can."

When it was announced that all teaching and learning would be moving to a remote format, there was no time to traverse the planning cycle where methods for transitioning our courses to an online environment could be robustly designed, executed, and assessed. Instead, our response to the move was more reactive; we immediately packed our on-campus offices and opened shop in our living rooms (or "home offices"). Although this chapter is in response to the sudden shift to remote learning and consultations due to COVID-19, that is not the only context where the following approaches may be helpful. Every year we work with instructors whose lives shift in unexpected ways, requiring our work with them to shift as well. Cancer diagnoses, family caretaking responsibilities, new jobs, the effects of climate change, and world events can all lead to the need to switch to remote work mid-project or mid-semester. To ease some of the burden that comes with an unexpected pivot to remote learning, instructional designers can provide guidance on resetting our expectations, designing more resilient courses, and introducing pedagogies that are grounded in care.

Resetting Our Expectations

The first and most vital thing instructional designers can do in the face of crisis is to reset our own expectations. We saw this in the immediate response to COVID-19 in the language used to describe what was happening. The question became, "Are we pivoting to *online* learning?" For instructional designers, online learning is a very structured and intentional process with backward design, learning objectives, aligned assessments, and selectively incorporating technology to tie the whole experience together. But the immediate shift required an immediate response.

We called our solution *remote* teaching in an effort to clearly distinguish what we were doing in reaction from the carefully curated online experiences we work to create (Gardner, 2020). And when no one was looking, we sometimes called it "panic-gogy" under our breath (Kamenetz, 2020). Everyone was asked to move all classes from entire campuses online overnight. And just like that, the typical 40-hour work week for instructional designers became 60 hours to 80 hours while we slowly realized that we would also be responsible for homeschooling our children at the same time. Our expectations need to change to match the reality of our situation.

Changing Our Expectations of Others

To continue working in this ever-changing context instructional designers need to reset their expectations on what instructors can and should be doing when it comes to transitioning online. Or to put it more bluntly, we need to lower our expectations because life doesn't pause in the middle of a crisis, and nobody learns well in a crisis (Lederman, 2020). People can only handle so much at a time, and badgering folks about the measurability of the verbs in their learning objectives isn't going to help anyone. But what can be helpful is restructuring how we approach our consultations.

Changing how designers meet with instructors can help bring a better rhythm to the work of both parties. Shorter meetings that focus on one or two next steps can help designers better manage the influx of consultations along with helping to avoid overwhelming instructors with responsibilities. Hour-long, casual meetings are a luxury unattainable in times of crisis. I would recommend designers limit their consultations to 30 minutes, and that includes a 5-minute buffer between meetings for the designer to catch their breath. With a shortened meeting time, the temptation will be to just get down to business and rush through as much content as possible. Resist this temptation. Spend those first 5 minutes trying to connect with your instructor, letting them know that despite feeling isolated and overwhelmed they are not alone. This isn't just trust building, it's valuing the people over the project. In the time left, find the one or two tangible next steps the instructor can take to feel less overwhelmed by their new responsibilities. One very tangible step can be to drop what can be dropped.

During those first 2 weeks of the pivot I was asked one question over and over again in various phrasings: "Is it okay to drop this major assessment?" Sometimes people just need to hear that it's okay to change plans. Designers can encourage instructors to drop those projects that they know are not going to work and, instead, assist in reconfiguring the instructional plan to emphasize the main goals for the course. Group projects can be great for learning but are challenging in the best of circumstances. Accordingly, group projects were often the first things to go when switching to remote teaching. I'm not implying we should drop collaboration and connection, not at all. If anything, connection should be maximized in crisis circumstances. I'm suggesting dropping or reducing the connections that are mediated by grades and points. The instructor isn't the only one feeling the tension of suddenly shifting to online or remote learning; every single learner will be feeling it, too. By altering the assessments and narrowing the focus of course content, designers can help instructors continue to move forward with their courses but in a manner that is less likely to leave their learners behind. It also frees up time in the course. In the same way designers can check in with instructors during consultations to let them know they may be isolated but they are not alone, instructors can use some of that time to connect with their learners who will also be feeling alone and scattered to the winds. Humanizing online learning is always important. Humanizing remote learning may be critical.

Removing barriers to online access is also a very practical approach to helping instructors go online in a hurry. Many universities use an online course quality rubric (i.e., Quality Matters) in association with developing online courses. It's not uncommon for universities to require passing these quality reviews for an instructor to be allowed to teach a course online. The question becomes, "Do we have the same course quality expectations for remote teaching that we have for online teaching?" I would argue no. This goes back to our earlier assertion that remote teaching is not the same creature as online teaching. One approach could be to boil down your current course design rubric to its most critical elements, the ones that have the most impact on the learner's experience. For example, when we took this approach on our campus, we identified that having instructions for every assignment is a critical component. It seems almost too basic of an element. Online, however, having complete and explicit instructions for assignments is far more critical, because it is less feasible to answer questions or make clarifications in the moment like you can in a face-to-face classroom. And if an instructor has never had to write out complete assignment instructions, what they use for in-person classes might not work very well for remote instruction.

Changing Expectations of Ourselves

You are a skilled and diligent instructional designer. You are not a miracle worker. Do not pretend you can fly in and rescue all the instructors and their learners from the chaos that comes from an unplanned shift to remote teaching and learning. The best you might be able to do is help a lot of instructors get prepared to teach online in a hurry. Recycling the resources you already have is a good place to start.

When the announcement came at my (Quinn's) university that we would be shifting all in-person classes to online, my team had exactly 9 days to come up with a program to take hundreds of instructors at four different campuses through that transition. We started with the most basic goal: "What would help an instructor who has never been online feel confident enough to keep teaching in a remote context?" Then each member of the team started digging through the online course design programs our different campuses already had in existence and stripped them for parts. We were able to construct about 75% of our brand new 4-week course from components of online content we already had. The rest we wrote over the next few days as we pooled resources and created accompanying graphics. The most challenging part (not counting dealing with provosts and deans and directors who all have conflicting demands of this program) was figuring out what we could realistically ask instructors to do in such a short time. Requiring measurable learning objectives did not make the list, but a plan for connecting and communicating with learners did. While it would have been ideal to make a course specifically tailored to this audience, the reality was that we had 9 days. But we got our course created, affectionately named it Start Here, and took 870 faculty through the process of pivoting online. But that kind of deeply stressful work comes with a price tag.

On the eve of its launch I had a very tense conversation with my supervisor. I told him I was taking some time off effective immediately. It could be vacation or quitting, his choice. The stress of this project was crushing to everyone on the team. I am no miracle worker; I got crushed, too. Creating Start Here was a brutal 9-day sprint that beat the design team to a pulp. I don't tell this story to offer a model in self-care; I did a pretty poor job of responding to my circumstances. I say it because it's the truth. Nothing about emergency pivoting online is easy—not for instructors, learners, or instructional designers.

Designing More Resilient Courses

Now that we have had time to adjust to the extreme changes that accompany working from home, we can think more clearly about how best to prepare our instructors to be ready with a resilient teaching mind-set. We can begin tackling questions such as, "How do we equip instructors, regardless of experience level, to design courses that are flexible and adaptable to changing circumstances without sacrificing the rigor of the learning experience?" There is no one perfect solution that will solve every course (re)design problem. Still, there are several promising frameworks that a designer can utilize to help guide instructors in creating a curriculum that is adaptable to almost any situation. The OPEN CoLab at Plymouth State University gives us the Adaptability, Connection, and Equity (ACE) framework. Vanderbilt University's Center for Teaching is in its fifth year of the Online Course Design Institute (OCDI). The University of Michigan's Center of Academic Innovation created a 4-week massive open online course (MOOC) called Resilient Teaching Through Times of Crisis and Change. Here, we'll provide a broad-stroke overview of each framework. These three frameworks can offer guidance for instructional designers on how to help instructors create more resilient online courses.

ACE Framework

It's tough to know how to proceed when the normal teaching routine is upended by the unexpected. One robust tool that the instructional designer can recommend to the frazzled faculty member as they plan is the open-source ACE framework (Open CoLAB, n.d.; available at https://colab.plymouthcreate.net/ace/). Developed at Plymouth State University's Open Learning & Teaching Collaborative, ACE stands for adaptability, connection, and equity, and it is a value-based approach that allows us to build flexibility into our courses on the front end so that when the unexpected

Figure 19.1

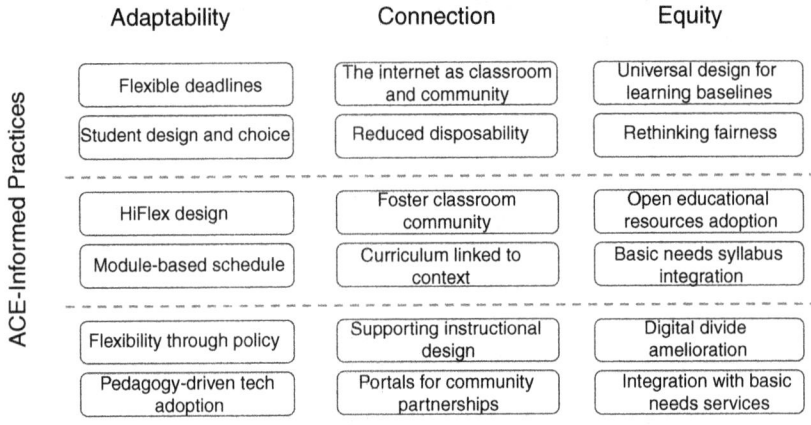

happens (i.e., COVID-19, learner emergencies), instructors are prepared to keep moving forward. The framework is laid out in a matrix that consists of three columns representing the three values (Figure 19.1). The body of the matrix is composed of rows of ACE-informed practices subdivided into three levels: assignment, course, and institution. Adaptability focuses on designing learning experiences that can be easily modified to meet the distinct needs of learners within different modalities. Connection encourages the prioritization of the learners' need for community engagement regardless of the setting of the learning space. Because all learners' lives are not created equal, equity challenges us to consider the potential barriers that our students might face when things go awry and factor into our planning how instructors can still provide them with the learning experience they deserve.

There are three levels from which one can choose to engage with the framework depending on personal needs, time, and circumstances. Level 1 is a beginning-level course checklist that can be used by the designer to support the instructor as they check the alignment of their courses against the ACE values. For example, to gauge how adaptable their courses are to sudden change, the instructor can reflect on whether they have a course model plan in place that accounts for the delivery of the course content in different modalities. Additionally, the instructor might also think about whether they have included contingencies in their course design, whether learners can easily find what they need, or if they have some alternative assignments in mind. Level 2 of the framework is designed for those who have more time to build in flexibility and follows the "Rule of 2s." The designer guides instructors to select two course or assignment-level practices within each value category on which to focus as they plan their course. This way the instructor can work specifically on high-priority areas without the overexertion of redesigning an entire course in multiple modalities. Level 3 is a self-paced, immersive experience in that for several weeks the user takes a deep dive into each of the assignment and course-level practices. The instructor selects a value area to explore at either the assignment or course-level. Flexible deadlines are an example of an assignment-level practice that fall within the adaptability column. The CoLab has licensed their ACE framework through Creative Commons, making it available to anyone wishing to learn more or implement at their own universities.

OCDI

Vanderbilt University's Center for Teaching (n.d.) provides another model for responding to the unexpected using adaptive course design, which is the intentional design of courses that can adapt to changing circumstances. The virtual, 2-week OCDI prepares faculty, postdocs, and graduate students to teach a fully online class (visit https://cft.vanderbilt.edu/ocdi/). It requires a commitment of 4 hours per day for 10 weekdays of asynchronous (learning management system [LMS] modules) and synchronous (Zoom) engagement. To avoid the disruption in teaching that took place with the sudden move to remote teaching caused by the COVID-19 pandemic, the institute encourages participants to design their courses such that all essential learning experiences and assessments take place in the online environment. Whether they start the semester online or on campus or a mix of both, they will be prepared to make a sudden pivot without sacrificing significant course elements.

Grounded in the backward design approach of instructional development, institute participants spend time developing course plans and learning and practicing the skills to build online modules. Additionally, they strategize about how to promote authentic interactions with and among their students in an equitable fashion, and they learn how to select and integrate appropriate online teaching tools into their courses. An important takeaway for participants of the institute, as noted in a blog post by Derek Bruff (director of Vanderbilt University Center for Teaching), is that there is not a one-to-one conversion of the classroom experience to the online environment. He stresses that this move "involves a rethinking of the goals of the course and finding useful ways to approach those goals using online methods and tools" (Bruff, 2020, para. 5). Bruff also cautions that we do not underestimate the utility of asynchronous online activities and suggests that participants consider how they can leverage the online learning space for the most critical elements of their courses.

Resilient Teaching Through Times of Crisis and Change

As defined by Rebecca Quintana (learning experience design lead at the University of Michigan), *resilient teaching* is "the ability to facilitate learning experiences that are designed to be adaptable to fluctuating conditions and disruptions" (Quintana, n.d., para. 1). As a response to instructor needs stemming from the COVID-19 crisis, the University of Michigan and Quintara (n.d.) introduced the Resilient Teaching Through Times of Crisis and Change MOOC (available at https://www.coursera.org/learn/resilient-teaching-through-times-of-crisis/home/welcome). Although created to address the teaching challenges that emerged with the global pandemic, Quintana introduces an adaptable framework that can be applied to any unexpected disruption that requires moving from one context to another. Well praised by participants, the course requires a commitment of approximately 15 hours over 4 weeks. Learners engage at their own pace with online readings, videos, and discussion prompts to identify the critical types of interactions they would like to promote in their courses while they learn how to develop a course plan built on the principles of resilient course design. The course walks learners through the fundamentals of resilient pedagogy while offering examples of courses designed and taught for extensibility (ability to foresee changes or additions to your course that may be possible or required), design for flexibility (ability to anticipate and respond to potential changes in a learning environment), and designing for redundancy (ability to analyze your course design plan and identify and create pieces that could perform similar operations). In the final week, participants are introduced to a complementary framework known as care-centered design, which is a model that considers the learners' needs as humans.

If anyone ever doubted the value of the instructional designer to the educational landscape before the onset of COVID-19, those doubts were forgotten as soon as campuses started closing. The ACE framework, OCDI, and the Resilient Teaching Through Times of Crisis and Change MOOC are just a few of the robust tools that allow the instructional designer to build flexible courses that can dodge and weave among changing circumstances.

Trauma-Informed Practices

Cathy Davidson (2020) talks about acknowledging that our learners will not have escaped the effects of higher education's remote learning pivot but will be returning to the courses from "a place of dislocation, anxiety, and trauma" (para. 1). Instructional designers can't negate all of the tensions facing our instructors and our learners, but by being aware of trauma-informed practices in higher education, we can help make a chaotic situation a little more stable.

Trauma-informed practices have been developed to help learners whose external stressors are overwhelming their internal resources. Many learners were coming to university classrooms with trauma in their lives before COVID-19. With a global pandemic, there will be countless more. Instructional designers can help create a supportive online learning environment by introducing instructors to some of the principles and practices of trauma-informed pedagogy. Shannon Davidson (2017) of Education Northwest has created a useful and in-depth guide for trauma-informed teaching practices in higher education. Four practices that are potentially helpful in online classes are empowering learners, checking in with learners, being sensitive to family structures, and identifying mentors and support systems (Davidson, 2017).

Designers can talk with instructors about creating opportunities in their courses to empower their learners by giving them choices and agency in their learning. This could be through assessment options, choosing content topics, or even setting their own due dates. The goal is to give the learners some sense of control in circumstances that rob them of other choices.

Checking in with their learners is another practice designers can suggest to instructors. It will take time from the regular class activities, but showing learners some sincere compassion will help provide the kind of environment that encourages learners to engage.

Remind the instructors to be sensitive to the family structures of their learners. It may be impossible for some learners to find an isolated space for synchronous classes. Instructors may also have learners who are caring for sick loved ones. With COVID-19 spreading as rapidly in the United States as it is, it's likely that all of the learners will have known someone who was infected. Many of them will have lost loved ones. And all of this is happening while they are trying to complete their statistics homework.

Finally, designers can help provide access to university support systems for learners. If designers keep an accurate list of university services like mental health support, food pantries, and Wi-Fi hotspots, that will help put those helplines in the hands of the people who can get them into the hands of learners across the university. These trauma-informed practices are a step toward creating online experiences grounded in a pedagogy of care.

Back to Normal

I'm not sure there is going to be a "back to normal" for our universities. And given the inequities in higher education that COVID-19 has exacerbated, I don't want to go back to *that* normal. Robin DeRosa (2020) stated the truth about resetting expectations with the following tweet:

> If we're remote in the Fall, and we plan all summer, we may feel like we're facilitating online learning more than we're continuing emergency remote teaching. BUT our students are still likely to come to us as emergency remote learners. That should inform our planning.

No matter how much time instructors have to prepare for remote teaching, the fact is that many learners are not there because they chose online learning. This realization should inform how learner-centered instructional designers help instructors to reset their teaching approaches. It's going to be difficult. It's going to be incomplete. It's going to be frustrating. Nobody signed up for emergency remote teaching, but here we are.

References

Bruff, D. (2020, July 1). *Adaptive course design: Preparing for fall 2020.* Vanderbilt University. https://cft.vanderbilt.edu/2020/07/adaptive-course-design-preparing-for-fall-2020/

Center for Teaching. (n.d.). *Online Course Design Institute.* Vanderbilt University. https://cft.vanderbilt.edu/ocdi/

Davidson, C. (2020, May 11). *The single most essential requirement in designing a fall online course.* HASTAC. https://www.hastac.org/blogs/cathy-davidson/2020/05/11/single-most-essential-requirement-designing-fall-online-course

Davidson, S. (2017). *Trauma-informed practices for postsecondary education: A guide.* Education Northwest. https://educationnorthwest.org/sites/default/files/resources/trauma-informed-practices-postsecondary-508.pdf

DeRosa, R. [@actualham]. (2020, May 10). *If we're remote in the fall, and we plan all summer, we may feel like we're facilitating online learning* [Tweet]. Twitter. https://twitter.com/actualham/status/1259514675030405123?s=11

Gardner, L. (2020, March 20). Covid-19 has forced higher ed to pivot to online learning. Here are 7 takeaways so far. *The Chronicle of Higher Education.* https://www.chronicle.com/article/Covid-19-Has-Forced-Higher-Ed/248297

Kamenetz, A. (2020, March 19). 'Panic-gogy': Teaching online classes during the coronavirus pandemic. NPR. https://www.npr.org/2020/03/19/817885991/panic-gogy-teaching-online-classes-during-the-coronavirus-pandemic

Lederman, D. (2020, June 3). Crisis and opportunity for faculty development. *Inside Higher Ed*. https://www.insidehighered.com/digital-learning/article/2020/06/03/how-new-one-person-teaching-center-navigating-moment-peril-and

Open CoLAB. (n.d.). *ACE framework*. Plymouth State University. https://colab.plymouthcreate.net/ace/.

Quintara, R. (n.d.). *Resilient teaching through times of crisis and change* Coursera. Retrieved July 2020 from https://www.coursera.org/learn/resilient-teaching-through-times-of-crisis/home/welcome

The temptation in any profession is to learn just enough to be dangerous.

CONCLUSION

A Day in the Life

Jerod Quinn

So you have read through this whole book, and now one solitary question rages in your mind as you begin reading this conclusion: Can I really do all these things in every online class I work on? Yes, my friend, you can.

But you won't, and not for a lack of passion or possibly even skill. It is because instructional design work is not work in isolation. You don't have complete control; you have collaboration instead. You have to meet the instructors where they are, and sometimes they are not where you would like them to be. Some collaborations will be laborious, and some will spark new and deep friendships. But every project will have opportunities for many of the ideas in these chapters, these threads, to be expressed and woven together to create a new learning experience.

This conclusion wraps up the conversation by looking at how these threads are expressed in the daily work of instructional design, from project management to meeting juggling to professional development, and I offer a call for community building with instructional designers across universities. I talk about specific opportunities for professional development that pay dividends, like teaching an online class, and make a plea for instructional designers to collaborate among campuses and across institutions. Finally, I offer encouragement to not only dig deeper into the frameworks presented in this book but also explore and create a framework for critical instructional design.

Designing a System

I've had the good fortune to meet and befriend instructional designers from all over the country. Two very frequent topics of conversation are (a) sharing approaches for getting ever increasing amounts of work done and (b) how to be more effective in our work without sacrificing human connection to the gods of efficiency. Several approaches that lead to doing effective instructional design work without being devoured by it have resulted from these conversations.

Instructional designers are systematic thinkers by nature or at least by training. Efficient and effective course design means working in a systematic fashion through backward design or an alternative approach. But each university has its own instructional design context and priorities, so there is no definitive system for keeping on top of your work that will apply on the east coast, west coast, and the no coast in between. Although rooted in similarities, our work is too contextual for universal approaches. You need to craft your own work management system. I encourage instructional designers to respond to this challenge by beginning at the same place we ask our instructors to begin: at the end.

To paraphrase Fink (2003), 2 years after your course design collaboration is over, what do you want the instructor to know and be able to do from your work together? This is an effective point to begin thinking about your project management needs as a designer and how you can shape your system to meet those needs. I encourage you to start with exploring your collaboration with instructors instead of the details of project management because the heart of our work is with people. My answer to this objective's question is that I want the instructors to see me as an ally in creating learning experiences that serve their learners. I also want them to recognize there is help in getting the work of course building done. Finally, I want them to see me as a design and pedagogical resource that will compassionately push them toward more learner-centered teaching approaches.

Although these are not the only objectives of my work, they are the most valuable ones. There are three approaches designers can use to reach these objectives, which form the foundation of my project management system. Although they appear to be amazingly basic ideas, I am continually surprised at how many instructional design colleagues have not made space in their project management approaches for such foundational practices. It seems that just trying to keep your head above water can keep you from seeing the practices that would really let you swim.

Notes, Overcommunication, and Making Room

Although my project management style has changed over the years, which currently is an adaptation of an agile approach (Pope-Ruark, 2017), the three core practices have remained constant.

The first of these practices is the simplest: Take notes and review them. It sounds like something so banal that it shouldn't be said in a serious conversation about workflow. Instructional designers juggle projects constantly, and by taking notes during meetings about ideas and decisions, designers can better manage the direction of the course design. A crucial and often overlooked step is later reviewing the notes in the context of the whole project. Without a paper trail, designers will end up repeating conversations and forgetting design decisions made in collaboration with the instructor. But this is not just about project management—it's about trust. Taking notes communicates that the designers take their collaboration with instructors seriously and demonstrates to instructors that designers see their time together as important enough to track. It's about the thread of building trust by valuing instructors (see chapter 3). Personally I take notes by hand in a small notebook. It's fast and allows me to write and also sketch ideas as they come to me. To me, having a computer screen between myself and the instructor feels like a barrier to our connection. After the meeting I type up my notes, review where we are in the project, and make a task list of the next things I need to do before the next meeting. Again, this simple practice can build trust and keep you on task, but I'm still shocked by how many designers don't make records of their work.

The second practice is overcommunicating with team members. Designers are not the only team members balancing work loads. I have yet to design a course with an instructor whose only responsibility at the moment is designing that online course. An example of overcommunicating is including an agenda on the meeting invitation and always providing the opportunity for other team members to add items. Another approach is at the end of each meeting, recap the decisions made and decide what work each team member needs to do before the next meeting. These are easy practices that are often disregarded because they seem so minor, but they have major impacts on helping collaborators know about and meet expectations. Again, the focus isn't just on the project; these are examples of the thread of setting boundaries on the scope of our work as designers (see chapter 4).

The third practice is making room for reading. I can't tell you how many times a colleague has seen me with a book or journal article and said something like, "I wish I had time to read." I never know how to reply to statements like that. My compassionate side recognizes the difficulties of workloads, and there are times when reading seems like an out-of-reach luxury. But my cynical side just hears, "I've got my bag of instructional design tricks and they are good enough. I'm happy being complacent." Instructors are depending on designers to stay connected with research on teaching and learning. This goes back to the thread of being grounded in evidence-based practice (see chapter 6). No, you can't keep on top of every new idea and development in online course design, but there are always new ideas to explore. In the busier seasons of my work I block out time on the calendar to read instructional design-related materials. Sometimes it's a book I'm interested in, and sometimes it is a journal article that will help me execute a new approach in an online course. Having a consistent flow of new ideas can help keep your mind sharp and inspire creativity. You will never find time to read that next book or journal article—you need to make time.

Professional Development

When I landed my first instructional design job, it was immediately clear to me that I was the least knowledgeable person in the room. It's a tough job being the least competent, but someone's got to do it, right? The director saw my values and my passion and decided that my abilities as a designer could be developed. My coworkers took the time to mentor me and teach me the skills I would need for this work. They also modeled how to seek opportunities to keep growing and learning from other professionals in the field. The temptation in any profession is to learn just enough to be dangerous. Not dangerous in the fun, experimental way but in the way that sets up instructors to fail by pushing half-baked advice. The trouble is that we are all half-baked in certain areas. As you may recall, few individuals engage in deliberate professional practice in their careers once they hit a comfortable level of competence (Ericsson, 1996). But there are professional development paths that pay dividends for the investment of time.

Find Your People

This book is in existence because I found and got involved in a professional network, because I found my people. Most of the contributors of the chapters in this book are people I met and learned from at conferences and then developed friendships with. Those whom I didn't meet at conferences are people recommended by other colleagues who met them at conferences. The most valuable thing instructional designers can do to intentionally develop their expertise is get involved with a national and a regional network of colleagues. This can be a terrifying thought to my fellow introverts.

I'm intentionally avoiding the term *networking* because for me it conjures up images of people in suits flipping business cards at each other while saying words and phrases like *synergy* and *paradigm shifts*. That's not what I'm talking about. I'm talking about joining a community where you can learn from and care about the work of others. It's finding a place where you can contribute to the conversations as well as learn from them.

There is no easy way to do this. You have to try different conferences and organizations until you find one that fits. I tried about a half dozen different conferences before I found my people. One sign that I was in the right place was not only a sense of shared values but also that I never once had to explain what an instructional designer does. Two fantastic organizations, among many worth investigating, are the Professional and Organizational Development Network in Higher Education (POD Network, https://podnetwork.org) and the Online Learning Consortium (OLC, https://onlinelearningconsortium.org). But don't overlook the value of regional conferences and groups. Find out what conferences instructional designers in your state attend and go there too. A few years back I found myself working on an online course that required a hands-on laboratory component. Neither I nor the instructor had ever designed anything like that. I will admit to a certain degree of panic. A couple of years prior I had met a designer at a regional conference who had redesigned a 1,200-student freshman organic chemistry course in which half of the students' laboratory experiments were conducted outside the university laboratory rooms. I called her up, and she generously offered support and guidance for my online labs project. That's what I mean by finding a community. It's not padding your followers on social media but connecting with like-minded people with similar values in an effort to create learner-centered experiences that reach beyond our own campuses.

Teach an Online Class

If you have never taught an online course before, beg, plead, and lobby for the opportunity. Being an online instructor is a completely different experience from being an online learner. Although it is not a requirement to be an excellent instructional designer, you will learn things that are difficult to internalize in any other way. Things like grading.

There are countless creative and effective ideas for assignments in online courses. Early in my career I was certain that instructors should do all of them in every course. If they are effective, evidence-based practices why wouldn't you want to do all of them? The answer is because the instructor has to grade them. Grading and offering thoughtful, formative feedback take time. Having to experience that process myself made me far more thoughtful about the amount and types of assessments I encourage instructors to use in their online courses. When instructors want to discuss their frustrations with getting learners to engage in a discussion forum, you experience a certain amount of credibility and camaraderie in being able to say, "I know, there was one particular semester where I failed miserably at getting my own learners to engage."

Be a Research Partner

You don't need a PhD to be a researcher. The quantitative and qualitative research training a person receives in a doctoral program goes far in helping to understand and guide research agendas, but it's not the only path. Working with instructors is another path to researching the design decisions in online courses. Instructors are often interested in publishing, and designers are often interested in finding out if the course worked. Depending on your university, instructors may already have a background in research methods and are on the hunt for new research projects for their own professional ambitions. An instructional designer can learn the methods and approaches of research design by working with interested instructors and leaning on them for guidance and direction. Although a PhD isn't required, a willing instructor who can guide the research definitely is. My first two peer-reviewed research publications happened because I was able to work with interested instructors who already understood the data-gathering and publication process and welcomed the extra help in planning, reviewing literature, executing, and writing.

Designers who try working with instructors on research projects should pick their partner based on a relationship grounded in trust and respect (see chapter 3). Designers should be warned that the world of academic publishing is rife with insecurities and egos, and sharing research can be an extremely vulnerable process for an instructor. I recommend designers embrace the process of overcommunication, being explicit about what they know and don't know and what they can bring as a research partner even if it's just excitement and willingness to learn.

Critical Instructional Design

So far, I've offered some practical approaches to managing workloads, and then encouraged designers to seek meaningful professional development to refine their skills. Finally, I would like to introduce a framework that will challenge designers to continue in thoughtfulness and person-centered approaches to instructional design.

Academia, like all professions, has its own vocabulary. The word *critical* has a different connotation in academia from what it means outside academia. It doesn't mean to label something as bad or deficient; it means to look at something in a way that challenges assumptions, questions power structures, and asks whose voices are being excluded from the conversations. It's not an approach bent on the destruction or shaming of something but a process that is grounded in hope and deconstructs exclusionary systems to build ones where every voice is included. To put it in an instructional designer context, "Far too much work in educational technology starts with tools, when what we need to start with is humans" (Morris & Stommel, 2019, "What is critical digital pedagogy?" section). To be critical in our context is to start with people.

So what would a critical approach to teaching (pedagogy) look like when that teaching happens in an online (digital) course? According to Morris and Stommel (2019), "A Critical Digital Pedagogy demands that open and networked educational environments not be merely repositories of content; rather, they must create dialogues in which both students and teachers participate as full agents" ("What is critical digital pedagogy?" section). Online courses have earned a bad reputation for learning because so many of them have been created as merely digital repositories of slides and documents, content to be inflicted on the learners who dare sidestep the traditional classroom experience. A critical digital pedagogy takes into account that online learning is not a product to be purchased, and that people are active participants in their own learning by connecting with content and each other to construct new knowledge. This approach challenges tools and practices that dehumanize learners and removes their agency by inflicting compromising terms of service agreements or biased algorithms on them in the name of efficiency. To have a critical digital pedagogy is to recognize that online tools can help facilitate meaningful learning experiences, but the tools are not substitutes for the experiences.

In combination with critical digital pedagogy, instructional designers can also have a particular framework to guide a more person-centered approach to our work, which is critical instructional design. Morris (2019) described it as "an approach to online teaching and learning that creates a space where student agency and critical consciousness can be fostered in a way that grows knowledge and expertise in a given subject" ("A call for critical instructional design" section). Again, instructional designers play a unique role in education. We find ourselves as mediators between the student experience and the instructor's vision. Our influence in the educational lives of learners far outweighs our salary classifications. The directions we steer instructors and academic departments toward influence the experiences of thousands of learners across the university, far more than the reach of the typical faculty member. If we focus our efforts on technology, data analytics, rubrics, and alignment maps at the expense of being learner-centered, then the effects of those choices ripple across the university. But if our work is grounded in hope and the personhood of our learners, then the effects of those choices will also ripple across the university. Morris (2019) talks about critical instructional design as an approach that

> prioritizes collaboration, participation, social justice, learner agency, emergence, narrative, and relationships that nurture between students, and between teachers and students. It acknowledges that all learning today is necessarily hybrid [online and offline], and looks for opportunities to integrate learners' digital lives into their digitally-enhanced or fully online learning experiences. ("A call for critical instructional design" section)

That is the role of the learner-centered instructional designer, to use technology when it aids human connections and learning.

So how do you actually begin doing that? The primary approach is practical and straightforward. As Morris (2019) frames it, "Instead of saying, 'I've always done it this way,' we need to say, 'How should I do this now?' That is the first and, as far as I can imagine, the only best practice associated with critical instructional design" ("A call for critical instructional design" section). It's so tempting to find an approach or a system, and then uncritically wield that system like a hammer against anything that vaguely resembles a nail for the rest of time. But designers trying to work with a critical approach to online course design continue to ask if their practices, some of which they may have been using for years, are still the most effective and inclusive practices for online learning experiences. Maybe a rubric isn't the solution after all. Remember, this is a process and not a destination. It's a lifetime of learning and unlearning. It's work, but work that values people above all else is amazingly meaningful. At the expense of being too dramatic, it's our efforts that can help change lives and enable learners to move toward their dreams. We need to remember that.

Conclusion

This is the charge of this book: While defining your work as an instructional designer, build trust with the instructors you work with as you apply frameworks for teaching and learning, and as you take practical approaches to online course design, your work will always be built on integrity and guided by the question of what will best serve our learners. By providing readers with the voices of instructional designers from across the country, I hope this book has shown you that our field is full of sharp, passionate, and collaborative people. I hope to encourage you to keep learning and refining your skills and to point you toward places where you can find your people. Being a learner-centered instructional designer isn't the easiest path to stay on, but it can be a deeply meaningful one that makes an impact on people's lives, including our own.

References

Ericsson, K. A. (1996). The acquisition of expert performance: An introduction to some key issues. In K. A. Ericsson (Ed.), *The road to excellence: The acquisition of expert performance in the arts and sciences, sports, and games* (pp. 1–50). Erlbaum.

Fink, L. D. (2003). *Creating significant learning experiences: An integrated approach to designing college courses.* Jossey-Bass.

Morris, S. M. (2019). Critical instructional design. In S. M. Morris & J. Stommel (Eds.), *An urgency of teachers: The work of critical digital pedagogy* (pp. 131–142). Hybrid.

Morris, S. M., & Stommel, J. (2019). Critical digital pedagogy: A definition. In S. M. Morris & J. Stommel (Eds.), *An urgency of teachers: The work of critical digital pedagogy* (pp. 2–12). Hybrid.

Pope-Ruark, R. (2017). *Agile faculty: Practical strategies for managing research, service, and teaching.* The University of Chicago Press.

ANNOTATED BIBLIOGRAPHY

The following books and articles make multiple appearances throughout this edited volume. They are some of the most influential and most helpful resources for instructional designers working with faculty to create online courses and offer pedagogical insights into how people learn and practical approaches to implementing those insights in academia. The contributors to this volume have found these sources particularly helpful in their instructional design work, and we offer them as a source of encouragement and wisdom to other designers working in higher education.

Ambrose, S., Lovett, M., Bridges, M., DiPietro, M., & Norman, M. (2010). *How learning works: Seven research-based principles for smart teaching.* Jossey-Bass.

Ambrose et al. offer a practical overview of the science behind the practices that help people learn and apply new things. They discuss how prior knowledge, organizing knowledge, motivation, mastery, feedback, the course climate, and self-directed learning are connected to learning by explaining the research on each principle and then offering educators approaches to incorporate them into teaching and learning practices. This book provides a practical entry point into the research behind effective teaching and learning practices.

Barr, R. B., & Tagg, J. (1995). From teaching to learning: A new paradigm for undergraduate education. *Change: The Magazine of Higher Learning, 27*(6), 12–26. https://doi.org/10.1080/00091383.1995.10544672

Barr and Tagg highlight and encourage a foundational paradigm shift in higher education from a focus on providing instruction (instruction paradigm) to moving toward producing learning (learning paradigm) in whatever ways that work. Often cited as a pillar of the call for active learning approaches, this article isn't prescriptive on details of the process of producing learning but encourages educators to find that out in their own contexts. They state that the purpose of college is not to transfer information but to create environments and experiences for students to construct their own knowledge as cocreators. It's a foundational shift in how we think about the purpose of higher education and serves as a clarion call for educators to change their practices to what serves student learning most effectively.

Fink, L. D. (2003). *Creating significant learning experiences: An integrated approach to designing college courses.* Jossey-Bass.

Fink offers a detail-rich, integrated approach to designing college courses from start to finish. Part of the idea of integrated course design is that the experience should go beyond rote memorization and content coverage and connect a student's learning to life outside the classroom and to their individual self. This integrated approach uses Fink's taxonomy of significant learning to craft learning objectives in the categories of foundational knowledge, application, integration, human dimension, caring, and learning how to learn. Fink then goes into detail about crafting significant learning experiences and ends offering an approach to also change the way educators teach to be more integrated in practice, not just design. This book is a foundational work on designing courses that go beyond basic content coverage into crafting powerful learning environments.

Intentional Futures. (2016). *Instructional design in higher education: A report on the role, workflow, and experience of instructional designers.* https://intentionalfutures.com/static/instructional-design-in-higher-education-report-5129d9d1e6c988c254567f91f3ab0d2c.pdfPLS

Based on survey data of more than 800 instructional designers, Intentional Futures attempts to map the work responsibilities, tensions, and people who make up the field of instructional design in higher education. It categorizes the main responsibilities of designers into four themes—design, manage, train, and support—while citing the overarching tensions designers face in their work in building trust in collaboration with faculty. This article provides a detailed picture of what instructional design looks like in higher education along with demographics about designers. It says the biggest barriers to success in the work are lack of faculty buy-in, time, and lack of resources in funding and support.

Darby, F. (with Lang, J. M.). (2019). *Small teaching online: Applying learning science in online classes.* Jossey-Bass.

Darby extends the conservation from Lang's influential book, *Small Teaching: Everyday Lessons From the Science of Learning,* to the online context as she examines several small practices that educators can use online that have big impacts. Beginning with designing for learning, Darby discusses backward design, engagement, and technology tools. She then discusses the more person-centered perspectives about building community, giving feedback, and student persistence and success. Finally, she talks about motivating online learners and educators through autonomy, connections, and professional development for online educators. Darby offers practical approaches for all different areas of online learning that instructional designers can use during consultations with faculty to help build trust and create stronger courses.

Linder, K., & Hayes, C. (2018). *High-impact practices in online education: Research and best practices.* Stylus.

In this edited collection, Linder and Hayes draw together diverse perspectives on what it means to translate high-impact practices to the online environment. With a chapter devoted to each of the 11 high-impact practices, the collection offers literature reviews on the scholarship of high-impact practices online, practical strategies and tips for translating high-impact practices to online modalities, and transparent discussions of some of the obstacles involved with implementing high-impact practices in online classrooms.

Mayer, R. E. (2008). Applying the science of learning: Evidence-based principles for the design of multimedia instruction. *American Psychologist, 63*(8), 760–769. https://doi.org/10.1037/0003-066x.63.8.760

Mayer, one of the leading researchers of multimedia instruction, offers 10 principles of multimedia instructional design as he works to connect the theoretical aspects of learning to practical application in instruction. Mayer's first five principles aim to reduce extraneous cognitive processing that interferes with multimedia learning, basically overloading the cogitative capacities of the learner with unnecessary information. He then details three principles for handling essential processing, which describe how to help learners make sense of large amounts of necessary information. The last two principles deal with helping learners engage in generative processing, which means helping learners to create their knowledge. These principles help instructional designers and other educators to plan and design instructional multimedia for richer learning experiences.

Wiggins, G., & McTighe, J. (2006). *Understanding by design* (2nd ed.). Pearson Education.

Wiggins and McTighe's work explains backward design as a process to create intentional courses that oppose the "twin sins of design" (p. 16)—activity-focused teaching and content-focused teaching—by focusing on learning instead of teaching. They explain the process of backward design in education and the six facets of understanding. They also encourage practitioners to frame their goals in terms of "essential questions" (p. 105), which spark connections between the classroom and the life experiences of learners. They end the book by explaining how backward design can be used as a curriculum framework. This is a practical book complete with guides, examples, and worksheets for readers to use in their contexts.

Winkelmes, M. A., Boyle, A., & Tapp, S. (Eds.). (2019). *Transparent design in higher education teaching and leadership*. Stylus.

In this edited guide, Winkelmes et al. explain the effectiveness of the transparency framework in various contexts in higher education. The transparency framework provides the organizing structure of task, purpose, and criteria with examples for educators to use when they create assignment descriptions. This framework has proven to be an equitable practice that has a low time investment, with valuable results for all learners by increasing confidence, belonging, and metacognitive skill development across disciplines and across levels of learner expertise. The first section of the book explains the practice of using the framework and the research on its effectiveness. The second section offers guidance to instructional developers working with faculty in higher education to implement the practice. The last section expands the usefulness of the framework beyond the classroom into larger areas of academia.

EDITOR AND CONTRIBUTORS

Editor

Jerod Quinn is an instructional designer for the course design and technology department at the University of Missouri, where he works with faculty designing and creating online classes. He has been working as an instructional designer for almost a decade and even longer in higher education. He has taught online classes in instructional design and face-to-face classes in educational technology. Leaning on his education, online teaching experience, and professional network, he works with faculty to create significant learning experiences online, face-to-face, and blended across disciplines. He's been a Professional and Organizational Development (POD) Network member for several years and is currently in pursuit of a PhD in educational psychology with an emphasis in quantitative research from the University of Missouri. He holds an MEd in educational technology: learning systems design and development.

Contributors

Josie G. Baudier is the director of the Center for Excellence in Teaching and Learning at Georgia Highlands College. Baudier holds an MS in instructional technology and is currently working to complete her EdD in curriculum and instruction, learning and development. She began her career in faculty development as an instructional designer and enjoys supporting faculty in their teaching through workshops and consultations focused on learner-centered education. In addition, Baudier is a certified national reviewer of online courses for the Quality Matters Program and a certified facilitator for Quality Matters professional development. She has taught part-time in education and first-year experience courses in all modalities. Before working in higher education, she taught in the K–12 environment in traditional and nontraditional settings. Her experience and philosophy, developed during her K–12 career, are easily transferable to her role in faculty development and supporting faculty. Baudier enjoys seeing all students develop into autonomous learners along with embedding motivation theory and a growth mindset in faculty development.

Danilo M. Baylen is a tenured professor of instructional technology in the department of educational technology and foundations at the University of West Georgia. Baylen completed graduate degrees in instructional technology, elementary studies, library and information studies, and counseling. Prior to his faculty position, he worked as an instructional designer, information technology services director, and faculty developer in several higher education institutions. He teaches, conducts research, and publishes on effective technology integration practices, visual and media literacy education, creative thinking, and collaborative learning. He is coeditor of *Essentials of Teaching and Integrating Visual and Media Literacy* (Springer, 2015) and received the Association for Educational Communications and Technology 2016 publication award. Currently, he serves as editor-in-chief of *The Book of Selected Readings of the International Visual Literacy Association*. In addition, he sits on multiple editorial boards, including *TechTrends, To Improve the Academy, Quarterly Review of Distance Education, Journal of International Students*, and *WVSU Research Journal*.

Emily Goldstein is the assistant director and instructional designer at the University of Missouri St. Louis. A results-oriented team leader, instructional designer, and web developer and technologist, she enjoys working with faculty in many capacities to define their instructional goals, develop courses that meet quality guidelines for instruction, and deliver engaging and interactive experiences to learners. Goldstein's current interests include promoting awareness of open educational resources and open access publishing through campus initiatives. Goldstein is cochair of the Focus on Teaching and Technology Conference, a regional Midwestern conference that reflects emerging trends in technology applications in higher education and shared expertise in online teaching experiences and strategies. She received her MA in agricultural education from the University of Missouri Columbia.

Christopher Grabau is an instructional developer for the Reinert Center for Transformative Teaching and Learning at Saint Louis University. With more than 20 years of experience working in higher education, Grabau consults with faculty, graduate students, and teaching staff on instructional design elements, course design, and thoughtful uses of instructional technologies. Grabau holds an MA in counseling and a PhD in education foundations. He has taught courses in educational psychology and has presented at national conferences on faculty development and course design strategies.

Jonathan Gratch is an assistant professor in the department of mathematics and computer science at Texas Woman's University and teaches courses related to media, digital graphics, informatics, and educational technology. His research interests include virtual worlds, game-based learning, multimedia in education, and emerging technologies. His current fields of study focus on the application of virtual reality for teaching and learning social awareness, the use of media for enhancing critical thinking and problem-solving through project-based learning, and the development of experiential learning using technology in distance education.

Linda Haynes is an associate professor of instructional technology in the department of educational technology and foundations at University of West Georgia. She earned her doctorate in instructional design and development from the University of South Alabama. While at the University of West Georgia, Haynes served as associate dean (2009–2011) in the College of Education and as instructional technology program coordinator (2012–2014). Graduate courses taught for the instructional technology program included assessment, instructional multimedia design and development, instructional technology issues, and global learning and collaboration. She also received several grant awards from the U.S. Department of Education and the Alabama Department of Education for evaluation studies of professional development activities. Other externally funded projects involved several validity studies of instruments to measure leadership effectiveness and teacher performance through the Georgia Department of Education. Finally, she served as a peer reviewer for the Quality Matters Quality Assurance System for Online Course Design.

Johanna Inman began working in the field of instructional design as an instructional technology consultant at Temple University in 2008, later becoming assistant director and then director of instructional technology at the Center for the Advancement of Teaching. In these roles, Inman created and facilitated a wide range of professional development programs, mentored faculty from disciplines and ranks across Temple University's 17 schools and colleges, and coordinated and managed a six-credit teaching in higher education certificate. Inman has presented extensively at regional and national conferences on teaching in higher education and is an active member of the Professional and Organizational Development (POD) Network. In addition to her work in educational development, Inman has more than 18 years of teaching experience. She has taught a variety of courses, including survey, studio, and capstone courses in the visual arts; writing-intensive courses; first-year seminars; and general education courses. For the past 6 years, she has taught an online graduate seminar about technology and teaching in higher education at Temple University. Inman earned her MFA, summa cum laude, from Tyler School of Art and is now an EdD candidate in higher education in the College of Education at Temple University. In 2019 Inman became inaugural director for a newly envisioned Teaching and Learning Center at Drexel University in Philadelphia, Pennsylvania.

Kathryn E. Linder is an avid writer and researcher with a passion for process and peeking behind the scenes at what it takes to be a successful academic. Currently, she directs the Oregon State University Ecampus Research Unit and is a certified work and life coach through the International Coach Federation. She is the creator of the *You've Got This* podcast and also hosts a weekly interview-based podcast called *Research in Action*. Her latest book is *Managing Your Professional Identity Online: A Guide for Higher Education* (Stylus, 2018).

Tammy M. McCoy is the teaching assistant (TA) development and future faculty specialist for the Center for Teaching and Learning (CTL). In this capacity, she works closely with graduate students and postdoctoral scholars interested in pursuing careers in college teaching through TA training and support, academic career development programs, and training and certification in college teaching. McCoy earned her doctorate and completed a postdoc in materials science and engineering at Georgia Tech. She also earned a master of science in materials engineering from Auburn University and a bachelor in mechanical engineering from Mississippi State University. Prior to beginning her current position, McCoy taught science at a local high school, was an instructor in the Department of Chemistry and Biochemistry at Spelman College and was an adjunct instructor in the Department of Mathematics, Computer Science, and Engineering at Georgia Perimeter College.

Carl S. Moore is currently the assistant chief academic officer at the University of the District of Columbia (UDC). He also serves as certificate faculty in Temple University's teaching in higher education certificate program, teaching faculty for University of Southern California's Equity Institute, and a workshop facilitator for the Online Learning Consortium. He is also frequently an invited speaker and consultant on inclusion, leadership, and faculty development and teaching- and learning-related topics. He has a doctorate in urban education from Temple University and a master of arts degree from the Ohio State University in higher education administration. His dissertation investigated how exemplary college faculty employ universal design for learning principles in their teaching practices. Moore has been teaching for more than 14 years. Along his path, he has served and maintained appointments across the faculty classification gamut, serving in instructional, adjunct, and tenure-track faculty roles. He has also created and instructed a variety of courses in education at The Ohio State University, Temple University, Cabrini College, and Arcadia University in face-to-face and online formats. For the past several years, Moore has dedicated his career to advancing the field of faculty development by serving as a department chair at UDC, assistant director of the Teaching and Learning Center at Temple University, and cochair of the Professional Organizational Development (POD) Network Conference. Alongside his career in academic affairs, Moore has also served in a number of student services leadership roles charged with enhancing student success. These roles entailed work in advising, retention, multicultural affairs, and the federal TRIO programs. As a self-described techie and advocate for mission alignment, his passions lie in using technology to enhance student outcomes at the course and institutional levels.

German E. Vargas Ramos is a learning designer for the Center for Teaching and Learning at Otterbein University in Westerville, Ohio, and a PhD candidate in the math, science, and learning technologies program of the College of Education at the University of Massachusetts, Amherst. He has a BA in English from the University of Puerto Rico at Mayagüez and an MEd in learning media and technologies from the University of Massachusetts Amherst. His research focuses on sociocultural theories of learning, critical literacy, and inclusive instructional design.

Shannon Riggs serves as the executive director of course development and learning innovation for Oregon State University Ecampus. Riggs's nearly 20 years of experience in higher education include traditional classroom instruction, online instruction, online course development, curriculum development, faculty development, instructional design, and leadership in institutions, including community colleges and private and public colleges and universities all over the United States and in Canada. Riggs writes about online course development and teaching and higher education administration and leadership and is the author of *Thrive Online: A New Approach for College Educators* (Stylus, 2020).

Bonni Stachowiak has the privilege of speaking with exceptional educators on a weekly basis as the host of the *Teaching in Higher Ed* podcast. Since 2014 her podcast has provided a space to explore the art and science of being more effective at facilitating learning. *Teaching in Higher Ed* also explores how to improve productivity, so faculty can have more peace in their lives and be even more present for their students. Stachowiak is the dean of teaching and learning at Vanguard University of Southern California. She's also an associate professor of business and management and teaches a few times a year in an educational leadership doctoral program. She's been teaching in-person, blended, and online courses throughout her entire career in higher education. Stachowiak and her husband are parents of two curious kids who regularly shape their perspectives on teaching and learning.

Traci Stromie is an instructional designer at the Center for Excellence in Teaching and Learning at Kennesaw State University. In her role as an instructional designer, Stromie creates and facilitates workshops about teaching and technology-enhanced learning, consults with faculty about integrating research-based pedagogy and practices into their curricula, and supports instructors in designing courses delivered in all modalities. An advocate for lifelong learning, Stromie is passionate about integrating a growth mind-set and research in educational development services and workshops. In addition to her role at the center, she is a part-time instructor for the Department of First-Year and Transition Studies.

Annie Tremonte is a long-time educator who is currently a digital learning coach in a public school district outside Seattle, Washington. She is honored to work with teachers every day to design learning opportunities to equitably empower all students. She has an MEd in digital education leadership from Seattle Pacific University. For the past few years, Tremonte has been an adjunct professor in this same program. In this role, she uses digital learning environments to expand educators' best practices, trading coverage of content for practices that build community and highlight students' voices to drive autonomous thinking and learning. As an adjunct professor, she focuses on supporting the development of graduate students to implement these practices in their own field of work.

Rayne Vieger is an elearning and open educational resources (OER) academic librarian for the University of Oregon, where she leads the library's initiatives in online learning and OER. This role brings together digital scholarship with digital pedagogy through instructional design, open education, educational technology, and the integration of faculty-based digital scholarship and research into teaching and learning. Vieger enjoys providing instructional design services and faculty development opportunities related to best practices in the online and hybrid learning environments and the adoption and creation of OER. Prior to this, Vieger served as an assistant director of instructional design for Oregon State University Ecampus, where she led a talented team of instructional designers in the design and delivery of fully online and hybrid degree programs. After earning a BA in English literature and an MS in library and information science from the University of North Texas, she spent 7 years working in the field of higher educational instructional design and faculty development at the University of Florida and Oregon State University.

Tom Warhover is an associate professor at the Missouri School of Journalism. He teaches classes in reporting and fact-checking and an online-only semantics class where only words and other images are tossed. Warhover was executive editor of the *Columbia Missourian*, a community newspaper managed by editor professors and staffed by students. He was chair of the print and digital news faculty. He has worked for *The Virginian-Pilot* newspaper as a reporter and editor. On nights and weekends, he coauthored a journalism textbook, *Getting the Whole Story: Reporting and Writing the News* (The Guilford Press, 2002).

David Wicks is an associate professor at Seattle Pacific University's School of Education. Prior to that, he spent 15 years as the director of Seattle Pacific University's instructional technology services department. He chairs the digital education leadership graduate program with alumni serving in educational technology leadership roles in K–12, higher education, and educational technology companies. He designed the curriculum and the instructional model used in the digital education leadership graduate's flexible online program. Wicks currently serves on the editorial board for the Teaching Online Pedagogical Repository and is the higher education representative for the Northwest Council for Computer Education.

Olena Zhadko is currently director of online education at Lehman College, City University of New York. She has nearly 15 years of experience in the field of educational technology and in advancing teaching and learning with technology. She has successfully worked at three academic centers by providing leadership and assistance in articulating what constitutes effective teaching, implementing it, and infusing best practices into curriculum development, delivery, and assessment through the effective use of technology. In her current role as Lehman College's senior administrator, she is charged with the oversight of all facets of online instruction. She has a PhD in teaching and learning, as well as the drive for advancing teaching and learning with technology.

INDEX

accessibility, 19, 50, 111, 190, 196
accountability, 180
ACE framework, 227, 228
active
   definition, 5
ADDIE, 30
affective network, 98
agenda, 4, 111, 196, 237
   meeting, 53
agile, 224
alignment, 51, 73, 84, 94, 112, 137, 139, 158, 228, 241
annotation
   digital, 142, 143
assessment
   authentic, 1, 2, 8, 9, 27, 32, 33, 34, 119, 120, 213
   backward design, 17, 31
assignment
   collaborative, 85
   video, 207, 208
   wrappers, 134
asynchronous, 71, 86, 87, 89, 94, 156, 191, 198, 202, 203, 205, 206, 218
   definition, 86
audio, 43, 166, 167, 168, 171, 172, 190, 194, 197, 217, 218
authentic
   definition, 32
authenticity, 111, 112, 114, 183, 203
   definition, 112

autonomy, 32, 33, 44, 87, 119, 122, 142, 198
   motivation, 87

backward design, 17, 24, 27, 31, 33, 111, 114, 224
   definition, 15
blog, 65, 76, 142, 144
blogs, 70, 156, 215
boundaries, 4, 7, 42, 45, 49, 139, 143, 225
burnout, 35, 54

camera
   synchronous, 194
CAST, 98, 100
chat, 195
chunking, 168, 171
coach, 20, 42
cognition, 119, 121
collaboration, 8, 13, 14, 15, 17, 28, 36, 39, 40, 42, 45, 111, 143, 177, 178, 179, 180, 181, 182, 183, 184, 185, 192, 196, 197, 202, 206, 214, 225, 235, 237, 241
community
   learning, 202
   professional, 235, 238
concierge, 7, 13, 15, 18, 23, 24
   definition, 13
consciousness
   critical, 108, 110

constructivist, 5, 40
consultation, 7, 27, 28, 29, 30, 33, 34, 35, 36, 43, 56, 117, 190
   model, 27
container, 153
cooperative, 178
copyright, 19
COVID-19, 223, 224, 229, 230, 231
creativity, 3, 20, 33, 122, 196, 239
critical
   perspectives, 69
critical digital pedagogy, 241
critical instructional design, 240, 241, 242
critically relevant pedagogy, 95
culturally responsive, 95

decoding the disciplines, 135
digital natives, 145, 147
digital immigrants, 145, 147
discussion
   seminar style, 204
   small-group, 205
diversity, 8, 98, 99, 177, 182, 190, 208
Domain of One's Own, 141
dual coding, 168, 171

education
   critical, 107, 108
embed, 141
empathy, 40, 42
environment
   supportive, 119, 123
evaluation
   peer, 184
evaluations
   midsemester, 124
evidence-based, 1, 7, 28, 34, 71, 72, 225, 239
   medicine, 71
   teaching, 72
   trust, 7
expectancy-value theory, 118
expectations, 224
   high, 219
expert blind spot, 88
expository, 5
extrinsic, 91, 118
   definition, 118

failure
   learning, 84
feedback, 18, 20, 45, 66, 69, 75, 84, 86, 101, 102, 113, 120, 122, 124, 125, 131, 134, 135, 137, 144, 154, 156, 181, 185, 191, 194, 196, 198, 212, 217, 218, 220, 239
   formative, 20, 84, 101, 102, 124, 185, 192, 196, 239

group work. *See* collaboration
groups, 182

high-impact practices, 202
humanistic
   psychology, 40
hybrid, 13, 24, 56, 93, 103, 241
hypothesis, 143, 144

icebreaker, 2, 61, 215
imposter syndrome, 70
inclusion
   assessment, 101
   power, 96
inclusive, 93, 94, 95, 96, 97, 98, 99, 101, 103, 109, 110, 111, 178, 190, 197, 209, 242
   synchronous, 190
inclusive teaching, 93, 94

interdependence, 180
intersectionality, 96
intrinsic, 118
  definition, 118
introduction, 179
  icebreakers, 62

knowledge
  prior, 131

layer
  dynamic, 158, 159, 161
  static, 158, 159
learner-centered, 3, 4, 7, 19, 28, 29, 33, 40, 41, 46, 86, 87, 94, 182, 198, 220, 223, 232, 236, 239
  definition, 4
  teaching, 1, 4
learning
  active, 4, 5, 19, 33, 102, 120, 132, 157, 216
  remote, 223, 224, 232
listening
  active, 28, 42
  definition, 43
literacy
  digital, 145

management
  project, 18, 235, 236, 237
manager
  concierge, 18
mastery, 82, 83, 84, 86, 88, 89, 90, 144, 181, 196
memory, 54, 82, 84, 86, 88, 89, 90, 168
metacognition, 8, 35, 102, 128, 129, 130, 132, 136
  definition, 129
microaggressions, 99, 109, 113

definition, 99
microphone, 194, 195
motivation, 23, 33, 44, 87, 103, 116, 118, 119, 120, 121, 122, 123, 124, 125, 166, 209
multimedia, 43, 50, 88, 96, 101, 158, 165, 166, 167, 168, 169, 171, 208, 220
  artifact, 165
  discussion, 207

network
  professional, 239
neurodiversity, 98

objectives, 4, 5, 6, 8, 9, 26, 28, 31, 32, 33, 34, 59, 60, 62, 63, 88, 99, 103, 104, 110, 111, 113, 117, 119, 120, 121, 125, 132, 136, 140, 142, 156, 178, 179, 181, 182, 197, 213, 236
  measurable, 6
Online Course Design Institute (OCDI), 229
open educational resources, 50
overcommunicating, 237

paradigms, 63
PBL. *See* problem-based learning
pedagogy, 1, 4, 15, 19, 24, 27, 36, 50, 51, 60, 62, 65, 70, 95, 104, 107, 136, 214, 240
  critical, 95
person-centered, 40, 240, 241
plus-one, 103
postcard, 65
praxis, 108, 110
pretraining, 167
principle
  coherence, 167, 171
  contiguity, 166

modality, 166
multimedia, 166
personalization, 167, 171
redundancy, 167
prior knowledge,, 82, 83, 86, 89, 90
privilege, 96, 107, 108, 109, 110, 112, 113, 114
problem-based learning, 102, 181
proficiency
  digital, 157
project management, 18
project-based, 160

Quality Matters, 20, 34, 88, 90, 225
quiz
  video, 173

rapport, 19, 41, 42, 43, 71, 77, 119, 171
reciprocity, 215, 216
recognition network, 98
record
  synchronous, 197
reflection, 4, 8, 28, 34, 35, 75, 100, 104, 110, 129, 131, 132, 133, 134, 136, 137, 156, 197, 209
  community-based, 134
  solitary, 133
Representation, 100
research-based. *See* evidence-based
residents
  online, 145
resilient, 227, 230
responsiveness, 111, 198, 219
  definition, 113
roles
  project, 183

rubric
  course design, 20
  course quality, 20

SAM, 30
SAMR, 98
scaffold, 2, 94, 104, 140, 144, 153, 156, 178, 181
schedule, 154
schemas, 84
scope creep
  objectives, 6
segmenting, 167
self-efficacy, 118, 119, 121, 122
self-evaluation, 184
self-questioning, 132
SGID. *See* small group instructional diagnosis
signature pedagogies
  definition, 46
situational factors, 94
skepticism, 62
skillset, 52, 54
small group instructional diagnosis, 125
social justice, 107, 109, 110, 111, 113, 114, 241
social learning, 82, 85, 86, 87, 89, 90
social presence
  definition, 189
Socratic, 61
stereotype threats, 46
strategic network, 98
stressful, 226
summative, 83, 84
syllabus, 49, 52, 90, 112, 136, 151, 153, 178
  decolonize, 112

synchronous, 71, 86, 87, 94, 156, 188, 189, 190, 191, 192, 193, 194, 195, 196, 197, 198, 199, 219

taxonomy, 32, 60, 179
  Bloom's, 60, 179
  Fink's, 32
teaching
  peer, 189
template
  email, 52, 55
TPACK, 72, 73, 74
transcription, 190
transcripts, 172, 196
transparency, 111, 114, 121, 122, 196
  definition, 113
transparent, 85, 121, 143, 178
trauma-informed practices, 231
trust, 2, 7, 14, 18, 23, 24, 28, 29, 36, 39, 40, 41, 42, 43, 44, 46, 60, 62, 72, 119, 121, 179, 180, 192, 194, 204, 237, 240, 242
  social, 204

UDL. *See* universal design for learning
universal design for learning, 8, 93, 220, 228
universal design principles. *See* universal design for learning

value
  definition, 118
video
  assignments, 172
  presentation, 170
  talking head, 170
visitors
  online, 145
visuals
  student-created, 209

Whiteness, 107, 108, 109, 114
  definition, 108
wikis, 70, 156, 215
WordPress, 142, 144

zone of proximal development, 83

Also available from Stylus

The Productive Online and Offline Professor

A Practical Guide

Bonni Stachowiak

Series Foreword by Kathryn E. Linder

Foreword by Robert Talbert

"Stachowiak has written a book on productivity like none other I've read. Productivity, within her framework, is grounded in priorities and purpose and allows us to demonstrate care for the people in our lives and for the relationships that matter. Even the technology-timid will find heaps of ideas to put into practice."—**Isabeau Iqbal**; *Senior Educational Developer, Centre for Teaching, Learning and Technology; The University of British Columbia*

High-Impact Practices in Online Education

Research and Best Practices

Edited by Kathryn E. Linder and Chrysanthemum Mattison Hayes

Foreword by Kelvin Thompson

"*High-Impact Practices in Online Education* asks the right questions about online teaching and learning. This collection offers grounded, practical suggestions for evolving online pedagogy toward a purposeful form of teaching that offers possibilities beyond anything we've done until now."—**Matthew Reed**, *Vice President for Learning, Brookdale Community College*

22883 Quicksilver Drive
Sterling, VA 20166-2019   Subscribe to our e-mail alerts: www.Styluspub.com